Resonant Minds

Resonant Minds

The Transformative Power of Music, One Note at a Time

Sara Leila Sherman
Morton Sherman

ROWMAN & LITTLEFIELD
Lanham • Boulder • New York • London

Rowman & Littlefield
Bloomsbury Publishing Inc, 1385 Broadway, New York, NY 10018, USA
Bloomsbury Publishing Plc, 50 Bedford Square, London, WC1B 3DP, UK
Bloomsbury Publishing Ireland, 29 Earlsfort Terrace, Dublin 2, D02 AY28, Ireland
www.rowman.com

Copyright © 2025 by Sara L. Sherman and Morton Sherman

All rights reserved. No part of this publication may be: i) reproduced or transmitted in any form, electronic or mechanical, including photocopying, recording or by means of any information storage or retrieval system without prior permission in writing from the publishers; or ii) used or reproduced in any way for the training, development or operation of artificial intelligence (AI) technologies, including generative AI technologies. The rights holders expressly reserve this publication from the text and data mining exception as per Article 4(3) of the Digital Single Market Directive (EU) 2019/790.

British Library Cataloguing in Publication Information Available

Library of Congress Cataloging-in-Publication Data
Names: Sherman, Sara Leila, 1985– author. | Sherman, Mort, 1949– author.
Title: Resonant minds : the transformative power of music, one note at a time / Sara L. Sherman, Morton Sherman.
Description: Lanham : Rowman & Littlefield, 2025. | Includes bibliographical references. | Summary: "Resonant Minds: The Transformative Power of Music, One Note at a Time explores how music shapes our cognitive, emotional, and social experiences. Through research, practical insights, and stories, the book highlights music's role in enhancing executive functions and building resilient minds by integrating music into daily life to foster connection and growth for all ages"— Provided by publisher.
Identifiers: LCCN 2024056577 (print) | LCCN 2024056578 (ebook) | ISBN 9781475874952 (cloth) | ISBN 9781475874969 (paperback) | ISBN 9781475874976 (epub)
Subjects: LCSH: Music—Psychological aspects. | Music—Social aspects. | Conduct of life.
Classification: LCC ML3838 .S515 2025 (print) | LCC ML3838 (ebook) | DDC 781.1/1—dc23/eng/20250117
LC record available at https://lccn.loc.gov/2024056577
LC ebook record available at https://lccn.loc.gov/2024056578

For product safety related questions contact productsafety@bloomsbury.com.

♾️™ The paper used in this publication meets the minimum requirements of American National Standard for Information Sciences—Permanence of Paper for Printed Library Materials, ANSI/NISO Z39.48-1992.

To our family, to life . . .

You just call out my name, and you know wherever I am, I'll come running.— Carole King

You are my sunshine . . .

Contents

Foreword   xiii

Prelude   xv

1   Fantasia   1
      Threads   2
      "Shake It Off"   2
      For Each of Us   3
      Yes, And   4
      The Pink Radio, Kazoos, and Competition   5
      Resonance   7
      What If I'm Happy Just the Way I Am?   8
      What's *the* Motivation?   9
      Listen to Music; Open Your Minds: A Movement . . .   10
      Guiding Principles   10

2   Sotto Voce   13
      We Are the World   13
      The Power and Presence of Music   14
      Intentional and Unintentional Music   15
      Research and We Feel the Beat   16
      Listen to the Music: Open Your Mind   17
      Historical and Evolutionary Perspectives   20
      The Profound Connection   20
      Questions for Reflection   20
      The Transformative Nature of Music   21
      Playlists for Whom?   22
      Breaking the Fourth Wall   24

3	Rubato: Embracing the Way It Is	27
	Threads	27
	Enhancing Awareness	27
	Music as an Anchor	28
	Questions for Reflection	29
	Connections	29
	Mindful . . . Mindfulness	30
	Too Much of a Good Thing?	31
	The Science of Balance	32
	Our Friend, George	32
	George's Story, Revisited	33
	Music as a Tool for Mindful Action	33
	The Neuroscientist with an Operatic Heart	34
	A Practical Focus for Attention	35
4	Themes and Variations	39
	Music as a Necessity, Not a Luxury: Themes and Variations Using Music	39
	Threads	39
	Benjamin Franklin: Music as Mindful Invention	40
	Franklin D. Roosevelt: Folk Music and National Resilience	40
	John F. Kennedy: Music as Cultural Diplomacy	41
	Abraham Lincoln: Music as Morale and Purpose in Wartime	41
	Musical Microecosystems	42
	Music as a Necessity, Not a Luxury	43
	Take Two	45
	The Songs of Families	46
	Music and Mindful Intention: A Lasting Legacy	46
5	Forte: Building on Possibilities	49
	Threads	49
	The Familiar . . . a Starting Place	49
	Opportunities . . . Music Everywhere	50
	A Leader's Conversation about Music	55
6	Tacet: Focus, Centering as an Essential Disposition	61
	Threads	61
	Becoming Artists of Sound	61
	Why Focus?	63
	Focus Is a Significant Concern for Learning and Living	64
	Notes from the Classroom	65
	Tailoring Music to Class Needs	66
	Movement Breaks and Engagement	66

Creativity and Music in Learning	67
Overcoming Challenges and Finding Resources	68
The Autopilot Experience	68
Some Thoughts about Active and Purposeful Passive Listening	69
Kids and Music as a Tool for Focus	70
Breathing with Bach: Two Approaches	70
From Automatic to Purposeful: Stories of Connection	71
Observations and Experiences	71
Tools for Focus and Relaxation	72
Practical Strategies	72
Sample Curriculums	73

7 Legato: Understanding the Long Arc of Mindful Actions — 77
- Threads — 77
- The Long Arc of Music — 77
- "Songs in the Key of Life" — 79
- What's Implicit Memory Got to Do with It? — 81
- How Does This Work? — 82
- Music Activates the Brain — 83
- Practical Applications and Activities — 85

8 Counterpoint: Executive Function — 87
- Using Skills to Take Mindful Action — 87
- Threads — 87
- Using Executive Function Skills — 88
- How I Discovered the Importance of Executive Function Skills and Their Connection to Music — 89
- What Are Executive Function Skills? — 92
- What's Under the "Umbrella"? The Four Components of Foundational Executive Function Skills — 92
- Why Are Executive Function Skills so Important? — 93
- Early Childhood and Adolescence Are Prime Times for the Development of EF Skills — 94
- What EF Skills Are *Not* — 95
- Ef Skills and Music — 96
- Does Learning Music Help Develop Executive Function Skills? — 97
- Am I Surprised That the Gains Are Modest? — 98
- The Time to Act Is Now — 99

9 Ostinato: Developing Mindful Habits for Life — 101
- Threads — 101
- Music and Mindfulness: How Music Speaks to Us — 103
- The Neuroscience Research — 103
- Mindful Listening with Habits of Mind — 103

	Listening with Understanding and Empathy	104
	Thinking Interdependently	104
	Remaining Open to Continuous Learning	105
	Ideas for Mindful Listening Interdependently	105
	The Thread of Habits and Imagination	106
10	Tutti: Putting It All Together: Community, Emotions, and Connections	111
	Threads	111
	The Power of Music in Building Community: From Neanderthals to Modern Grooves	111
	Mindful Action, Music, and Community Building: An Evolutionary Perspective	114
	Putting It All Together	115
	The Science of Groove: Synchronizing Hearts and Minds	116
	Drum It Out: The Power of the Beat	117
	The Dance of Community: Movement, Music, and the Magic of Connection	118
	We Like to Move It: The Power of Music and Movement	121
	Practical Application: Movement and Community Building through Music	121
	Reflective Journaling	123
11	Espressivo: Playing with Expression	125
	Threads	125
	The Universal Language	125
	The Emotional Language of Music	127
	Kids Feel It: Understanding Music and Emotion through a Child's Perspective	127
	Emotional Balance and Cognitive Resilience	130
	Continuing the Thread through Time	130
	Exploring the Connection Between Music and Spirituality	132
	The Harmonious Power of Music	134
	Emotional Reset with Music	135
12	Conducting: Leading through Resonance	139
	Threads	139
	All about Nurturing	139
	We Are All Leaders	141
	Notes from the Kitchen	142
	Building Focus and Reducing Stress	143
	Music as a Tool for Building Community	144
	Shining Eyes	145
	How Do You Know It's Working?	145

	Resonance in Leadership	146
	Music as a Tool for Leadership and Motivational Strategies	147
	Mindfulness and Leadership Qualities	148
	Leaders Who Use Music in Their Leadership Practices	148
	Raising the Baton	149
13	Harmony: Transcending Barriers; Creating Opportunities	151
	Threads	151
	What Is Your Book about, Mommy?	152
	Music and Socioeconomic Barriers: A Historical Perspective	152
	Technological Shifts and Financial Burdens	153
	Music Education and Western Bias	153
	The Modern Digital Divide	153
	Now What?	154
	The Modern Mindfulness Divide	155
	The Universal Language of Music: Accessibility beyond Economic Barriers	155
	Music in Diverse Socioeconomic Communities	156
	Music in Neurodivergent Classrooms: A Tool for Focus and Connection	157
	Resonance in Open Doors	160
	Breaking Barriers through Music and Mindfulness	162
	Practical Applications	163
14	Coda: Now What, So What?	165
	Threads	165
	Go to Sleep!	165
	So What about AI?	167
	Harmony of Tomorrow	169
	The Frustrating Silence	170
	So, What If?	172
	Building a Mindful Musical Movement	173
	Music at Home: Creating a Personal Ecosystem	174
	Music in Public Spaces: A Community Affair	174
	A Movement of *Resonant Minds*	175
	AI Is a Tool to Help Build Mindful Action	176
	Play On	177
Acknowledgments		179
Bibliography		183
About the Authors		193

Foreword

Why not just live in the moment, especially if it has a good beat?

Goldie Hawn, *A Lotus Grows in the Mud*
(Berkeley Books, 2005)

Mindfulness has been a profound guide throughout my dancing career, shaping not only the way I move but also how I engage with my own body, my emotions, and the energy surrounding me. Dance, in its most powerful form, is not just about technical execution; it is a journey of self-awareness and presence. From the beginning of my training, mindfulness allowed me to be deeply connected to every movement, breath, and nuance of the music I danced to. This practice helped me learn what it was to stay in the present moment.

Mindfulness taught me to tune into my body—to listen to its needs, respect its limits, and nurture its strengths. I learned to appreciate the subtleties of each muscle's engagement and each joint's articulation. I embodied them, allowing my mind and body to become one in the dance.

Music has always been at the heart of my connection to movement, largely because of my father. He was a violin player, and from a young age, I was immersed in the sound of strings that filled our home. The music that surrounded me became the backdrop to my childhood, and as my father played, I instinctively danced. The sound of the violin swelled through the air, and my body responded naturally, fluidly, to every note and rhythm.

My father's violin became the foundation for how I learned to interpret music through my body. Every time I danced, I felt as if I was collaborating with the sound, not just moving to it but moving with it, letting the music guide my steps.

I found that the practice of mindfulness allowed me to remain connected to that childlike joy I felt when I first danced alongside my father's violin, always reminding me that dance, at its core, is about joy, about feeling the energy in the room, in the music, and within myself. I used to call it the joy of moving the molecules in the air with intention, creating ripples of energy that extend far beyond my own body. I could feel it in every movement, in every interaction between music and motion.

The music that once filled our home became the foundation for my love of movement, my love of music, and the deep secret of mindfulness.

Goldie Hawn

Prelude

Resonant Minds explores the profound impact of the purposeful use of music on focus and cognitive, emotional, and social experiences. Through the use of executive functions now which enable memory attachments and lead to positive habits, music may be a universal connector that transcends barriers, nurturing leadership, community building, and cultural exploration. Offering practical strategies for integrating music into daily life through mindful action, *Resonant Minds* offers insights for parents, educators, and anyone interested in the deeper role of music in personal growth and societal well-being, particularly with fast-paced technological development (figure 0.1).

Figure 0.1. Reflections. *Photograph courtesy of Debra Sherman.*

OUR PRELUDE

WE LOVE MUSIC

"To take the simplest example: one man laughs, and another, who hears, becomes merry; or a man weeps, and another, who hears, feels sorrow. A man is excited or irritated, and another man, seeing him, comes to a similar state of mind."[1]

"We are accustomed to understand art to be only what we hear and see in theaters, concerts, and exhibitions, together with buildings, statues, poems, novels . . . But all this is but the smallest part of the art by which we communicate with each other in life. All human life is filled with works of art of every kind—from cradlesong, jest, mimicry, the ornamentation of houses, dress, and utensils, up to church services, buildings, monuments, and triumphal processions. It is all artistic activity."[2]

WHAT IS . . . ANY OF THIS, REALLY?

Jumping and horsing around as a toddler, Sara often joined her sisters on Mort's back. Mom's job was to pick the music that we would all sing, competing to see who could be the loudest. Sometimes Bette Midler was a favorite music selection, especially "Otto Titsling." As Mort whinnied, the musical carousing ended with everyone collapsing and giggling on the floor or with rousing rides on their hobby horses to the "William Tell Overture."

As Sara listened to her sisters' lessons, Adena on the violin and Rachel on the piano, she wanted in on the fun. Sara would bounce to the piano and play with her nose and toes, and sometimes her fingers and elbows. She also had a small keyboard, a toddler-sized violin, a plastic drum, a tambourine, and a kazoo.

Two family favorites were flashlight tag and drumming on the table, seeing if other family members could guess the tune. Flashlight tag is played in lots of homes. How about a variation: flashlight tag with creepy Halloween music in the background? Maybe that's a way for parents getting a few quiet moments in the dark while the children are giggling in closets somewhere.

No doubt in our minds that this was all excellent preparation for a classical musician!

By itself, music is wonderful, exciting, serious, mood-setting, and worth studying. However, music doesn't take a breath, make a sound, or look beyond the notes on the paper without some human making it happen.

Music is an anchor that connects and makes us feel. It can be serious, fun, romantic, stirring, subtle, and even boring, depending on our needs and intentions.

Some earliest musical memories include seeing *Les Miserable* as a family multiple times, then reenacting it at home, fighting over who would get to act out which parts. Early morning car rides to school were fueled by blasting "Bohemian Rhapsody" by Queen, with headbanging and air guitar, to boost our moods to get ready for the day.

How did we as a family bring those notes off the page into joy, fun, and serious study?

Mort has been wondering for a while about the connection that we all have to music. Why, at one of his retirement parties, did he hand out kazoos to everyone to join in playing "You Are My Sunshine" followed by Carol King's, "You've Got a Friend?" Serious music is played in a joyful way, and sometimes joyful music is played in a serious way. Music has given us and our families countless moments of happiness and connection.

"ODE TO JOY"

Sun was beaming through the car windows, music blasting, heart full. The car ride included singing the last movement of Beethoven's Ninth Symphony ("Ode to Joy") at the top of our lungs, ignoring the German words, and making up a language complete with animal sounds.

On repeat, this was how Mort drove ten-year-old Sara to her first sleep-away piano camp. After nearly fifty minutes of orchestral music, the recording's tenor proudly interrupts, saying, "Oh friends, no more of these sounds! Let us sing more cheerful songs more full of joy!" Finding joy in music and interacting with all genres of music, breaking that fourth wall in performances started here, oinking like a pig to "Ode to Joy."

Could Sara have ever come to these moments of exuberant expression in a traditional approach to classical music? Beethoven is a classical composer; it's serious music!

WONDERFULLY FRÖHLICH!

Conductors aren't just the leaders of an orchestra. They are teachers in the classroom, principals in the school, parents to their children, coaches to the team, and supervisors to their colleagues. We are all conductors of our own orchestra. We are all leaders. Your orchestra might be filled with students, athletes, your own kids, or even your synapses and neural pathways.

Too often we look at classical music, or at the conductor and the musicians on a platform or stage, separate from how the rest of us live. The musicians' study and talent are admirable. We want to hear and feel their music—to be accessible, to learn from it, and to join others in a community of understanding. Music should have its moment on the stage and be part of our lives after we leave a concert.

Music is everywhere—in your fingertips, in your brain, in lullabies, on the radio, and playing during your spin class. Since music is so ubiquitous, we believe it is a significant lever to take mindful action. This is not just the quiet moments at a classical concert or the excitement of singing and waving cell phones at a country festival—this lever for mindful action is about what happens after the music fades, in the silence between the notes, when the real reflection begins.

We share our music with one another, and we love sharing our music with families and friends. With that foundation of love and eagerness to share, we wonder, "Now what, so what?" It's a question woven throughout this book. We should be more mindful; now what? Music can help us be more resonant and present in our lives; good, so what?

When Sara was thirteen, she heard Marta Argerich perform Schumann's "Piano Concerto" and was brought to tears. Unsure of why she was crying, she just knew it was the most beautiful and emotionally stirring experience she had ever had. How wonderful it would be if we could all share these shouts of approval, clapping of hands, or tears with neighbors and friends.

Mozart for Munchkins, an interactive concert series based in NYC, is asked all the time, "What if my child cries?" The reply is often, "Maybe that's an early sign they don't resonate with Debussy!" Or, "What if my child starts to clap or dance?" The response: "Fantastic! This is an interactive performance."

At the beginning of each show with children of all ages (babies too!), caregivers are gently reminded to stay present. If kids are asked to sway, adults, please help! If the caregivers are engaged, the more likely their children will be as well.

Mozart for Munchkins is but one of many organizations across the world that want the audience to feel, to move, to become infected in the best possible way by the music.

MAGICAL MOMENT

Growing up with classical music, Sara loved her music. The shouts, claps, and cries were not part of how she was taught to play or perform. She knew music well after years of lessons, traveling the world for music, and attending concerts. There was always that magical moment: the first tuning note, the dimmed lights, and the hush as the conductor stepped on stage. The moment felt remarkable, almost untouchable. Now, she realizes that this moment isn't just hers—it's universal, shared by all who love music. Whether it's the jazz band stepping on stage or the hush as a pop star picks up the microphone, that same magic is felt across genres.

However, not everyone's experience at a classical music concert is so magical. "Be quiet! Stay in your seats! Don't move!" Someone who might be getting over a cold will be given looks first for coughing, then more intense glares for the crinkling that follows as they're desperately trying to open a cough drop as softly as possible (which always seems to make it louder).

Why are we like this? According to Nielsen Music Reports, 1 percent of the world listens to classical music with a whopping 0.1 percent increase from 2017 to 2021.[3] A tenth of a percentage increase across the world! Another report from 2022 shows that number at 22 percent, but it is highly misleading, as the survey was conducted only in America and Great Britain.[4] Hardly a global reflection.

Why bring up the magic for only a few listeners as we begin a conversation about the intentional use of music in our lives? This view of the classical music world is important to highlight the challenges facing an essential art form and to think about what might be applied to other forms of music.

Music Is for Everyone. But Do We Really Make Music for Everyone?

Sara, a classically trained pianist, spent her early years steeped in the traditional world of conservatory training. As a young child, she had opportunities to perform around the world as a solo pianist, chamber musician, and soloist with orchestras. Yet, all these performances were steeped in the traditional "lights down, be quiet, get in your seats" culture.

As she matured as a musician, Sara began to question this approach, seeking to understand the *why* behind the *do*. Nervously, she asked her teachers this very question, seeking to gain clarity. During her undergraduate studies, she was told, "Have you listened to all my recordings? Do it like this." None of this is to take away the brilliance of her great mentors across the world. The recordings *were* amazing! But the *why* isn't solved by listening to recordings alone.

In high school, eager to develop stronger fingers and technique, she was met with a "later; let's focus on songs for now." Frustrated, knowing technique was one of her greatest weaknesses, she looked elsewhere. At a summer music festival in Ukraine, fellow students, just a few years older, secretly gave her technique lessons. They barely spoke English, and someone had to stand on "watch" to make sure her teacher wouldn't catch them. They could barely communicate through language, but the music and passion were language enough.

This all sounds absurd, doesn't it? As curious minds, parents, educators, and individuals, we know that "because I told you so" is never a mindful answer. Sara learned from these experiences that music and the pedagogy of teaching need to nurture thoughtful, empathetic individuals.

Of all the music opportunities available to young classical musicians, many conservatories continue to offer narrow perspectives. Students are often confined to degrees that are siloed by their specific instrument or genre, where they study the history of their particular field and are trained within rigid performance traditions—"Sit down, be quiet" concerts being the norm. Limitations show up in concert halls, conservatories, private lessons, and judgmental mindsets across the world.

This does not help the one percent of classical music lovers increase their audience to even two percent.

Sara had the honor of studying with renowned clarinetist and Klezmer musician, David Kraukaer. During their first lesson together, he handed her a lead sheet—a piece of paper with just chords and a melody. Her reaction? "Where are the rest of the notes?" The skill of improvisation—playing what you feel based on chords and melody—was so foreign to the strict discipline of classical music, it was terrifying. But then it was exciting.

In 2010, Sara helped create the first Klezmer Chamber music group at the Manhattan School of Music. This ensemble, composed of jazz musicians, classical musicians, and a composer/violinist, broke down barriers. People clapped during the concert, not just at the end of a piece, creating a sense of community and interaction. Some even danced! This was a new performance experience for Sara, one that wouldn't have been possible if she hadn't sought out ways to express herself beyond the written notes. One of Sara's sisters, Rachel, a special education teacher, calls this "going beyond the paper."

BEYOND THE NOTES

Making music accessible to everyone means making it participatory, not just a passive listening experience. Often, this is done in pre-concert talks, when you have that amazing conductor who might talk about the piece before a concert. But once that oboe starts, you better open your cough drops quickly and "sit down, be quiet."

During grad school, Sara often called Mort, caught up in the question: What is art, really? A canvas filled with bold solid colors by Rothko, a porcelain urinal signed "R. Mutt" by Duchamp, Marina Abramovic sitting across from people who had lined up for hours just to stare at her in silence—is this art? Have you ever seen Victor Borge's phonetic punctuation (so good!) or his solo interpretations of a Mozart aria? How about PD Bach, turning a symphony into a baseball game: "The basses are off!" Speaking of baseball, what about the artful way a pitcher practices day in and day out—is that precise execution of throwing a baseball art?

Whether or not these fall under the conventional idea of art, they make us *feel something*. They spark conversation, connection—even debates about whether or not they *are* art. That's still a way of connecting!

The quotes used at the beginning of this introduction by Tolstoy provide a view of art as something far beyond the confines of galleries, theaters, and concert halls. They remind us that art is, at its core, about *connection*.

Art is that whisper in your ear, a secret passed from one heart to another, transcending time and space. Whether the brushstrokes on a canvas, the lullaby sung to a child, the twist of words in a poem, or the spontaneous rhythm of a drum circle, art exists in every corner of human interaction. It's not just about what we see or hear, but about what we feel—those moments when something stirs within, and we're not quite the same as we were before.

Maybe art is less about *what it is* and more about *what it does*. For us, art is an invitation to be part of something greater, to feel connected in a way that words alone can't quite capture.

Art, by ourselves, for ourselves? Sure. We sing alone in the shower, or whistle a happy tune, or blast music in the car when no one's around. Yet, even as we sing alone in the car, we might be thinking of someone we want to share that song with, or even imagining singing it to them. There is something about our wanting to feel connected and to share that universal language of music. Even Michelangelo had thirteen or so painters helping with the Sistine Chapel. You are not alone.

This "glorious infection" of resonant minds can move beyond siloed ideologies and a reluctance to change.

If there's music within us, how do we find the music in ourselves that connects us more deeply to others? Things resonate differently with each of us—one size does not fit all.

TUNING TO A

Some of us were fortunate to grow up immersed in classical music—attending lessons, sitting in ornate concert halls, and creating vivid memories of what a concert is "supposed" to be. There are deep-rooted traditions and expected behaviors at classical music concerts: The audience shuffles to their seats, browses program notes, and settles in. Once the oboe sounds an A—the tuning note for all instruments to synchronize—the concertmaster joins, and then the rest of the orchestra. An exciting moment of anticipation signals the start of something special. There are often no words, but that signal note commands: "Sit down! Be quiet! The performance is about to start."

Learning these silent cues and knowing when to follow them takes great discipline—moments of mindfulness that come from regularly attending concerts. How many actually experienced these musical traditions as children? How many parents feel comfortable taking their children to a classical concert? How many adults attend if they didn't grow up with this tradition? We know the numbers are underwhelming.

Sure, discipline is important for growth, but classical music's challenges aren't just a lack of discipline—it's the deafening alienation it creates. The classical music world has erected walls that push away young audiences and newcomers, training them to be silent, not to respond, and certainly not to engage. Clap between movements? Prepare to be met with glares that could freeze an iceberg. Is spontaneity an enemy to be crushed rather than a natural, joyful response to art?

Classical music isn't alone in its rigidity. Other genres, too, can become confined by their own unspoken rules. Jazz, for instance, is rooted in improvisation and free expression; yet, there's still an understanding in some concert venues that the audience should "know" when to respond—when to snap their fingers in approval or when to hold back applause until the solo is done.

Even in pop music, where fans are encouraged to sing along and wave their cell phones in the air, there are moments of expectation. A quiet ballad may call for reflection, but anyone who cheers or sings out of sync during that moment can get side-eye from their neighbors. And at hip-hop shows, the energy can be electric, but there's often an invisible line between crowd participation and moments when you're just expected to listen. All genres, in their own way, create these layers of expectation that can unintentionally create distance between the art and the audience, even as they establish respectful audience protocols.

A child starts clapping to Gershwin. Instead of celebrating that spark of joy and engagement, we shush them. The message is clear: you don't belong unless you play by our strict rules. We know we are being harsh. But really? Was it always this way between the performers and the audience? No. An excerpt from a letter by Mozart on July 3, 1778, gives us an appreciation of his joy with the audience:

> The audience were quite carried away. There was a tremendous burst of applause (after the first movement). But as I knew when I wrote it what effect it would surely produce, I introduced the opening passage again at the closing and there were shouts (of approval).

I began (the allegro) with two violins only, softly for the first eight bars, followed instantly by a forte. The audience, as I expected, said, "Sssssh!" at the soft beginning, and when they heard the forte, began at once to clap their hands.[5]

The joyful principle Mozart wrote about often applies across music genres. During Grateful Dead or Phish concerts, the line between performer and audience often dissolves entirely. Fans dance, sing, and even follow the band from city to city, turning each performance into a shared experience. Gospel music encourages participation; often, it is not just encouraged, but expected. These genres thrive on engagement, where breaking the "rules" is encouraged.

Leonard Bernstein championed this approach. The seeds of this book started decades ago after Sara read one of his biographies (with Mort!), learned of his *Young People's Concerts,* and watched countless videos of him conducting, teaching, and sharing his love of music. Sara then worked at the Cook Music Library at Indiana University, which holds Leonard Bernstein's archives. During her breaks, she would wander through the aisles deep in the basement archives, looking through his scores and his notes.

Bernstein said, "Music can name the unnameable and communicate the unknowable."[6] Not only was he a brilliant musician, he was a communicator, a connector. Bernstein's philosophy of music as an active, joyful force resonates here. He believed music wasn't just for the concert hall—it was for everyone, in everyday life.

Rigidity has a time and a place, important in its own way. There is that silence between the notes and the quiet movements that gives the audience a chance to reflect, to read the program notes, and to think about what's coming next. But Mozart's note doesn't have this feeling of rigidity for everyone. If we want to make music for everyone, or at least significantly increase the audience, let's tear down these walls and make the art form accessible, participatory, and, most importantly, alive.

In conversations with talented musicians, one shared, "I don't believe in all that mindfulness business." But why not give it a try? Another Broadway musician, intrigued after a show, responded with curiosity and openness, calling it, "Some deep shit!"

Yes, yes it is. Specialization in any field, whether as a Broadway musician, surgeon, MLB player, principal, or educator, is important. We can't become the best versions of ourselves without exploring what else is out there and constantly asking, "What can we do differently to better ourselves and others?"

This siloed mentality doesn't set anyone up for the "now what, so what" of life. Staying curious, pushing boundaries, and exploring new ways of expression are essential to break free from the 1 percent trap. To make art infectious from the audience to the performer, we must constantly, listen, reflect, and adjust.

Okay, we made our point about classical music, which we love. How about if we replaced "classical" with "jazz" or "musical theater" in every paragraph above?

If someone really loves jazz or classical music, shouldn't that suffice? We said earlier that music is for everyone, but not all music is for everyone. The compelling and exciting possibility for us is that so many listen to and love their music. Now all we have to do is expand their listening just a bit, think about the moods and moments of their music, and tweak their playlists ever so slightly. And then, repeat.

We wonder how to reach families in pockets of poverty or others who live in environments without much exposure to different kinds of music. According to the U.S. Census Bureau, in 2021 around 11.6 million children in the United States lived in poverty, representing 16 percent of all children. Approximately 9.2 percent of families in the United States are living below the poverty line.[7]

These families have music in their lives. No doubt about that. How about if we take all the science and practical wisdom that we have and apply the best of what we know to our neighbors in need? Might it be that the schools these children attend have already cut their music programs? Where and how do they get the opportunity for mindful moments through music?

Mort grew up in a family in which both parents worked hard during the Depression years. His dad did not graduate from high school. It was certainly not the same experience Sara had growing up.

In two generations, the family evolved . . . that word shouldn't be seen as a pejorative—from the life of a gifted mechanic to the life of a remarkable musician. The mechanic, father of five sons, asked as he held up his large, never-entirely-free-of-grease hands, "When you get older, do you want hands that look like this? Being a mechanic is tough but a good life. You can make decisions about your lives. Go to college, be a mechanic, or learn a trade. Make good choices."

That was an extraordinary, compelling, and mindful moment.

What was the spark that brought some in that family to love music and literature? It certainly wasn't in school where Mort auditioned to play the French Horn in third grade and was immediately directed to the drums. However, somewhere along the way, there was a connection made. Was it spiritual, religious, or the tunes on the radio? Maybe in the protest music of the sixties.

The family didn't go to concerts, and the brothers didn't have exposure to that level of live music until college. Graduation from record players to stereos seemed to happen when they married. We may never know for sure what was the musical spark.

And it doesn't make much difference except to think about how many little boys and girls there are out there who would benefit from a mindful spark that we can help create.

Our questions about the mindful spark are foundational to our work. If music is within us and all around us, how do we intentionally build experiences and develop communities that lead to reciprocal, mindful actions that expand and deepen our life experience?

NOTES

1. Leo Tolstoy, *What Is Art?*, trans. Aylmer Maude (Hackett Publishing Company, Inc., 1996), 121–122.

2. Tolstoy, *What Is Art?*, 43–44.

3. Nielsen Music/MRC Data, *Nielsen Music Reports*, 2017–2021, https://www.nielsen.com/.

4. IFPI, "Global Music Report 2022: State of the Industry," *International Federation of the Phonographic Industry*, 2022, https://luminatedata.com/.

5. Wolfgang Amadeus Mozart, *The Letters of Mozart and His Family*, edited and translated by Emily Anderson (Penguin Books, 1966), 495.

6. Leonard Bernstein, *The Joy of Music* (Simon & Schuster, 1959).

7. "Income and Poverty in the United States: 2021," U.S. Census Bureau, last modified September 13, 2022, https://www.census.gov/library/publications/2022/demo/p60-276.html.

Chapter 1

Fantasia

The human voice has, in a way, music in it. It's in the delivery, the diction, the feeling. That's why music in movies can reach people so deeply. —Walt Disney[1]

Animation offers a medium of storytelling and visual entertainment which can bring pleasure and information to people of all ages everywhere in the world. And this may be particularly true in music, which is international. —Walt Disney[2]

Figure 1.1. Juneteenth celebration, West Village 2021. *Courtesy of* ©*2025 Juan Patino Photography.*

THREADS

- Music connects the pieces of the long arc of life.
- The importance and the difference of this book is the cobbled kaleidoscope of stories, research, experience, and dreams into a vision of mindful action through music, not just theory.

The intentional use of music shapes our cognitive, emotional, and social experiences. *Resonant Minds* captures the profound ways music influences our brain, our communities, and our ability to connect and nurture. Building from the familiar, including passive listening to mindful action, expanding and deepening the influence of music on ourselves and our communities.

No matter how we access music, it has a profound influence on ourselves and those around us. This book explores the intersection of music, mindful action, and community. We encourage a movement—one that connects music, mindful action, executive function, and technology, intentionally creating the long arc of life through music.

"SHAKE IT OFF"

Hey, "Shake It Off"! Even Taylor Swift has music in her mind saying that "it's going to be alright."[3] We know that the players are going to play, but she can't stop grooving. This song can be found with the youngest listeners dancing and singing inspired by Rosita (their favorite pig) from *Sing*, or with Treasure Trunk Theatre's dance teacher leading a performance with eight-year-old Swifties, or a child asking Alexa to play "Shake It Off" when their parents are upset—music has always been a dynamic force, not just a backdrop in our lives.

"Happy Birthday" has the same tune in almost all languages. "Twinkle, Twinkle Little Star" and the "ABC's" share the same melody. Even Mozart wrote twelve variations on the theme of "Twinkle Twinkle"! The tune is so familiar across languages and cultures because it brings people together. We don't pick "Battle Hymn of the Republic" for birthdays, but we might play "When the Saints Come Marching In" to capture the joyous spirit of celebration. These selections are intentional.

Music goes beyond enjoyment, enhancing executive functions such as planning, decision-making, and problem-solving, engaging various neural pathways. Whether the emotional depth of a favorite song or the cognitive sharpening that comes from memorizing a song, music helps us build stronger, more resilient minds. A powerful tool for learning and personal growth, music significantly improves focus and cognitive flexibility.

The power of music isn't just for us as individuals. Music is a universal connector that transcends socioeconomic barriers and bridges the gap among English language learners, in both neurotypical and neurodivergent minds. Through stories, research, and practical insights, *Resonant Minds* shows how music used deliberately and purposefully can be a tool for nurturing leadership, community building, and exploring diverse cultural perspectives. The reader is challenged to consider the role of music in creating inclusive spaces where everyone, regardless of background or ability, can participate and thrive.

Seventy-six trombones . . . a parade for July 4th, Pride March in the West Village, Chinese New Year Parade, Thanksgiving, Rose Bowl parade . . . we love our marching bands (figure 1.1). Even before you see the bands, you hear them, and something in you changes—you tap your feet, smile, and anticipate their arrival. The rhythm, the energy, it links us all together.

Whether we're playing or just enjoying the music and atmosphere, the groove links us, creating community through swaying bodies and smiling faces.

The link is everywhere! From Mickey Mouse conducting dancing mops to *The Sorcerer's Apprentice* or Bugs Bunny's fingers flailing across the piano keys to Liszt's "Hungarian Rhapsody" or the phenomena of Ms. Rachel and the new songs for the youngest listeners she composes with her husband, featuring Elmo or Broadway musicians. No way these scenes pull us in without the music. Music's power in storytelling makes these moments unforgettable.

FOR EACH OF US

Phones, fancy watches, Alexas, Google Home devices, laptops, smart TVs—the ways we consume music are ever-growing and constantly changing. How many devices do you have? How many apps are on those devices?

At this distinct moment in human development, the nexus among these elements creates exciting, endless possibilities.

Imagine teachers playing a song to quiet a classroom or to teach a history lesson. Picture yourself using music to reflect on your own emotions. Think of the ways music can build positivity in your community or personal life. So many ways to use music to create meaningful change. So much possibility.

If you're a parent reading this book, we're talking about your children. If you're a teacher, we're talking about your classroom. If you're a leader of any kind, you'll see how these concepts ripple out, impacting everyone in your sphere.

Using music intentionally starts with us and continues outward, touching all those around us. The banker, the candlestick maker, the grocer, the librarian, the curious mind, the business executive . . . everyone!

This book provides actionable strategies for using music in your everyday life. Not just for entertainment, but as a growth tool. Music to support learning, emotional well-being, and social connection. Approaching music in this way is not just for musicians or music lovers; it is for anyone interested in understanding the deeper impact of music on our lives and society, and the intersection of music, mindfulness, and community.

Connecting through music and sound is limitless, and the divisions among us blur through shared musical moments. Guidance is offered on integrating music into daily routines, educational settings, and community activities, making it accessible and relevant for all ages.

QR codes are used throughout the book to provide sample music and suggested activities. The use of QR codes is our way of keeping these ideas alive as we develop a dynamic effort to learn and act together.

YES, AND

Nearly every day by nearly everyone with whom we shared the ideas of this book nearly all have been excited about the concepts, yet still wondered about the *and* . . . "What makes your ideas any different?"

Mark Twain suggests: "There is no such thing as a new idea. It is impossible. We simply take a lot of old ideas and put them into a sort of mental kaleidoscope. We give them a turn and they make new and curious combinations. We keep on turning and making new combinations indefinitely; but they are the same old pieces of colored glass that have been in use through all the ages."[4]

What is new is the way we have cobbled together a kaleidoscope of stories, research, experience, and dreams into what we hope resonates as a lens to opening our minds to what's possible. The turn of each piece that you read provokes new images to think about as you continuously construct and reconstruct your view of the world.

Without getting too caught up in whether these are new pieces of glass or advancements on the glass we can already see and know about, our kaleidoscope view and the answers to the "AND?" are based on exciting and "can't be ignored" forward-to-the-future perspectives:

- The science and practice of music supporting focus, improving cognition, building communities, shaping culture, and creating joy are in sync. Music has been an essential part of our lives for thousands of years.
- We know that we can build on the familiar to mindfully be active, participating users and listeners of music.
- Neuroscience, executive function, and habits of mind serve as our map.

- Motivation through one person, one small group, one network, and then another working together will build a large network of practitioners who share, learn, and grow together.
- Technologies such as AI, are tools with breakthrough promise of generating entirely new and easy ways of finding and creating personalized and customized music.
- We believe in the good will of humankind, who want to be part of a symphony of life that helps create that more perfect union.

THE PINK RADIO, KAZOOS, AND COMPETITION

The pink transistor radio clock was tuned to the classical station as Sara fell asleep at night. The bright red numbers on the clock glared at her as she tried to stay awake, but the sounds of Beethoven, Chopin, and Debussy would soothe her to sleep.

Her mom, a pillar of strength, love, and patience, would sing "Scarlet Ribbons" or "Scarborough Fair" on repeat until she fell asleep. If not singing, she would guide a meditation starting at the toes, ending at the head, thinking of each body part and letting it "fall asleep." Now, Sara and her children do this, but they've added a moment of gratitude, "Thank you, hands, that I was able to write, eat, and hold my stuffed animal when I was sad today!"

Have you ever been in a room of over fifty adults, playing kazoos? We mentioned earlier that kazoo magic was part of one of Mort's going away parties as the entire room joined in on "You Are My Sunshine." What a wonderful way to create such a sense of community in a room, even those that were shy joining in on the fun.

An absolute rule when competing regularly as a child was that no one could talk to Sara on the way to, before, and after an audition. She would play through Chopin, Beethoven, and Scriabin, from memory, seeing the music with eyes closed, fingers twitching along. At fourteen years old, in Alushta, Ukraine, on stage with Chopin's "Third Scherzo" and windows wide open during the summer heat, the monks' chants began loud and clear from the monastery down the road. Sara's breath was shaky, and it was like watching someone else at the piano.

As the notes cascaded from high to low over and over again, the monks chant repeated. The show had to go on. She fumbled through the rest of the piece, unable to stay focused on fingers and sounds coming out from piano to the audience. Focus and mindfulness were still developing skills, as they are throughout life.

We will talk about classical, country, gospel, and jazz music but that's not all. This type of mindful action and music that ranges from joy to focus and emotions to community building isn't possible without acknowledging the moments of dancing around the kitchen table with Sara's mother, sisters, and three-year-old niece, wooden spoons and spatulas in hand singing "Build Me Up Buttercup" until they were sweaty and laughing.

Using music for mindful action can be a learned behavior with countless benefits.

The possibilities . . .

We honor the remarkable practitioners, scientists, and mindfulness leaders who help us lead centered, positive, nonjudgmental lives. We want to move to active and dynamic use of music to expand through mindful behavior.

The possibility exists to combine the "why" of music with the "why" of mindful behavior.

Sitting and staring at a wall is not for everyone. Getting into the Lotus position does not work for most of us. Although mindfulness may seem ubiquitous, only about 14 percent of adults in the United States regularly practice meditation, with numbers ranging from 10 to 20 percent in other Western regions.[5] In contrast, The International Federation of the Phonographic Industry's 2021 report stated that 76 percent of the world listens to music daily. This means we have a powerful tool at our fingertips—music—as a unique practice of presence. By intentionally incorporating music into our daily lives, we open the door to limitless potential for positive impact, benefiting each and every one of us.[6]

You don't need to be a student of music nor a musician nor a mindfulness practitioner. Music is within us, an untapped reservoir of possibilities to help shape how we live and how we might impact others. Music is a metaphor for living.

What if we treat music like sports fans nurture the community at games?

Matt, an enthusiastic sports fan, described the mental component of watching a game: "There's an escalated state of mind, a slow build-up that gets more interesting." He noted that, unlike concerts where excitement is sustained, sports events are unpredictable. With five minutes left in the game, fans are engaged, imagining potential plays and outcomes. This shared experience creates a strong sense of community, as fans, often strangers, cheer together and bond over their shared passion.

Sports fans form a "we," with players becoming part of their extended family and friends. The community that forms around a sports team is enduring, uniting fans through the highs and lows of wins and losses. At a concert, whether it's for Bruce Springsteen, Beyoncé, or a small jazz band in the park, the shared excitement and emotional connection is powerful. You don't have to know the person next to you to feel that shared energy.

Imagine if we could recreate that same sense of community and connection with music in our daily lives—at home, at school, or even at work. Consider the fervor of fans who have attended countless shows of the same performance. This isn't about duplicating their behavior but understanding what drives their community spirit and expanding on it.

"And they're off with a four note theme! The beginning is always very exciting, folks." PDQ Bach is this wonderfully comedic figure created by Peter Schickele, who mashes up classical music with humorous twists. Moments are created when you listen to an orchestra, expecting something grand, and then out pops a kazoo solo. Onstage you might find a referee, cheerleaders, or even kids in the audience fist pumping to Beethoven's Fifth Symphony.

Resonance! Music can mix with anything—even the world of sports broadcasting. Music has the ability to be a shared experience, to break down barriers, and to connect people from all walks of life. Whether it's at a baseball game, a concert, or even while listening to a favorite song on the subway, music brings us together in ways we sometimes don't even notice.

Just like the way a conductor subtly shapes a performance with a nod, smile, or wave of the hand, we can shape our lives by being mindful about the music we surround ourselves with. We'll explore how to make resonance part of our daily rituals, and create more spaces where music helps us feel connected—to ourselves and to others.

RESONANCE

The thread of resonance is the link among the parts of this book and our work. Resonance is not just a musical term; it's a way of life. How we treat ourselves, how we interact with others, and how music vibrates through every part of our lives—that's resonance . . . musical, personal, and interpersonal resonance. Pulse, timbre, vibrations synchronized. Life.

In popular music, show tunes, gospel, country . . . resonance is a thread in music, how we relate to music, and how we relate to one another. This word resonance captures so well the leadership concepts of empathy—the connection an entertainer feels with an audience, the cheers a politician receives after delivering a powerful speech, or even the deep, wonderful embrace between a grandmother and her grandson.

Movies and popular media resonate with us. A terrific example of resonant messaging through media is the movie *Network*. The lead character shares his frustration with society through his television news show and encourages listeners to throw open the windows and hear him.

I'm as mad as hell, and I'm not going to take this anymore.[7]

We aim to create a movement, not based on being mad as hell, but in optimism encouraged by widespread practice and ongoing research in this field.

We believe that the use of mindful action combined with the intrinsic power of music has the potential for great impact. The use of executive function and emerging technologies expand and deepen the use of music as a way of life to focus, build community, and lift spirits for ourselves and others.

Our sense is that generally we do want to be at peace, not moved to shouting angry epitaphs out the window. We know that mindful action through music will not solve the problems of the world. At the same time, we can't sit idly by and just hope for something to come along to improve our lot as humans. We can control our path to a different life. That's what this book is about.

We are inspired by the lofty aspirations of our preamble to the Constitution of the United States . . . what amazing fifty-two words:

> We the People of the United States, in Order to form a more perfect Union, establish Justice, ensure domestic Tranquility, provide for the common defense, promote the general Welfare, and secure the Blessings of Liberty to ourselves and our Posterity, do ordain and establish this Constitution for the United States of America.

Our hope is to contribute to the more perfect union, that music and mindful action can promote tranquility, general welfare, and the blessings of liberty.

We start with the familiar and build on the traditional definitions of these words.

Mindfulness is about creating a state of presence that goes beyond traditional meditative practices. It involves bringing awareness through mindful action, which in turn expands focus, strengthens communities, enhances executive functions, nurtures leadership, strengthens emotional awareness, and builds positive habits through memory associations.

WHAT IF I'M HAPPY JUST THE WAY I AM?

Why change? This question is core to our theory of action. How do we move from what's comfortable to what's possible? Much has been written about motivation, building, and sustaining culture, moving from our level of familiarity and comfort to a broader perspective.

Maybe we have our heads in the clouds, yet we are convinced that music is a natural, already widespread lever for change when actively and purposefully used.

We know we're not alone with questions of motivation. Just ask parents how they help their children see the need to take the dishes to the sink after a meal, pick up their clothes when they change, eat a salad, go for a walk, drink enough water, or do homework.

How in the world do we expect people to change on a dime and start using executive function skills, mindful action through music to focus, build community, be calmer, and create a better world. What's the motivation?

Many of us have great intentions. That's why so many people make New Year's resolutions. And don't keep them. Or when we hear the alarm go off early in the morning because we set it to get up and out the door for a walk. Instead, we go back to sleep. Diets, exercise, and so much more that we think about, but just don't get to.

WHAT'S *THE* MOTIVATION?

A shared belief among many is that the best way to motivate is with rewards like money—the carrot-and-stick approach. That's a mistake, says Daniel H. Pink (author of *To Sell Is Human: The Surprising Truth about Motivating Others*). He asserts that the secret to high performance and satisfaction—at work, at school, and at home—is the deeply human need to direct our own lives, to learn and create new things, and to do better by ourselves and our world. He examines the three elements of true motivation—autonomy, mastery, and purpose.[8]

We want to create a movement, but we are realistic about how slowly we turn, one step at a time, one note at a time.

Motivation is often built through being part of communities, large and small. We have spoken to sports fans who connect with their teams, who are energized by the connections with other fans, and with the details of the sport and the players. We've thought about how to "hook" people into this movement, when so many other initiatives about health and exercise and mindfulness have not made it to scale.

We emotionally, enthusiastically, wholeheartedly believe that what can make this effort different is that it is based on music, already part of our lives. The resonance with life experiences is the opportunity and the difference maker.

Who/what are the influencers?

What tunes can we play, do you need to hear? Music is the lever, the key, the motivator.

LISTEN TO MUSIC; OPEN YOUR MINDS: A MOVEMENT . . .

We aim to create a movement toward more resonant minds, understanding that meaningful change occurs slowly and personally. This book is not a simple how-to guide for a better life and world. Instead, it serves as an emphatic call to mind, urging us to build on the resources already at our fingertips to deepen and expand our life experiences.

In today's world, we risk becoming narrower individuals, trapped in routines and reinforced by technology that feeds us only the familiar. We are encouraged to buy products we already own, listen to songs that echo the ones we've always heard, and support political candidates who play to the tunes already lodged in our heads. This siloed existence limits us, driven by paths we've already walked and experiences we've already lived.

We can do better.

"Put on your oxygen mask first, then help children." Recognizing and respecting the familiar, our journey begins with the individual. Focusing on how music enhances concentration and active listening in turn allows us to engage more deeply with the world and understand our cognitive functioning.

As we expand from the individual to the collective, music acts as a thread that weaves us together. A packed concert, where total strangers are suddenly singing in unison or a song that brings tears at a memorial service—music strengthens social bonds allowing for empathy through shared experiences.

Singular experiences may serve as a basis for creating lifelong threads that build communities.

Movement and music create rhythms of wellness that improve our physical and emotional health. Music also informs leadership, whether in boardrooms, classrooms, or homes. As we navigate a rapidly evolving technological landscape, we examine how AI expands our musical horizons, offering personalized experiences that challenge and enrich us.

From the personal to the communal, and from history's greatest leaders to tomorrow's tech innovations, we invite exploration of music as a lever, a dynamic force for positive change, inspiring ways of thinking, living, and connecting. Together, we will discover how music can help us lead more expansive and resonant lives.

GUIDING PRINCIPLES

As cobblers piecing together work from a broad array of experiences and science, we have developed some core working principles. We start with the belief that there is the deep human condition of wanting to improve, to learn, and to grow through life:

- Start from where people are. Respect with nonjudgment—for ourselves and others.
- Music as a part of our everyday lives: we can connect to it and use music purposefully.
- Science and practice: substantive research supports core principles of arts and mindfulness.
- Mindful action—learning is reciprocal, cyclical, and lifelong.
- There is a nexus of music, mindful action and taking positive action:
  - Creating habits of mind and behavior.
  - Executive functions are the skills which help us take mindful actions.
  - Motivation is developed one person at a time, with the goal of creating expanding communities.
- Technology tools offer promise to collect, curate, and create the dynamic playlists of our lives.

NOTES

1. "Walt Disney's Words: Quotations of Walt Disney," compiled by Kathy Puckett, 2001, p. 24.
2. Kathy Merlock Jackson, ed., *Walt Disney: Conversations* (University Press of Mississippi, 2006), 32.
3. Taylor Swift, "Shake It Off," Max Martin and Shellback, August 19, 2014, Big Machine Records, 6, 2014, compact disc.
4. Albert Bigelow Paine, *Mark Twain: A Biography: The Personal and Literary Life of Samuel Langhorne Clemens, Vol. 3* (Harper & Brothers, 1912), 1343.
5. "National Health Interview Survey 2017," National Center for Complementary and Integrative Health, last modified September 15, 2024.
6. IFPI, "Engaging with Music 2021," *International Federation of the Phonographic Industry*, 2021, https://www.ifpi.org/wp-content/uploads/2021/10/IFPI-Engaging-with-Music-report.pdf.
7. *Network*, directed by Sidney Lumet (Metro-Goldwyn-Mayer, 1976), https://www.youtube.com/watch?v=ZwMVMbmQBug.
8. Daniel H. Pink, *To Sell Is Human: The Surprising Truth about Moving Others* (Riverhead Books, 2012).

Chapter 2

Sotto Voce

Music gives a soul to the universe, wings to the mind, flight to the imagination and life to everything. —Plato

To live on a day-to-day basis is insufficient. We need to transcend, transport, and escape. We need meaning, understanding, and explanation. We need to see overall patterns in our lives. We need hope, the sense of a future, and the freedom to get beyond ourselves . . . in states of mind that allow us to rise above our immediate surroundings and see the beauty and value of the world we live in.[1]

Threads:

- What is music? The beat of our hearts, the rhythm of our feet, the tone of our voices, the hum of the refrigerator, the peace of an exhale—there is music everywhere and within us. This chapter dives into the basics of music and mindfulness, our personal relationships to this work and its importance.
- We live in a feedback loop of the familiar. We can be the conductors of the music of our lives.

WE ARE THE WORLD

Amanda's day starts early. She walks down three flights from her apartment, choosing to avoid the elevator and the overhead soft jazz. Just elevator music, right? The kind of ambient sound that's there but not really there, just filling the silence.

The radio in the cab is playing a pop hit, not one she likes or listens to carefully. She sometimes takes the bus, but she is in a rush today.

Afternoons for Amanda are loaded with snacks and high energy playlists on her headphones.

A local gathering place has an open mic that evening. Amanda leans back, smiles with friends, and encourages others to belt out a song. Some select slow, melancholy songs while others jump around on the low stage, laughing and shaking to the tune. The small audience joins in.

Beyond Amanda, we find salsa music blaring as children run through fire hydrants in Washington Heights. The familiar tune of Mario plays as the video game begins, unchanged since 1985. Political rally chants echo, advocating for equal rights or supporting union workers on strike. The sounds of fiddle and guitar fill the air at the end of a long day for a bluegrass jam. These diverse musical scenes paint a vibrant picture of our collective experiences.

Birds calling to each other, the drone of fans, the drip of a faucet. All sounds, but music? It depends on who you ask.

Sure, it can be music, and even used with intent. The soundtrack at a spa, playing classical music with a waterfall overlay to bring on calm and ease. Someone mindfully picked that music just for your massage! You can thank them or growl at them later, depending on whether or not it resonated with you.

For the purpose of *Resonant Minds*, music is an intentionally composed piece of music that evokes focus, emotion, community, and connection.

THE POWER AND PRESENCE OF MUSIC

Music isn't just sound—it's the silence between the sounds, the tension of waiting for the next note, the breath held in anticipation. Think of these moments:

- The steady hum of the dishwasher, background to a Sunday afternoon.
- The soft lull of a baby's heartbeat on an ultrasound.
- The click-clack of keys on a laptop as ideas come to life.
- The rhythmic chopping of vegetables while cooking dinner.

These sounds form the everyday symphony that surrounds us, shaping our moods and memories. We all experience music differently. For some, the sound of a saxophone echoing through the subway is calming. For others, it's a reminder of a busy, overwhelming day.

Do you have a story similar to Amanda's of your life surrounded by music? Perhaps driving to work, dropping off the kids, and putting on a purposeful playlist while cooking dinner. Maybe after a long day working the night shift at the hospital, you find yourself zoning out to the music on your drive home and thinking about the white noise that will aid you to sleep as the sun rises. These stories are all about us.

But what's undeniable is that music—and sound—embodies emotion, presence, joy, and love. It's a universal language, weaving invisible threads between people.

Composer and conductor Michael Tilson Thomas once asked, "What happens when the music stops?" Our thoughts and emotions don't stop with the last note. Music lingers, it creates moods that stretch beyond the melody. What sticks after the music stops? A memory? A feeling? The power of music lives on in how it shapes us after the final chord has been struck.[2]

INTENTIONAL AND UNINTENTIONAL MUSIC

There's a distinction between music that's intentionally composed and sounds that exist in the background of our lives.

Unintentional sounds might be beyond our control and form the backdrop of our everyday lives—the honk of a car horn, the drip of a leaky faucet—are just part of the noise we live with.

Purposeful and intentional music, on the other hand, is created with a clear intent: a well-rehearsed orchestra performance, a movement break in a classroom.

Eleven-year-old Madison asked, "What's your book about?" Before we could explain beyond "using music purposefully," Madison, with her curious mind, interrupted. "Where does white noise fit into all of this? And what about brown noise, pink noise, and all those sound machine options?"

Great question! Do these sounds even count as music? Babies and kids often drift off to sleep with sound machines humming away, and let's be honest, plenty of adults rely on them too. You'll find them in doctors' offices, filling the quiet between patient rooms.

While sound machines aren't music in the traditional sense, they definitely serve a purpose. They help us relax, block out distractions, and create the right environment for sleep. It's more of a steady wash of ambient noise.

Music, on the other hand, has layers—rhythm, pitch, timbre—that pull us into active, intentional listening. White noise, though, is more passive, just part of the background. It still does its job, but we aren't consciously tuning in to the individual sounds the way we do with music.

At 3 a.m., Naomi, half-asleep, picks up her crying daughter and sits in the rocking chair. The white noise machine fills the room, creating a calming backdrop. The wash of sound is a soothing balm for both of them, a constant since the baby was born.

While waking up in the middle of the night isn't fun, the white noise calms her daughter and reduces Naomi's anxiety about being tired for work the next day. White noise itself is an indescribable sound—not high or low, but a whoosh of constant static, yet more pleasant than what we think of when we think of in-between radio stations.

So, does this qualify as music in the traditional sense? No, dear Madison, but it is still important to recognize the significant impact that sound machines have on both adults and children with their constant auditory environment.

RESEARCH AND WE FEEL THE BEAT

> I feel it in my fingers, I feel it in my toes
> Well, love is all around me and so the feeling grows[3]

We sing to one another. We dance with each other. We fall in love, we celebrate, we recover, and we mourn to music.

Music is an essential part of our lives.

Many under thirty turn to social media to hear new music and to share what they're listening to. Others still turn to radio, movies, and television to hear and learn music. Regardless of how or where we access or listen to music, what is clear about music is that it is everywhere and for nearly everyone.

Science may lag behind the practice but what we do know about music is significant. Some comparisons are in tune with science, practice, and experience of the intentional use of music. For example, there is little doubt that exercise is good for you. Attention to core muscles is known to be important. Going for a walk, for example, helps with balance and stamina. Doing crossword puzzles and Wordle are accepted as wonderful ways to stimulate cognitive abilities.

We know to wear warm clothes when it's cold out, drink plenty of fluids when it's hot out, cover our mouth when we sneeze, and read, laugh, and play a little each day.

Our goal is to have the majesty and beauty of music understood and used in the same way. Not to be overly simplistic, but mindful use of music is good for us as individuals and for us as neighbors. What if we could teach the world to sing in perfect harmony, to open minds in order to mindfully listen to music?

Perhaps because music is so ubiquitous, so much a part of our lives, we take it for granted. We should accept music mindfully used as a necessary part of our lives, just as we do with eating well or exercising.

How about a world where right next to the posters that say "read," we create posters that call for us to listen to music? How about a QR code on those posters that would take us to sample playlists or to AI technology that generates music for you?

LISTEN TO THE MUSIC: OPEN YOUR MIND

Music is often siloed into personal tastes. Of course, the familiar is comfortable!

Over the years, schools have tried to teach music appreciation, exposing students to an increased canon. Projects like the Lincoln Center Institute have worked to bring students and teachers closer to the arts through participation. Across the country community bands, pop-up music in parks, big concerts with thousands of fans, and smaller, quieter classical audiences all share music with their audiences and with each other. How wonderful!

Music and culture go together. From a square dance, grass dance, salsa . . . whatever state or country you might live in or visit, there are beautiful sounds that make us human and individual. We are absolutely supporting and encouraging more music that is personal, cultural, and shared. Let's create and connect.

Arts educators have recognized the need for a more holistic and nurturing approach. This encourages individuals to discover and express themselves freely. We advocate for a deliberate expansion of our musical interests. Can you already hear the rock folks cringing about listening to opera? Or the country folks smiling politely when offered the chance to listen to jazz? This is where intentional use of music can make a difference.

By building on what we already know and love, we can expand beyond the genres we love to build an expanded playlist for our lives. Mindful action helps us remain nonjudgmental, open to other music, and embracing the possibilities of something new.

It's like Plato's *Allegory of the Cave* where those who were only exposed to the reality of the shadows on the walls are blinded by the sun once they go outside. We don't want to blind anyone. Eyes can be open and minds can be expanded all the while keeping sight on the world around us.

Our culture reinforces narrow tastes. The music field categorizes in hopes of recognizing all forms of music and honoring the artists who contribute so wonderfully to our lives. At the same time, the list of Grammy Awards categories underscores the expansive, well-defined, narrow bands of music, with thirty-six categories, including some really interesting ones:

- Dance/Electronic
- New Age, Ambient, or Chant
- Improvised Jazz Solo
- Roots Gospel Album
- Regional Mexican Music Album (Including Tejano)
- Regional Roots Music

When you ask someone what kind of music they like, a response may be country and some R & B. Our hope is to have responses that include those answers and to go beyond in search of broader playlists, constructively seeking an expanded listening of the world around us so that the expanded awareness of music's possibilities can mindfully lead to use of music throughout our days and lives.

Have you ever asked a musician what they do? Often, the responses are usually specific: "I'm a drummer," or "I play on Broadway." There are those who answer that they are musicians. We wonder if the level of specificity reveals a mindset and a focus rather than approaching music in a broader way. Being a musician is so much more than the instrument played or the stages on which they perform. Wandering through Central Park in New York, the parks in Portland, or the street corners in New Orleans can be magical. Just jamming, smiling, feeling one another's beats and moods, these musicians capture the moment and transcend the specific.

Musicians, teachers, chefs, nurses, police, firemen, and all of us can be nurturers. Musicians are connectors of sounds that have the ability to stir emotions and connect us. The genre or the style of music is the entry point and can lead to the imaginative and universal elements that impact listeners. The pitches, rhythm, and instrumentation are just instructions. The musician individualizes the sounds and has the ability to break down traditional boundaries and create profound, lasting impacts.

Let's be careful about the familiar being too narrow a focus. You have to start somewhere. Our hope is to build from what we know—often called the what—to the broader potential of music the why of music.

A global report on how people around the world enjoy and engage with music is based on the responses of more than 44,000 people in twenty-two countries.[4] The report is the largest music study of its kind. The facts are staggering:

- Seventy-six percent of respondents listen to music daily.
- People listen to an average of 20.1 hours of music a week (up from 18.4 hours in 2021).
- Music is already used for mental health: 69 percent of people say music is important to their mental health, while 68 percent say that music is important when they exercise.

How much of this music is background? How much is listened to with purposeful, active listening? Are the songs preselected based on previous likes by algorithms from Apple Music and Spotify, or are people requesting specific songs?

Seventy-six percent of people listen to music every day! That's incredible. Now, we're looking to make that listening part of a contemplative practice, a flow. To pair the way we listen to music with mindful action.

Music has the potential to aid Alzheimer's patients make connections, improve school readiness and language development, enhance memory and logic, and help us become more mindful of our own bodies. Despite its potential, music is often underutilized in our everyday lives.

Ben Zander, a deeply insightful conductor, tells a story in his TED Talk titled "Classical Music with Shining Eyes" of two shoe salespeople who visit a foreign culture. One reports that the news is bad: the local population does not wear shoes. The other person reports that there is a glorious opportunity: the local population does not wear shoes . . . yet! Zander then goes on to wonder what would have happened if Martin Luther King had stood on the steps of the Lincoln Memorial and said I have a dream today, but it's not for everyone. How antivisionary that would have been. Our dream is for everyone. Not classical music, but *your* music, ever-expanding.

We are of the mind that there is a glorious opportunity to scale as never before, to make connections generally overlooked, and to develop a culture—one song and one person at a time—that is committed to a better world.

Sure, we are encouraging the dynamic listening to music, being aware of choices, and purposefully bringing music into your life. However, this is not all we are recommending. Playlists for life are a way to access personally meaningful music. We encourage going beyond the confines of the familiar. Most of us want to grow, to create a more joyful and positive world for ourselves and others, and to use tools which make all this possible. This is the why.

The use of the term "playlist" is just the starting point. Our proposition is that music and mindful action lead to playlists for life. How we interact with music that impacts how we engage with ourselves and others—a ripple effect that extends far beyond simple listening. By learning to actively listen, we can bring new awareness to our experience with music, connecting more deeply with the breath and rhythm of each piece.

HISTORICAL AND EVOLUTIONARY PERSPECTIVES

Music has been documented to have been around for over 40,000 years. Early humans made music with purpose. The cognitive and emotional engagement required for music-making aligns with mindfulness principles, promoting presence and emotional well-being. The communal aspect of music fosters social cohesion, communication, and cultural transmission, essential for group survival and identity.

The earliest known written music comes from ancient Mesopotamia, around 1400 B.C., with the "Hurrian Hymn No. 6" being one of the oldest surviving examples of written music. That's over 3,400 years ago!

THE PROFOUND CONNECTION

Music, whether major or minor, fast or slow, played by a solo instrument or a full orchestra, doesn't just change how we feel—it impacts our neurological systems. A simple song can make us smile and simultaneously lower blood pressure.

Why is our society so deeply connected to music, and how can we purposefully use it? Consider a time when you were deeply impacted by music. What were you doing? Here are some common experiences:

- Driving with the windows down.
- First slow dance.
- A holiday tune.
- A walk accompanied by the sounds of nature.

Music is always with us, always accessible in our minds, providing a soundtrack to our lives. By integrating music and mindful action we can create a powerful tool for emotional regulation, community building, and overall well-being. Whether through purposeful listening or active engagement, music can enhance our mindfulness practice and enrich our daily lives.

The profound connection happens when it plays on in our hearts and minds. Does it ever stop?

QUESTIONS FOR REFLECTION

1. When was the last time you were deeply moved by a piece of music? What were you doing?

2. Can you recall a moment when a song connected you to a specific memory or emotion?
3. How does the background music in your daily life affect your mood and focus?
4. What sounds form the soundtrack of your life? How do they make you feel?
5. Have you ever used music intentionally to change your emotional state or mindset? How did it work?

THE TRANSFORMATIVE NATURE OF MUSIC

With closed eyes and a cleansing breath, you may find yourself transported by the memory of a sound, a song, or a familiar voice. Our personal soundtracks, like the melodies of our lives, are woven from these moments of resonance and remembrance.

The arts have been healers from the beginning of time. For tens of thousands of years the arts have been used to heal, build communities, discover a sense of self, and find meaning in our lives. It's not just music; it's the impact of the arts on humans.

> You know the transformative power of art. You've gotten lost in music, in a painting, in a movie or a play, and you felt something shift within you. You've read a book, so compelling that you pressed it into the hands of a friend; you've heard a song so moving, you listened to it over and over, memorizing every word. The arts bring joy. Inspiration. Well-being. Understanding. Even salvation. And while these experiences may not be easy to explain, you've always known they are real and true.

But we now have scientific proof that the arts are essential to our very survival.[5]

Music is important, helping in:

- Stress Reduction: Mindful listening to music offers a simple yet effective way to alleviate stress and promote relaxation.
- Emotional Regulation: Music has the power to evoke a wide range of emotions, providing a safe space for exploring and processing feelings.
- Enhanced Well-Being: Cultivating mindfulness through music promotes overall well-being by creating a deeper connection to oneself and the present moment.
- Improved Relationships: Sharing music with others can strengthen social connections and promote a sense of community.

We learn daily about advances in neuroscience and the brain. As neuroscience informs the field of "neuroarts," we gain exciting scientific evidence that supports what we've long observed about the powerful effects of music and the arts on children and families, opening up even more possibilities.

PLAYLISTS FOR WHOM?

The program team for Mozart for Munchkins led a school's professional learning day as part of a music and mindfulness program. It featured an amazing mix of music. Folk tunes, classical, and jazz . . . a complete repertoire! However, not everyone felt that way.

In a debrief after the session, the principal was upset. "What about pop music?" The visceral reaction was to bite back, "We're Mozart for Munchkins! During the program folk tunes and a mention of Taylor Swift were included. Not enough?" The program team deliberately paused, took a breath, and let those thoughts pass as they re-evaluated how to connect through music.

The next assembly was with neurodivergent students in both middle and high school. Some were nonverbal, and some were in wheelchairs. In these situations, it's uncertain how the students will react until the playing starts. With the same principal, thought leader practitioner and several teachers, the planning team hopped on a call and listened.

Breathing with Bach is for everyone; however, shying away from pop music is not inclusive of all music. If music is for everybody, doesn't that include all types of music? The next assembly, the program contained classical, jazz, "We Will Rock You," Taylor Swift favorites, "Happy" by Will Pharrell, and musical choices ready to swap on the spot if the musicians were not connecting with the students.

Just because music is for everyone, it doesn't mean our musical choices will have the same impact and purpose for everyone. Throughout this book, we will name pieces and we will give you QR codes connected to playlists, but just because a piece resonates with us, we recognize it might not be the same fit for you. We want you to take our suggestions and make them your own. It's about becoming the conductor of your own playlists, the symphony of your own lives.

- Identify the Purpose: What is your goal? This could be to help with focus during study time, to calm anxiety before bed, or to energize and uplift during the day.
- Choose the Right Music: Select music that supports the intended purpose.
  - Calming Music: Soft, slow-paced music with minimal lyrics can help reduce anxiety and promote relaxation. Classical music, world music

with sustained sounds, ambient music, and certain types of jazz are good options.
- Focus Music: Instrumental music, such as classical piano pieces or lo-fi beats, can enhance concentration and reduce distractions.
- Energizing Music: Upbeat, rhythmic music can boost energy levels and improve mood. Genres like pop, rock, and certain types of jazz can be effective.
- Emotional Regulation Music: Music that reflects or shifts emotional states can help in processing and regulating emotions. This can include blues, folk, or any genre that resonates emotionally.
* Create a Structured Playlist: Organize the playlist in a way that gradually transitions through different emotional or physiological states.
* Incorporate Mindfulness Practices: Combine the playlist with specific mindful action prompts.
* Test and Adjust: Monitor the effects of the playlist as you listen. Pay attention to how the music influences your mood, focus, and overall well-being. Adjust the playlist as needed.

Tips for Teachers and Parents

* Use Technology: Utilize music streaming services to create and share playlists.
* Mindful Listening Sessions: Set aside time for mindful listening sessions where children or students focus entirely on the music. Encourage them to notice the different instruments, rhythms, and how the music makes them feel.
* Engage in Music-Making: Encourage children to create their own music as a form of mindful action. Simple activities like drumming, humming, or playing basic instruments can be very effective.
* Combine Music with Movement: Use music for mindful movement practices like yoga or dance.
* Storytelling with Music: Integrate music into storytelling or reading time.
* Teach Emotional Vocabulary: Use music as a tool to teach children about emotions. Discuss how different pieces of music make them feel and why.

Example Playlists

* Calming Playlist for Bedtime
    1. "Clair de Lune" by Claude Debussy.
    2. "Weightless" by Marconi Union.
    3. "Nocturne in E-flat Major" by Frédéric Chopin.
    4. "Ambient 1: Music for Airports" by Brian Eno.

- Focus Playlist for Study Time
  1. "Spring" from *The Four Seasons* by Antonio Vivaldi.
  2. "Gymnopédie No. 1" by Erik Satie.
  3. "Canon in D" by Johann Pachelbel.
  4. "Lo-Fi Beats" by Various Artists.
- Energizing Playlist for Morning Routine
  1. "Here Comes the Sun" by The Beatles.
  2. "Happy" by Pharrell Williams.
  3. "Uptown Funk" by Mark Ronson ft. Bruno Mars.
  4. "Shake It Off" by Taylor Swift.
- Emotional Regulation Playlist
  1. "A Change Is Gonna Come" by Sam Cooke.
  2. "Lean on Me" by Bill Withers.
  3. "Let It Be" by The Beatles.
  4. "Don't Worry, Be Happy" by Bobby McFerrin.

BREAKING THE FOURTH WALL

When Mozart for Munchkins began, most concerts were introduced with this message: "If your children make noise or cry, don't get up and leave! We want children to express themselves and experience the music. If a child cries during Debussy but doesn't during Gershwin, think of it as expressing their musical preferences."

How many concerts have you attended where you had to sit quietly, listen attentively, let your mind wander, then got restless and checked your watch several times? While there is a time and place for this type of performance, which we deeply respect and admire, we wanted to step out of that box and create a bigger box by making music accessible for all ages and audiences. This meant breaking down the fourth wall—the invisible boundary between the audience and performer—and transforming the performance into a collaboration. A collective experience of music where everyone feels, thinks, acts, and creates a sense of community.

The first concert in this series took place in December 2017. Unsure of how the audience would react, the program creators were both nervous and excited. Then it happened. During Mozart's Violin Concerto in A Major, the violinist walked into the audience. The wall was broken. Children approached the performer (carefully!) and together, they brought Mozart into the audience. There were no invisible boundaries anymore. There was just music, people, and a shared experience.

A little girl, maybe two years old, looked on in wonder and lifted her hand to the violin. Once this wall was broken, we continued to move and exist purposefully in the audience. During "Flight of the Bumblebee," parents and grandparents like Mort! lifted their children in the air, spinning in circles and buzzing like bees around the room. The joy, laughter, and release of oxytocin were palpable. This is why the fourth wall is deliberately broken: for the connection, awe, and community that happen in those magical moments.

A playlist had been created and music selected to capture the energy and build the community. Our premise was that you can do this anytime for yourself and for others. It's not just who we are but the possibilities within all of us.

By breaking the fourth wall, everyone is invited to be part of the performance, creating a unique and unforgettable musical experience that transcends traditional boundaries and creates a sense of belonging and shared joy.

As the conductors of our minds and, in turn, those we interact with daily, we often get stuck within our own walls. What if we consciously break down that fourth wall to connect with others? Even better, connect through music and feel a deeper sense of connection with those around us.

NOTES

1. Oliver Sacks, *Gratitude* (Pan Macmillan, 2015), 14.
2. Michael Tilson Thomas, "Music and Emotion through Time," TED2012 official TED Conference, March 2012, 19 min., 56 sec.
3. The Troggs, "Love Is All Around Me," October 1967, Lion Records, Track A, *Love Is All Around Me,* 1967, Vinyl.
4. IFPI, 2021, *Engaging with Music 2021*.
5. Susan Magsamen and Ivy Ross, *Your Brain on Art: How the Arts Transform Us* (Random House, 2023), ix.

Chapter 3

Rubato

Embracing the Way It Is

Listening is where love begins: listening to ourselves and then to our neighbors. —Fred Rogers[1]

THREADS

- What are the basics of music and mindfulness, our personal relationships to this work and its importance?
- What's the point of using music purposefully?
- What's in it for the audience?

ENHANCING AWARENESS

Ann was at her weekly piano lesson and had just finished playing a piece she had been working on for several weeks (figure 3.1). Before there was even time for feedback or a debrief, she said, "I have no clue what I just played."

This is a common occurrence during lessons, and it is even more frequent when asking students to do something very specific like, "Start from page two and play the left hand alone," only to have the student go back to the beginning of page one!

How many of you have had this experience? Not just with a child, but with colleagues, friends, or family? How frustrating and infuriating, but we all do it.

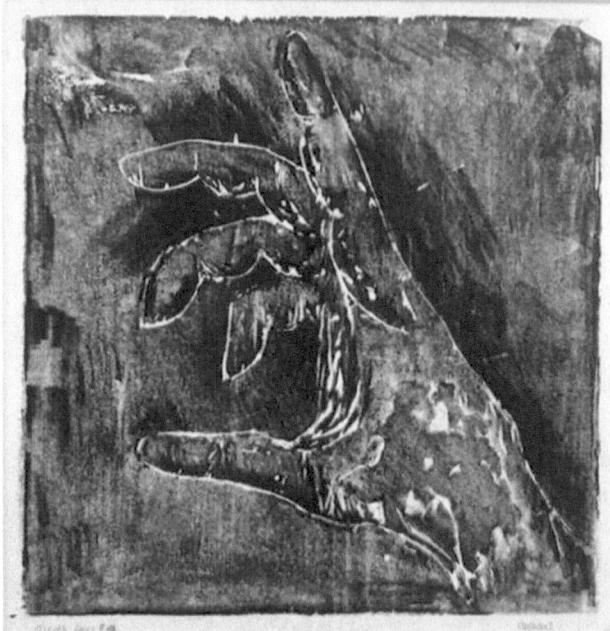

Figure 3.1. Embrace. *Original woodcut print by Debra Sherman.*

Why do you think this happens? Have you ever caught yourself zoning out in a meeting or during a conversation? How often do you realize you've been on "autopilot" and missed the last few minutes of dialogue?

Ann's realization that she was physically present but mentally elsewhere is a valuable lesson in communication—honest and clear. This occurrence can be caused due to an attention lapse (letting the mind wander), cognitive overload, auditory processing issues, and more.

Our minds naturally wander. It's part of what makes us healthy, adaptive, and creative. But the beauty of being mindful is that it helps us bring our attention back to the present. Music can be a tool to help with that. When we listen to music mindfully, it invites us into a deeper relationship with both the sounds and ourselves. We shift from passive listening—where the music washes over us—to active listening, where we engage, reflect, and connect.

MUSIC AS AN ANCHOR

We know that the sources of our music play a large role in staying on our listening paths. These familiar sources lead us to familiar patterns of music.

This brings up three essential questions:

- How might those familiar patterns be used as a base to purposefully bring that music to lighten our moods, help us focus, and connect with others?
- How do we expand our base of listening to go beyond the familiar?
- How do we seek and listen to other forms of music with an open mind?

This nexus, moving from relying on what's familiar to engaging mindfully with new sounds and experiences, is at the heart of mindful action in music. That deliberate intentional moment may be challenging and sometimes uncomfortable. That's what makes it so powerful.

We center on five key concepts associated with mindfulness: awareness, presence, acceptance, focus, and compassion. These ideas frame the shift from passive listening to a more deliberate, active experience of music.

QUESTIONS FOR REFLECTION

1. Have you ever been physically present in a conversation but mentally elsewhere? What caused this?
2. How often do you find yourself drifting off during meetings or lectures?
3. Can you recall a time when you were listening passively and missed important information? How did you handle it?
4. How do you balance passive listening with active listening in your daily interactions?
5. What strategies do you use to bring your focus back when you notice your mind has wandered?

CONNECTIONS

Classrooms across the world hum with energy—students chatter, papers rustle, chairs scrape. Then, a sharp clap breaks through the noise. The teacher raises her hand, and instantly, eyes snap forward. She pauses, letting the silence settle. A gentle chime rings, its resonance filling the room. "One, two, three . . . look at me," she says softly, her voice calm yet commanding. Slowly, the students shift in their seats, their focus drawn inward. The room stills, and the lesson begins.

Now that the teacher has the students' attention, are they really listening? Or are they automatons who sit there with a smile, politely looking, simply playing the game of dutiful students while actually sitting passively inside their heads? How do we get them from passive to active? From merely hearing to truly listening.

This is where music comes in. Not just background noise, but music that is used to intentionally shift anyone—students, parents, teachers—into a space of active engagement. Many may feel they don't know enough about music to use it mindfully, but music is already at our fingertips. Remember, 76 percent of us already listen to music everyday![2]

From the lullabies sung to us as babies, to songs in school, to the carefully selected tracks of our teenage years, music has always been there. The oldies that make us sing along and smile, and in the tunes that help us through tough times, music is always with us.

Music allows us to connect emotionally with ourselves and others, turning passive listeners into active participants. The key is to be mindful of these connections, to curate our musical experiences with intention. We just have to recognize and meaningfully corral the treasures already within our grasp, using music to set the tone and guide our emotions in purposeful ways.

MINDFUL . . . MINDFULNESS

Mindfulness is not a one-size-fits-all concept.

The Dalai Lama helps us understand individual responsibility. In *The Art of Happiness*, he connects the development of our minds with the thought that our destination in future lives is in our hands through the taking of responsibility for ourselves. No one else can help us.[3]

Music fits into this concept perfectly. When we listen with intention, music moves from a passive experience into an active, mindful experience.

Mindfulness is deeply personal as we each search to find what resonates. If we play with the word "mindfulness" we can come up with many variations. What resonates with you?

- Mindful.
- Mind. Full.
- Mindfull.
- Mindfulness.
- Mind. Full. Ness.

Each one brings its own nuance, its own rhythm. What stands out to you? What makes you pause?

Mindfulness could also be found in the rhythmic pounding of feet on the ground during a long run, the metronomic breath syncing with each step. The movement is hypnotic, grounding, and calming, creating space to become aware of thoughts and emotions. Mindfulness provides a positive path, offering clarity of mind. What's important is that we're present, practicing self-regulation and attention in ways that support our well-being.

Mindfulness is not absolute or rigid. Most importantly, mindfulness is how we take agency over our own thoughts, behaviors, and patterns, how to be and how to take action.

We all use mindful action during the day as we become aware of choices, from what shows to watch on TV to what time to go to sleep. As a skill, mindful action can be sharpened and improved in a purposeful fashion, always improving, leading to contemplative practice.

TOO MUCH OF A GOOD THING?

A slice of cake? Delicious. Four slices? Stomachache. Even foods we consider "healthy" can prove problematic in excess—just ask any five-year-old after an October apple-picking trip!

This same concept applies to so many other areas of life.

Exercise releases endorphins and feels good, but too much? Suddenly, you're waddling instead of walking, dealing with torn muscles, and your fitness tracker declares your training "unproductive" after a twelve-mile run. Too much to reap the benefits.

Connecting with family and friends is essential for maintaining relationships, combating loneliness, and feeling supported. But what happens when we procrastinate by texting or spend hours gossiping on calls, seeking opinions for every small decision? We risk losing ourselves.

So, can we overdo mindfulness? Can we overdo mindful use of music? We don't want to drive everyone nuts so that with every moment, every tune, we have to be intentional about choices, follow up, and connections. We absolutely want music as part of our lives: an escape, a moment of peace, something to share, and for just plain old fun.

Having music play from sunrise to sunset is not the answer! As we explore throughout the book, finding the right balance brings us to mindful action for different purposes.

The *New York Times* addressed this idea in their article, "Are We Talking Too Much about Mental Health?" Mental health has become a focal point for adolescents and teenagers, but teenagers also try to diagnose themselves using TikTok or Instagram. Researchers Lucy Foulkes and Jack Andrews from Oxford University warn against "prevalence inflation"—a tendency to over-interpret symptoms, which can lead to unnecessary or even harmful self-diagnosis.[4]

In the UK, typical mindfulness interventions in schools—like breathing, being aware of physical sensations, and focusing on the present—were tested with teens. The results were disappointing. In some cases, the interventions even seemed to do more harm than good. Dr. Foulkes remarked, "It's creating this message that teenagers are vulnerable, they're likely to have problems, and the solution is to outsource them to a professional."[5]

THE SCIENCE OF BALANCE

We should be aware of balance and perspective as mindful action. Mindfulness practices, when done in moderation, can enhance emotional regulation and focus by increasing activity in the prefrontal cortex and amygdala. Too much mindfulness—especially silent meditation—can have the opposite effect, leading to emotional blunting and dissociation, where both negative and positive emotions are dulled.

While mindfulness is valuable, it needs to be practiced with balance and intention, or there's the possibility of diminishing emotional experiences. Silent meditation, for example, can be helpful for some, but may not be suitable for everyone or in every situation.

We do not want the use of music in schools or use of mindful programs to fall into the trap of incomplete research, premature conclusion, or biased reactions. Instead of pulling these programs or claiming that mindfulness isn't beneficial in schools, we need to ask ourselves: Why didn't it work? What could we do better? How can we adapt by reflecting and making thoughtful changes to have a more meaningful impact?

OUR FRIEND, GEORGE

George is twelve years old. Winter break is over, and he's finally back at school. After weeks away, George is excited to see his friends, but he feels some nervousness too. Since September, George has been practicing mindfulness with his classmates every morning in homeroom. They meditate silently through guided practice.

"Everyone in their seats! Sit down and be quiet! Hands on your laps; no more talking," the teacher starts.

Such silence feels intense to George. Silence leaves room for thoughts to spiral. "What if my friends don't talk to me today? Why does everybody hate me? Why is no one sitting with me at lunch? How come I'm not as tall as my classmates?"

We've all been there. That uncomfortable silence where the mind wanders into anxiety. George isn't alone in feeling this way.

This doesn't mean mindfulness should be discarded. Instead, we should reflect and adjust based on individual needs and purposes.

And now, a better George story.

GEORGE'S STORY, REVISITED

George is still excited but nervous to be back after the break. This time, he's looking forward to the mindfulness practice because it helps the students connect and reset, but it's a little different now.

Once everyone is signed in to the homeroom, the teacher asks the class to vote on a song for their morning practice. The playlist is full of tunes the students suggested themselves—what a beautifully diverse mix!

- "drivers license" by Olivia Rodrigo
- "So What" by Miles Davis
- "Heat Waves" by Glass Animals
- "New Rules" by Dua Lipa
- "Believer" by Imagine Dragons
- "Dynamite" by BTS
- "Winter" by Vivaldi

That day, "Believer" wins. The playlist is kept for future sessions.

As the song plays, students are encouraged to actively listen and journal about their break. Journaling could be many things–writing, drawing, doodling, or staring into space. It's up to the individual to take their own mindful action, connecting to the music.

If students wish to share, they can, but it can also be a personal release. For George, who's often anxious about his thoughts, the music provides an outlet. He feels a sense of connection with his classmates through the shared experience, without needing to speak a word. The music anchors him, helping him release his thoughts in a way that feels natural and safe.

MUSIC AS A TOOL FOR MINDFUL ACTION

MindUP, developed over twenty years ago by the Goldie Hawn Foundation, continues to be an exceptional model for contemplative practice in education. Based on four pillars—neuroscience, positive psychology, mindful awareness, and social-emotional learning—MindUP promotes emotional literacy, focus, and self-regulation, giving students the tools to thrive both academically and emotionally.

Molly Cantor, associate professor and lab director in the Speech In Context Lab at University of British Columbia, is a lead in the field of psychology and educational development at MindUP. Emphasizing the importance of self-awareness, Molly compares the regular use of MindUp to "lifting weights in the prefrontal cortex." Further explaining that "it's the exercise of noticing and bringing attention back . . . lifting the weight of focus to create those neural connections."

According to Molly, focused attention practices, such as those found in MindUP, allow students to build executive functioning skills, which are critical for goal-setting, emotional regulation, and decision-making. For students who find silent meditation intimidating, she offers an alternative: "Music could be the anchor for some of these kids," making mindfulness more accessible and engaging.

In the same spirit, MindUP collaborated with Mozart for Munchkins to create MindUP for Music cards for educators. These cards have sample engagement prompts and use QR codes as links to the music. The cards are divided into Focus, Movement, Let's Talk about It (social-emotional literacy), Brain Facts, and Journey through Music (all the sections work together).

In addition to the cards, the two organizations collaborated on a concert at Hudson Yards, engaging hundreds of families, professional development days at the United Federation of Teachers, and the start of some brain break videos.

Through this reciprocal relationship between self-awareness and contemplative practice, students are able to become more present, less reactive, and more connected to both themselves and others. Nurturing individual growth and community building, MindUP's influence reaches far beyond the classroom.

THE NEUROSCIENTIST WITH AN OPERATIC HEART

How exactly does music affect the brain on a deeper level? At the fascinating intersection of art and science stands Dr. Indre Viskontas, a remarkable figure who brings together the worlds of neuroscience and music. Indre is not only an accomplished neuroscientist with expertise in memory and the brain's relationship to music, but also a trained opera singer with a deep love for the performing arts. With a PhD in Cognitive Neuroscience from UCLA, she has built a career studying how our brains respond to music and what makes it such a powerful tool for shaping human behavior.

Indre brings a dual perspective that allows her to understand music not just as an art form, but also as a scientifically validated tool for transformation.

Indre shared insights into how music taps into the brain's dopamine system—a critical neurochemical driver of motivation. Many of us think of dopamine as the "pleasure chemical," but Dr. Indre Viskontas says that its role is actually more complex. "Dopamine is one of the main neurochemicals involved in motivation. I would say it has a bigger role in motivation than in pleasure." This distinction is important because dopamine isn't just about feeling good—it's about pushing us to *do* something, to get out of our seats and take action.

Our concern is about motivating people through music, creating that spark that will have them do something. Indre clarified that, "there's a drive that dopamine creates—a craving for something, which I think is a much more powerful motivator than the actual experience of pleasure." It's that desire, that craving for something more, that keeps us engaged—not just the reward itself.

Music can tap into this system in many ways. When we listen to music, especially the kind that resonates with us emotionally, a dopamine trigger is released, helping us push through hard things—whether a difficult workout or simply staying focused during a mundane task. Music helps us overcome obstacles by increasing our general brain arousal and, as Indre shared, "makes hard things easier."

This insight has enormous implications for how we can use music as a motivational tool in our daily lives. It's not just about feeling good in the moment but using music to drive us toward long-term goals, to make challenging tasks feel less overwhelming, and to stay engaged even when the going gets tough. As Indre remarked, "Pleasure is the death of desire . . . and it's the desire that gets you out of your seat."

Understanding this deeper function of dopamine helps us to see music not just as something we enjoy, but as a tool we can use strategically to shape our lives and build resilience. Whether getting us moving physically or helping us focus mentally, music may be linked to the very core of what drives human behavior.

A PRACTICAL FOCUS FOR ATTENTION

Music, when used mindfully, can offer a practical focus for attention, much like George's experience. Through intentional mindful listening, music helps synchronize brain waves among listeners, bringing a sense of unity and collective focus. This shared experience allows students like George to feel connected and understood, without even needing to use words.

What if this type of mindful music listening was more prevalent?

We don't need to be limited by conventional ideas about what constitutes focus. Music, when used mindfully, can offer a path to emotional balance and cognitive engagement, enhancing our ability to connect with ourselves and others.

Like our cake, our exercise, our chatty phone calls. Balance.

Curated to fit an individual's mood or environment, music becomes a personalized and dynamic mindfulness experience. Mindfulness, when integrated into daily life with music, can enrich emotional well-being without overwhelming us.

We've all faced moments of self-doubt, imposter syndrome, or self-judgment. Think about George—his inner dialogue is so common, yet rarely discussed and often harder to overcome. Purposeful listening should be nonjudgmental, for both the listener and the performer. The point of mindful listening is presence, not perfection.

Purposeful listening should be nonjudgmental for the listener, the leader, the performer, and all those touched by the music when the point of listening is presence.

Negative thoughts will come and go, and the key is not to judge ourselves for them. Perhaps the musician missed a note in the live performance—maybe we cringe for a moment, but does that fleeting error diminish the emotional impact of the piece? We're all human, and mistakes are natural.

Reflection helps us consider our experiences and adjust practices to better suit our needs, making mindfulness beneficial rather than overwhelming. Inflection—the act of responding thoughtfully to those reflections—drives meaningful growth. Together, they form a dynamic process.

For George, and maybe for all of us, reflection means recognizing the need for a more engaging form of mindfulness. Inflection came in the form of adapting his mindfulness practice to include music, creating a more supportive environment for his emotional and cognitive development. This balance between reflection and inflection is key to creating meaningful and effective mindfulness practices that cater to diverse needs.

The intersection of mindfulness and music is not about doing more, but being more intentional. Using music as the tool to bring us back to mindfulness, fully present in ourselves. When it doesn't work, we reflect and adapt, becoming active creators, leaders, and participants in our own lives.

NOTES

1. Fred Rogers, *The World According to Mister Rogers: Important Things to Remember* (Hyperion Books, 2003), 93.
2. IFPI, "Engaging with Music 2021."

3. Dalai Lama and Howard C. Cutler, *The Art of Happiness: A Handbook for Living* (Riverhead Books, 1998).

4. Ellen Barry, "Are We Talking Too Much about Mental Health?" *New York Times*, last modified May 6, 2024, https://www.nytimes.com/2024/05/06/health/mental-health-schools.html.

5. Ellen Barry, "Are We Talking Too Much about Mental Health?"

Chapter 4

Themes and Variations

MUSIC AS A NECESSITY, NOT A LUXURY: THEMES AND VARIATIONS USING MUSIC

Music "brings us together, helping us reflect upon who we are, where we have come from, and what lies ahead." The arts and music transcend "languages, cultures, and borders" . . . and help "exchange ideas and styles and share in the artistic vibrancy born from diverse experiences and traditions." —President Obama[1]

THREADS

- Music is more than entertainment.
- History and the present use provide examples of how music has intentionally been used to shape environments, emotions, intentions, and actions.
- Are we making the most of music?

This chapter and the next present a legato view that music brings to our lives historically, in the present, and prospectively. Music is a necessity, not just a luxury.

While both chapters dive into history and culture, this chapter is about *how* music has been used outside of schools, for example, by presidents, hospitals, doctors, and the entertainment industry. The next chapter focuses on the possibilities of how music *can* be used in history and literature, connecting the cultural and emotional significance of the past with our present realities.

Music too often slips into the background, serving as filler rather than something deeply intentional. In places like offices, hospitals, and even our homes, music could be so much more—building community, healing emotions, and enhancing focus. When we consciously apply music, it has the potential not only to just impact our individual experiences but also entire communities.

BENJAMIN FRANKLIN: MUSIC AS MINDFUL INVENTION

On a quiet evening in 1761, Benjamin Franklin—a statesman, inventor, and musician—sits down to play his newly invented glass armonica. An invention born from the simple pleasure of making a goblet sing by running a finger along its edge.

Franklin's glass armonica was an instrument uniquely suited to mindfulness. Its gentle, calming sound was said to evoke deep emotions and encourage reflective thought. Even Franklin himself remarked on how much personal satisfaction the instrument brought him.

Wolfgang Amadeus Mozart and Ludwig van Beethoven, among others, even composed pieces specifically for the glass armonica, as its popularity grew across Europe.

Calming anxious patients in hospitals, the glass armonica's soothing tones were even thought to have therapeutic effects. This early recognition of music's potential to promote well-being is closely tied to Franklin's broader belief in the importance of music as a tool for building community and emotional harmony.

Though wildly popular for a time, the glass armonica eventually fell out of favor, partly due to rumors that its sound could drive listeners mad—a testament to its emotionally powerful and often eerie timbre. Even in the armonica's decline, the instrument shows how deeply music can impact the human mind. The glass armonica does still exist, with current models sounding like a pipe organ—ethereal and bright.

In this way, Franklin's legacy reflects the idea that music, when used with mindful intention, can serve as a powerful connector—both between individuals and within the larger community.

FRANKLIN D. ROOSEVELT: FOLK MUSIC AND NATIONAL RESILIENCE

Two centuries later, another Franklin—Franklin D. Roosevelt—was leading the country through one of its darkest times: the Great Depression. As economic hardship gripped the nation, Roosevelt understood that people needed more than policies and speeches to keep hope alive. They needed connection. They needed resilience. And music, especially folk music, became a cornerstone of his leadership.

During his famous fireside chats, Roosevelt spoke directly to the people, offering reassurance in the face of uncertainty. The broadcasts often began with musical preludes, setting a reflective and hopeful tone. While Roosevelt didn't initiate the Federal Music Project, he supported its mission as part of the larger Works Progress Administration (WPA). The Federal Music Project provided jobs for unemployed musicians and brought free concerts to the public, featuring folk songs that told the stories of ordinary Americans.

Songs like Woody Guthrie's "This Land is Your Land" captured the spirit of perseverance and solidarity. Music became a way for Americans to reflect on their struggles while staying grounded in the present and reminding them to look toward a brighter future. Roosevelt's mindful use of music helped calm a nation's collective anxiety and offered an emotional balm during hard times.

JOHN F. KENNEDY: MUSIC AS CULTURAL DIPLOMACY

In the 1960s, President John F. Kennedy continued the tradition of using music as a powerful connector. He invited musicians from all over the world, from classical to jazz, to perform at the White House. By using music as a connector, it became a bridge between cultures and as a way to highlight the value of diversity.

One of the most memorable White House performances was by renowned cellist Pablo Casals in 1962. Casals's performance was not just a musical event; it was a symbolic gesture of peace and cultural exchange during the height of the Cold War. As Kennedy once remarked, "The life of the arts is very close to the center of a nation's purpose."[2] For him, music was a mindful way of promoting unity, both at home and abroad.

Perhaps Kennedy's most impactful use of music with intention came in his support of the Civil Rights Movement. Artists like Harry Belafonte and Marian Anderson, who were both vocal advocates for civil rights, performed at events tied to the Kennedy administration. Their performances created an emotional connection between the movement and the American people, using music as a form of mindful action to inspire empathy.

ABRAHAM LINCOLN: MUSIC AS MORALE AND PURPOSE IN WARTIME

Perhaps no president understood the power of music to build community during times of crisis more than Abraham Lincoln. During the Civil War,

Lincoln often turned to music to boost morale and inspire a sense of purpose among soldiers and civilians. Songs like "The Battle Hymn of the Republic" became rallying cries for the Union cause, reinforcing the moral righteousness of their fight.

Lincoln knew the value of mindful listening. Before battles, Union bands would play to calm the soldiers' nerves and prepare them mentally for the challenges ahead. As historian James McPherson notes, music played a crucial role in maintaining morale among the troops, reinforcing a sense of purpose and unity that was essential to the Union's ultimate victory.

Even in moments of triumph, Lincoln used music as a bridge for healing. After the Confederate surrender at Appomattox, Lincoln requested that the band play "Dixie," a Southern anthem saying, "That tune is now ours as much as theirs."[3] His gesture was symbolic—an attempt to reunite the divided nation through music. In that moment, Lincoln showed that mindful use of music could heal even the deepest wounds of division.

MUSICAL MICROECOSYSTEMS

Office buildings, banks, doctors' offices, and even our homes are distinct opportunities to establish tone, promote healing, evoke emotions, build community, and develop joy. Our lives are filled with natural moments of connection through music.

If we know music helps with focus and emotion, and even healing, shouldn't it have a greater presence? Sure, there's a television high on a wall in a patients' room for viewing pleasure. We can even tune in to a radio or streaming session from our hospital beds to hear a playlist created by others and considered to be good for most patients. But how mindful is that?

Music can be used to create micro ecosystems throughout our lives.

Some healthcare institutions are beginning to embrace this idea. At the MD Anderson Cancer Center, music is prescribed for patients as a therapeutic intervention. They have found that "intubated and even fully sedated patients under general anesthesia respond positively to prescribed music. The patient does not need to be conscious or aware. Simply being in the same room while the music plays lowers levels of stress biomarkers and improves hemodynamic stabilities."[4]

This is a huge step in integrating music into holistic care. New organizations like Social Prescribing USA are aiming to make social prescribing—referring patients to non-clinical activities like music therapy—available to every American by 2035. This innovate approach involves referring patients to non-clinical activities, including music, to improve mental and emotional health. Whether it's recommending participation in a local choir, suggesting therapeutic drumming, or even listening to a curated playlist, healthcare professionals are using music as a form of medicine to combat loneliness, anxiety, and depression.

In the UK, music has become a crucial element of social prescribing programs. Patients struggling with mental health issues are encouraged to engage in music groups, attend concerts, or even compose their own songs. These programs not only improve emotional well-being but also reconnect individuals back to a sense of community and purpose, much like Roosevelt did with folk music during the Depression.

MUSIC AS A NECESSITY, NOT A LUXURY

Oliver Sacks wrote, "Music can lift us out of depression or move us to tears—it is a remedy, a tonic, orange juice for the ear. But for many of my neurological patients, music is even more—it can provide access, even when no medication can, to movement, to speech, to life."[5]

We have no shortage of stories to share about the medical professionals and their gentle, loving care. There are fewer stories about the mindful use of music by the profession, but still ample examples exist.

Alan Goldblatt recently retired as a geriatric, hospice, and palliative care physician. Just writing that sentence fills us with awe and gratitude for a remarkable person, and for all those who care for our family and friends at the end of their lives.

Alan incorporated music into his care in a way that he believes can truly transform the experience of patients and their families during some of life's most difficult moments. His extensive experience with patients across all walks of life has shown him the power of music beyond mere entertainment. "Music can have an extraordinary effect on the well-being of patients and their families when they are facing advanced disease or death," Alan shared. He also explained how the team he works with strives to reach beyond the limits of traditional medical treatments, emphasizing that this healing is about more than just physical well-being.

"We work as a team, constantly trying to reach beyond the limits of medical treatments in order to provide a holistic path to 'healing.'" Recounting the profound effects he's seen as a doctor, Alan states that "even as a bystander, witnessing the calming effect of a live singer's voice at the bedside of a dying person evokes the deepest emotions." He describes these moments as "communication without words," which helps cleanse and focus the emotions surrounding those difficult bedside moments.

The gratitude of patients is one of the most powerful aspects of music therapy. Alan says, "For the responsive patients, the gratitude that radiates from the recipient is often evident, as words seem insufficient to compensate for the warmth and loving nature of this gift."

What exactly is music therapy? According to a study Alan references, music therapy offers concrete benefits. In a 2005 study by R. E. Hilliard, "six out of eleven studies showed significant outcomes which supported the value of music therapy," including positive effects such as pain reduction, reduced anxiety, and improved relaxation and energy levels.[6]

Alan outlines the methods music therapists use: "Music therapists use many methods to connect with their clients and families, such as assisted songwriting, improvisation, lyric analysis, singing, and instrument playing." He notes that therapists also use techniques such as guided imagery, helping patients deal with emotional challenges like anxiety, depression, and fear, while addressing physical symptoms like pain and shortness of breath.

Music therapy addresses the whole person—physically, emotionally, and spiritually. Alan shares how the spiritual element of music plays a unique role, offering "familiar rituals which can bring solace" and helping to ease the feeling of isolation that can worsen during illness.

> Kremena Bikov, RN, BSN, a hospice nurse shares a story on the unique power of music:
>
> "I feel that the effects of music on our patients have always been deeply personal, and witnessing that for me has been rare. What I can speak to more credibly is the effect music has had on me during such times.
>
> "We were about to compassionately extubate an elderly patient, whose daughter was bereft, crying inconsolably and, at times, hyperventilating (I needed to attend to her more at that time). As per the procedure, we had our music therapist present to play music during the extubation process.
>
> "She started, softly at first. Then as the ETT was being removed, she began playing more loudly in order to drown the sound associated with extubation. I felt grounded, relieved, and calmer for knowing that there was a gentler sound that this patient's daughter was perceiving at that moment.
>
> I also remember Claire, another certified music therapist, playing ukulele and singing beautifully at an extubation that was very similar, during the care of one of our very young pediatric patients—a baby boy, a few months old. I sat holding him while Georgia played soft melodies, adjusting in response to his reactions. The vibrations felt soothing and intimate, and enhanced the experience of the moment. Paradoxically, the whole atmosphere was imbued with a feeling of normalcy, as if a healthy baby was being rocked to sleep."

Dr. Goldblatt and Nurse Bikov lived experiences support the research of music leading to personal, emotional connections. They've learned that music can break down the vulnerability barriers that prevent communication and provide a space for meaningful and compassionate dialogue, even during the most difficult moments in life.

TAKE TWO

Hollywood has long understood the power of music. From the early days of animation, tv shows, movies—and music leads us to feel, to understand.

Before movies had words, they had music. Silent films relied on live or recorded scores to convey mood, exaggerate character movements, and set the tone. Music can purposefully even misdirect us ("Watch out, the bad guy is coming!" to "Just kidding, everyone is ok"). The composer and director intentionally pick music to steer the audience's emotions—whether heightening suspense or providing comic relief.

Hollywood's strategic use of music is a form of mindful storytelling. Specially curated sounds becomes the vehicle that carries the audience's emotions. This mirrors how music in educational and therapeutic settings can be used for focus, emotional awareness, and even to create purposeful moments of reflection. It's no coincidence that both the entertainment industry and mindfulness practices leverage music to cultivate an experience where the listener can become fully absorbed, grounded in the present moment.

Terry Thoren, the former CEO of Klasky Csupo, Inc.—the company that incubated *The Simpsons* and produced *Rugrats*, *The Wild Thornberrys*, and *Rocket Power*—is now the CEO of Wonder Media. Terry's ongoing work is based on his singular success and effective use of animation and music to connect with children to create healthy lifestyles.

When Terry and his team create animations, they build on the students' sense of what's familiar so that they can learn to describe what the characters say, what they see, and what they hear (the music and sound effects). Music enhances the animation experience by:

- setting the tone,
- supporting the narrative,
- adding personality,
- building tension, and
- highlighting moments.

Whether in animation or other media, a similar list can be generated to describe the importance of music. In chapter 9, a discussion with Shara Senderoff, explores how imagination and music merge with new technologies to enhance imagination and mindfulness.

THE SONGS OF FAMILIES

"Just give my love to mother, she'll know how much I love her, and tell her not to weep for me; for I know we'll meet again." These deeply sweet and troubling lines from the traditional American folk song "Just before the Battle, Mother" were written by George F. Root during the American Civil War.

Expressing a soldier's thoughts and emotions as he prepares for battle, this song reflects his love and concern for his mother. The words so strongly reflect the poignant feelings of soldiers facing the uncertainty of war and the deep emotional bonds they share with their loved ones that this song lasted for decades as a salute to soldiers and their families.

"From the Halls of Montezuma to the shores of Tripoli, we fight our country's battles in the air, on land, and sea." How many Marine mothers and fathers sing this song, bringing back so many memories? Semper fidelis. We guess that the songs of families included belting out this song. Ours sure did.

Although the memories of sweet songs and lullabies from childhood have faded for many of us, we know they are still in our memories somewhere. The songs reflected the moods and struggles of their time. As with many of us, we do not fully understand until later in life how meaningful family songs are.

Many of us have similar stories with our music and memories. Music is personal, creates emotions, and we are often in a passive / dynamic relationship to music. What if we built on those experiences more mindfully? Is it possible for us to go beyond the familiar, to find time to expand our playlists, to personalize those playlists by time of day, mood, or context? For example, we often ask our electronic friends to play oldies, or all news, or top hits, and then we say, "skip" when a song comes up that doesn't please us. That's a mindful action.

MUSIC AND MINDFUL INTENTION: A LASTING LEGACY

Whether you're a leader guiding a nation, a doctor prescribing an unconventional yet effective treatment, or a composer creating the next great film score, the message is the same: Music, when used with mindful intention, becomes more than just sound. Each note becomes a shared human experience that uplifts, heals, and connects.

As we reflect, it becomes clear that music, when used with mindful intention, has the power to transform not only individual lives but entire communities. Whether bringing people together in times of crisis or inspiring them to dream of a better future, music holds a unique place in the human experience—with still to be imagined potential.

NOTES

1. Barack Obama, Message to the World Choir Games, Shaoxing, China, 2010.
2. John F. Kennedy, "Remarks at Amherst College," October 26, 1963.
3. James M. McPherson, *Battle Cry of Freedom: The Civil War Era* (Oxford University Press, 1988).
4. Caroline Brennan, "What Is Music Medicine?" *Cancerwise*, October 31, 2023, https://www.mdanderson.org/cancerwise/what-is-music-medicine.h00-159622590.html.
5. Oliver Sacks, *Musicophilia: Tales of Music and the Brain* (Knopf, 2007), xi.
6. Russell E. Hilliard, "Music Therapy in Hospice and Palliative Care: A Review of the Empirical Data," *Evidence-based Complementary and Alternative Medicine* 2, no. 2 (2005): 173–178, https://doi.org/10.1093/ecam/neh076.

Chapter 5

Forte

Building on Possibilities

After silence, that which comes nearest to expressing the inexpressible is music. —Aldous Huxley[1]

THREADS

- Teachers and artists compose, deliberate, and curate.
- Resources to come back to these ideas time and time again. As the seasons change, we change and music changes.
- Our musical choices might not be yours, and that's okay.

THE FAMILIAR . . . A STARTING PLACE

Taylor Swift's song "Shake It Off" (yes, her again), has over three billion music video views as of the summer of 2024. What joy there is in watching the Swifties of the world and other wonderful, stirring, moving, exciting musical movements over the years. Wow, did people swoon over Frank Sinatra, fall in love with Elvis Presley, Kenny Chesney, Eminem, Sheryl Crow, Tevye, the Phantom, and dance along with Britney Spears! Not everyone liked them. Of course not. That's the point. Music is for everyone. But not all music is for everyone.

During an assembly for elementary school kids, the cello played long, flowing melodies while the piano mimicked the sparkling water in Camille Saint-Saëns's "The Swan." The students waved scarves in the air, creating swirls of color to match the ripples of water, moving them however they liked. As the piano notes cascaded down to the final chord, the brass section interrupted with a low note, cutting off the piano. From that low note came another, just a half step apart—the familiar *Jaws* theme, or as the kids recognized it, "Baby Shark."

The room erupted with singing, and the familiar hand motions to the song took over. There was laughter, dancing, and the band moved into the audience to sing with the kids. When it was all over, the band asked, "Now, why in the world did we interrupt the beautiful calm of 'The Swan'?"

Two notes played one after the other can signal to a whole room that the mood is changing. This doesn't mean the swaying sounds of "The Swan" are any less impactful, but it shows that every piece of music can have a purpose. Those simple two notes were a conversation, a bridge, a cue for a new, familiar song. They connected all of us.

"Baby Shark" is the first YouTube music video *ever* to reach 10 billion views.[2] Grandparents wonder how they can shake off that one! But the excitement and movement it brings to children all over the world is undeniable. Children request it. Parents play it. And everyone sings along. Moods are raised, smiles abound, and hand movements are universal. What if we could expand that feeling with other music, personalized by family? What a dream, what a possibility.

OPPORTUNITIES ... MUSIC EVERYWHERE

Presenting intentional moments of music, developing expanded playlists, and making connections to our exciting world are opportunities we are presented with each day in organizations, schools, and personal moments.

Early on in our time at elementary school we begin to learn our history—our own and that of the world. Because music is ubiquitous, too often thought of as an elective, not an essential subject, few of us have learned history that includes the music that helped shape cultures. Countries went to war, often led into battle by a fife and drum. How many of us have heard those tunes, let alone understood their role in rallying troops and uniting people?

Music and history are not parallel or separate; they are part of a whole.

Our national stage has many examples of music as an integral part of human rights, both cultural and political movements, that should be part of what we learn.

Music has always set the tone at presidential inaugurations, offering a glimpse into each administration's values. FDR used "Happy Days Are Here Again" in 1933, symbolizing hope during the Great Depression. Dwight D. Eisenhower's 1953 inauguration featured patriotic standards like "Hail to the

Chief." JFK invited Marian Anderson to sing the national anthem in 1961, a powerful moment during the civil rights era. Bill Clinton used Fleetwood Mac's "Don't Stop" at his 1993 inauguration, capturing optimism for the future. Barack Obama featured Aretha Franklin singing "My Country, 'Tis of Thee" in 2009, emphasizing unity. Ronald Reagan included "America the Beautiful" in 1981 to evoke national pride, while George W. Bush continued the patriotic theme with "God Bless America" in 2001. Joe Biden's 2021 inauguration featured "This Land Is Your Land" and "Amazing Grace," calling for unity and healing. These musical choices reflect each president's message and the mood of the nation at the time.

Before Marian Anderson was invited to sing for JFK, she was denied the right to perform at Constitution Hall by the Daughters of the American Revolution. Constitution Hall holds 3,702 audience members. Instead of walking away, she used her music to communicate her message for equal rights, standing on the steps of the Lincoln Memorial. That day, Anderson performed outdoors to an integrated audience of 75,000 people.

She opened with an emotional rendition of "My Country, 'Tis of Thee," followed by an aria from Donizetti's *La Favorite*, Schubert's "Ave Maria," and spirituals like "Gospel Train" and "Trampin." Her voice, the majestic notes, and compelling rhythms of her performance still resonate with us today, carrying powerful lessons of struggle, resilience, and enduring strength. Moments like these in history create connections and impact generations.

There are countless examples of what could be included in our curriculum. We can gain insight through the music and the musicians of different eras from the people of that time to the human struggles and joys. Music has strengthened and brought together communities for over 40,000 years. From the earliest documented flutes and drum circles to Beyoncé as a theme song for a presidential campaign, music has always been a powerful reflection of the human experience.

Music gives life to the pages of history books.

Incorporating the music and history of the time can make learning more engaging and memorable. We'll explore some sample lesson plans in the next chapter, but the answer is clear: history is more meaningful when we create associations with what is familiar. By making interdisciplinary connections, we not only make history come to life but enhance retention and understanding. The more connections we make, the deeper our learning experience becomes.

What of the literature we read? Of course there is a connection to music, even if we don't learn about it when we read books. We learn to analyze the prose, look for symbols, study syntax; yet, we do not hear the music of the time, or the music in the book. We have all taken a course or two in Shakespeare. Is there no music in his work? Hmph. What about:

Twelfth Night, "O Mistress Mine," Feste:
O mistress mine, where are you roaming? O, stay and hear; your true-love's coming, That can sing both high and low . . .
As You Like It, "Under the Greenwood Tree," Amiens:
Under the greenwood tree, Who loves to lie with me, And turn his merry note Unto the sweet bird's throat . . .
Othello, "Willow Song," Desdemona:
The poor soul sat sighing by a sycamore tree, Sing all a green willow; Her hand on her bosom, her head on her knee, Sing willow, willow, willow . . .
Henry VIII, "Orpheus with His Lute," a song performed during a masque:
Orpheus with his lute made trees, And the mountain tops that freeze, Bow themselves when he did sing . . .

Play on, William. Play on.

And not just Shakespeare. Music is more than a backdrop. As a driving force in literature, music plays an integral role in shaping themes, characters, and narratives. Music in literature often reflects inner landscapes and external realities, offering mindful experiences for characters and readers alike.

Isn't a reading list itself just like a playlist of books?

Literature and music are so wonderfully intertwined in so many great books, a short list was hard to make. So, here's the long reading list you never knew you needed:

- *The Great Gatsby* by F. Scott Fitzgerald (1925) features jazz music as a symbol of the era's decadence and the characters' pursuit of the American Dream.
- *Song of Solomon* by Toni Morrison (1977) references a biblical book, but within the novel, folk songs and oral traditions play a crucial role.
- *A Clockwork Orange* by Anthony Burgess (1962) shows the protagonist, Alex, as having an intense love for classical music, particularly Beethoven.
- *High Fidelity* by Nick Hornby (1995) is deeply infused with pop and rock music culture. The protagonist, Rob Fleming, is a record store owner who constantly references music as he navigates his relationships and personal growth.
- *Daisy Jones & The Six* by Taylor Jenkins Reid (2019) is presented as an oral history of a fictional 1970s rock band, Daisy Jones & The Six.
- *The Ensemble* by Aja Gabel (2018) follows the lives of four musicians in a string quartet over the course of nearly two decades.
- *The Music Shop* by Rachel Joyce (2017) tells the story of Frank, a music shop owner who has a unique talent for finding the perfect record to heal each of his customers' emotional wounds.

- *A Visit from the Goon Squad* by Jennifer Egan (2010) showcases music as a central motif in this Pulitzer Prize-winning novel. The characters' lives revolve around the music industry, and Egan uses rock and punk as a metaphor for rebellion, change, and the passage of time.
- *The Wind-Up Bird Chronicle* by Haruki Murakami (1994) continually references classical music, jazz, and pop songs shaping the surreal atmosphere. Music becomes a bridge between the ordinary and the fantastical, much like in Shakespeare's plays where songs transition between scenes and emotions.
- *Bel Canto* by Ann Patchett (2001) revolves around a hostage situation at a lavish party where a famous opera singer performs. Opera becomes a way for the hostages and captors to communicate beyond words, transcending their situation.
- *The Goldfinch* by Donna Tartt (2013) references classical music and opera, and music serves as an undercurrent to the characters' emotional turmoil and intellectual engagement.

We want to know our important historical figures as people, not stick figures. What music did they listen to? What music might have stirred them up or calmed them down? Let's hear the music of their lives and ask critical, analytical questions about how music might have affected them, or why they listened to certain music.

George Washington said, "Nothing is more agreeable, and ornamental, than good music."[3] What might he have enjoyed during his presidency? Insight to his musical preferences might give us greater understanding of our founding father. Since we don't have that, how about this as an imaginary playlist:

- "Yankee Doodle"
- "The British Grenadiers"
- "Greensleeves"
- "Chester" by William Billings
- "The Soldiers' Dance"
- "Amazing Grace"

Capturing the dramatic transformation of John Newton after surviving a violent storm at sea in 1748, "Amazing Grace" was written in 1772. The remarkable history of this song ties together so many important periods, a thread over time. The lyrics reflect his personal journey from a life of sin to redemption through God's grace.

One song, heard by Americans for over 250 years. Wow.

What if we created a playlist of "Amazing Grace" variations? Each version would capture the mood, culture, and emotions of its time—from gospel to bagpipes, to presidential memories and civil rights marches.

Thinking about the long arc of music stretching back through American history gives us chills. President George W. Bush referenced "Amazing Grace" in speeches and used the famous melody as connection during memorial services following the events of September 11, 2001.

From president to president: Barack Obama sang "Amazing Grace" during his eulogy for Reverend Clementa Pinckney in 2015, after the tragic Charleston church shooting.

And one song's impact continues . . . featured in films and television shows, often underscoring moments of emotional intensity or transformation, the hymn was part of films such as *Silkwood* (1983), *Coal Miner's Daughter* (1980), and *The Shawshank Redemption* (1994).

Although we don't know exactly what each president might have listened to, Barack Obama shares his musical playlists for each season on social media. Summer 2024 included eighty-eight songs from various groups and musicians such as the Rolling Stones and Etta James.

What if we could go back in time and check out Instagram post from all historical figures to see what they were listening to each year, and more importantly, why?

Yes, we know we are getting carried away, but isn't it fun to think about how music might have been included in our learning? How the words on the page could have taken fanciful and stirring flight to help us better understand.

We could continue writing about music in math, science, physical education, and sports.

Why, we wonder, is this such an occasional part of our education yet an integral part of our lives? To show we're not just screaming through a megaphone we constructed, how about some research support:

- Music can be used as a pedagogical tool to introduce and reinforce concepts in history, science, literature, and other subjects. A study published in the *Psychology of Music* found that music can significantly improve retention and recall of information when used in educational contexts.[4]
- Overemphasis on standardized testing often limits the broader cultural and artistic aspects of education. A study published in the *American Educational*

Research Journal points out that this focus can limit creativity and critical thinking.[5]
- A study published in the *Journal of Educational Psychology* concluded that incorporating music into lessons can capture students' interest and make learning more enjoyable, leading to better academic outcomes.[6]

Perhaps our curriculum is so text-based and state test focused that we have lost sight of how to expand what our students learn, excluding as core competencies the culture of the times. Our remarkable teachers are on their own to develop ways to bring learners into the curriculum. When a teacher starts a new unit, or gives the homework assignment for the next day, wouldn't we have a better chance of capturing the students' minds through music? We get excited about the possibilities of reversing the order of the curriculum, starting with music as a hook, the lever to history, science, literature, physical education, and much more!

A LEADER'S CONVERSATION ABOUT MUSIC

In a personal and touching conversation with Greg Hutchings, former superintendent of schools in Alexandria, VA, and Shaker Heights, OH, we talked about his playlist of gospel music. As we reflected on the history of enslaved people in our country, we came up with a few songs that might have been sung in the 1860s and in the following decades, but could not name one instance when the songs were part of the retelling of that history.

Imagine if part of the history of the 1860s included more than just dates and events—if it brought to life the experiences and voices of the people who lived during that time. During the 1860s, enslaved African Americans sang a variety of spirituals, work songs, and folk songs that were deeply rooted in their experiences of oppression, hope, resistance, and faith. These songs carried stories of struggle and resilience, providing emotional strength and a sense of community in the face of unimaginable hardship. A quick online search found five songs that enslaved people might have sung during that period:

- "Swing Low, Sweet Chariot" is a spiritual song believed to have been composed before 1862 by Wallace Willis, a Choctaw. The song speaks of hope and the longing for freedom, with "sweet chariot" symbolizing the Underground Railroad or the journey to heaven.
- "Wade in the Water" is a song of faith but also a coded message for escaping enslaved people. The lyrics are said to have been a guide for how to escape to avoid being tracked by dogs by traveling through water.

- "Go Down, Moses" symbolized the enslaved people's desire for liberation from bondage. The song was a rallying cry for resistance and hope.
- "Follow the Drinking Gourd" was perhaps a code for the Underground Railroad, with the "drinking gourd" referring to the Big Dipper constellation, which points to the North Star.
- "Steal Away (To Jesus)" is a song of religious devotion and a coded signal indicating an upcoming secret gathering or escape.

When we want to gain cultural awareness, understanding, and respect for one another, too often we rely on cultural awareness days or fairs. We bring in foods and traditions of our cultures to share with classmates or colleagues. That's all well and good, but not sufficient. What about weaving music and culture throughout the curriculum and office, not as an adjunct but as a core part of our knowledge.

There are remarkable opportunities for us to come together through music with purposeful inclusion in our schools, conversations, and connections. Even trained musicians! Here are several songs that might be used to build a playlist as part of contemporary discussions:

- "Alright" by Kendrick Lamar (2015), became an unofficial anthem for the Black Lives Matter movement with its message of resilience and hope.
- "Freedom" by Beyoncé ft. Kendrick Lamar (2016). R&B / Hip-Hop on Beyoncé's critically acclaimed album *Lemonade*.
- "Lift Every Voice and Sing." A gospel / spiritual song often referred to as the "Black National Anthem." The song, originally written in 1900 by James Weldon Johnson, continues to be a powerful symbol of strength and resistance.

Several states' published competencies explain how culture, music, and mindful action might be part of a social sciences approach to who we are as Americans. For example, The Virginia Standards of Learning, revised in 2023, include:

Grade 11: Virginia and United States History

The standards for Virginia and United States History expand upon the foundational knowledge and skills previously introduced to include the historical development of American ideas and institutions from the Age of Exploration to the present. While continuing to focus on political, geographic, and economic history, the standards provide students with a basic knowledge of American culture through a chronological survey of major issues, movements, people, and events in Virginia and United States history. As a foundation to develop historical thinking skills, students will apply social science skills to understand the challenges facing the development of the United States. These skills will support the investigation and evaluation of the fundamental political principles, events, people, and ideas that developed and fostered our American identity and led to our country's prominence in world affairs.

The door is wide open to include music and visual arts in understanding the people and the events of the time. We look at this as an invitation for a curriculum to include stories and culture of the time.

Our point is not to critique any state or business for its list of competencies. We want to offer possibilities to look at each other and to engage one another in a way which is core to nearly all humans . . . through music.

We can better understand our neighbors through music. Our Latino neighbors have certainly contributed to our American culture and continue to shape who we are. One of the top music videos worldwide is "Despacito" by Luis Fonsi featuring Daddy Yankee with over eight billion views on YouTube. Beyond the pop charts, Latino music encompasses rich traditions and diverse styles that tell stories of heritage and identity:

- "La Bamba"—a traditional Mexican folk song from the state of Veracruz that dates back to at least the eighteenth century and was popularized internationally by Ritchie Valens in 1958.
- Tango—founded in Buenos Aires, Argentina, and Montevideo, Uruguay, tango emerged in the late nineteenth century in working-class neighborhoods, beginning as a dance and musical form combining African, Native American, and European influences.
- Salsa—with roots in Cuba and Puerto Rico that developed in the 1960s and 1970s in New York City, salsa is a fusion of Cuban son, mambo, and other Afro-Cuban music styles, mixed with jazz and Puerto Rican influences.
- Reggaeton—a style of music that originated in Puerto Rico in the early 1990s, blending Latin Caribbean music styles such as reggae, dancehall, and hip-hop with Latin rhythms. The genre gained widespread popularity in the early 2000s with artists like Daddy Yankee ("Gasolina"), and later, with artists like Bad Bunny and J Balvin.

Music played a significant role in the United Farm Workers (UFW) movement, led by César Chávez, particularly during the grape pickers' strike in the 1960s. Songs were used to rally workers, raise morale, and spread the message of the movement:

- "De Colores" was a traditional Spanish folk song that became an anthem for the United Farm Workers.
- "No Nos Moverán" ("We Shall Not Be Moved") was originally a gospel hymn, before being adapted into Spanish and becoming a powerful protest song.
- "El Picket Sign" was written by El Teatro Campesino, a theater group founded by Luis Valdez.

Music is a vital tool for organizing, educating, and motivating. Helping to create a sense of community and purpose, reinforcing the values of solidarity and resistance, the songs associated with the UFW and César Chávez continue to be powerful symbols of the farmworker struggle and the broader fight for social justice.

Palestinian music reflects the region's rich cultural heritage, struggles, and hopes. Traditional folk music as well as contemporary styles address political and social issues. Some notable Palestinian artists and songs:

- "Ya Halali Ya Mali" by Mohammed Assaf, a singer from Gaza, gained international fame after winning *Arab Idol* in 2013.
- "Al Kufiyyeh 3arabeyeh" by Shadia Mansour, known as the "First Lady of Arabic Hip-Hop," is a Palestinian-British artist.
- "The Dream" by Rim Banna, who was a Palestinian singer and composer from Nazareth known for her modern interpretations of traditional Palestinian songs and lullabies.

We can continue to go around the world to make the point that music is an important way to gain understanding of ourselves, our culture, and of others. That quiet moment leading to mindful action is when we purposefully consider going beyond the familiar.

The possibilities are so exciting, almost endless, when we think about music in America, shaping our understanding of one another. What about exploring Israeli, Ukrainian, Somalian, French, Russian, and Chinese music? We could name every country's music! To look closely at what goes on in our schools is to see that we ask each other to learn the names and dates of key events, the broad social and economic reasons for the events, and to memorize some important language from key documents. Mindful action would give us pause to think about possibilities and build on what makes us groove.

NOTES

1. Aldous Huxley, *Music at Night and Other Essays* (Chatto & Windus, 1931), 19.
2. Sanj Atwal, "Baby Shark Becomes First YouTube Video to Reach 10 billion Views," Guinness World Book of Records, last modified January 19, 2022, https://www.guinnessworldrecords.com/news/2022/1/baby-shark-becomes-first-youtube-video-to-reach-10-billion-views-689527.
3. George Washington, "General Orders, June 4, 1777," in *The Writings of George Washington from the Original Manuscript Sources, 1745–1799, Vol. 8*, ed. John C. Fitzpatrick (United States Government Printing Office, 1931), 181–182.
4. Karen M. Ludke, Fernanda Ferreira, and Katie Overy, "Singing Can Facilitate Foreign Language Learning," *Psychology of Music* 42, no. 3 (January 2014): 389–403, https://doi.org/10.3758/s13421-013-0342-5.
5. Wayne Au, "High-Stakes Testing and Curricular Control: A Qualitative Metasynthesis," *American Educational Research Journal* 44, no. 3 (June/July 2007): 594–629, https://doi.org/10.3102/0013189X07306523.
6. Susan Hallam, "The Power of Music: Its Impact on the Intellectual, Social and Personal Development of Children and Young People," *International Journal of Music Education* 28, no. 3 (August 2010): 269–289, https://doi.org/10.1177/0255761410370658.

Chapter 6

Tacet

Focus, Centering as an Essential Disposition

You can't depend on your eyes when your imagination is out of focus.

—Mark Twain[1]

THREADS

- Music is our focus—purposeful action is our goal.
- Why do we need focus?
- Nurturing ourselves and others through purposeful action . . . trickle down, ripple effect.

Focus is important, even essential, in personal development, in educational settings, at home, and at work. By practicing active listening at home and in schools, individuals can improve their concentration and attention, leading to better executive functioning. In this chapter, we'll discuss how music can enhance focus and awareness by using strategies that create lasting habits. Through this lens, we're not just listening to music—we're becoming artists of sound (figure 6.1).

BECOMING ARTISTS OF SOUND

Early one Saturday morning, a diverse group of educators, neuroscientists, thought leaders, and artists gathered for a day of exploration at a Neuro-Arts conference. These thought leaders are often the presenters, so this was a rare opportunity to be an

Figure 6.1. *Courtesy of* Little Mozart Foundation, *photography by Juan Patino.*

audience member soaking in the knowledge and experiences shared by the practitioners.

The stage was set for an inspiring session featuring David Levanthal, the founding teacher and program director for Dance for PD, and the world-renowned soprano Renée Fleming. Both are not only brilliant artists but also passionate advocates for the healing power of the arts and the profound connection between mind and body.

As the attendees settled into their seats, Renée began by discussing the importance of diaphragmatic breathing. She led the audience through a series of inhales and exhales, grounding everyone in the rhythm of their bodies. In that moment, the room—filled with people from the Kennedy Center, the National Endowment for the Arts, neuroscientists, performers, and more—was united in this simple but powerful exercise.

Moments later, music began to play. David encouraged everyone to rise to their feet and become artists of sound. He guided their movements, suggesting they use their arms as paint brushes to "paint" the sounds they heard. As the music swelled, he encouraged more freeform movement, urging everyone to feel and react to the music in their own way. This exercise was not just about dance but about actively listening and being fully present, a lesson grounded in Renée's initial breathing exercise.

Smiles and nervous laughter preceded lots of movement as neuroscientists swayed alongside performers, and educators moved in rhythm with thought leaders. Each person in the room listened for cues, reacting as one, as they shared a transformative experience. This idea is reinforced by the therapeutic power of music, where sound and movement have been shown to improve attention and cognitive flexibility.[2]

This work is for everyone, not just children, and not just musicians or educators.

The remarkable collaborators who developed the NeuroArts Blueprint recognize the role between artists and scientists perfectly:

"Artists have always understood the power of the arts to heal and to help humans thrive. In many ways, science is now catching up, while adding new layers of knowledge, understanding, and application."[3]

We are bridging those gaps, providing opportunities and insights for application. This chapter will explore this bridging work between art and science and how we can apply focus as an essential skill for personal and communal growth.

WHY FOCUS?

A whole chapter on focus? Yes! The connection between sound, focus, and movement doesn't just apply to artists or professionals. It's relevant for everyone—children especially.

Grayson is an incredible seven-year-old with a huge, loving heart. He is bright, curious, loves to read—and like many kids–often ignores his mother multiple times a day. For months, his mom, Arianna, would get frustrated and use the typical annoyed parent phrases:

- "Pay attention!"
- "Look over here!"
- "Are you even listening to me?"

We can replace Arianna and Grayson's names with yours and millions of others. The point is that when we work hard mindfully to raise our children to focus, we use mindfulness terms to call their attention. Some of the phrases that parents and guardians use:

- Mind your manners.
- Turn your listening ears on.
- Mind me now . . .

- Look at me; focus on what I'm saying.
- Be on your best behavior.
- Work smarter, not harder.
- Mind your own beeswax!

You know the old story asking how you get to Carnegie Hall . . . practice, lots of practice. We know that's accurate but not a sufficient answer. We've used language like the above and lots more with emphasis countless times, but does it make a difference? Could it make a more designed difference if these ideas are used alongside music to create new associations with focus?

Integrating music into daily routines enhances executive functions like decision-making and problem-solving. Just as athletes train their bodies, music can train the brain to focus. Through repetition and patterns, we can use music as a vehicle for promoting mindful actions in ourselves and others.

The more we understand our thought patterns—our metacognition—the more effectively we can manage our mental states. Through consistent practice and through thinking of music as a tool in our toolkit, we can train our brains to smoothly navigate these transitions between active and passive listening, making us more adaptable and resilient.

FOCUS IS A SIGNIFICANT CONCERN FOR LEARNING AND LIVING

Well, isn't that obvious?

A spring 2024 NCES survey indicated that 76 percent of public schools reported a negative impact on student learning and behaviors due to a lack of focus.[4]

Excuse us for being a bit prickly about these findings. Just go into any school and talk to the students and teachers. Talk to parents and guardians. Talk to employers. Developing and maintaining focus is a concern.

Yet there are many examples of being focused: Simon Biles at the Olympics (in fact, any of the Olympians), a nurse taking blood pressure, a gamer sitting at the screen for hours, mah jong players, a piano player, a little leaguer at bat, and on!

We *can* focus. Individuals and groups focus. Is the survey question asked in a way that reflects the nature of learning and the needs of today's learners? Maybe the questions in the national survey reflect a disconnect with school or with learners' distractions with other, more engaging and connected (small community) activities.

If we can agree that focus is important and that there are many, many examples of focus throughout our lives, maybe the question is, how do we improve focus in our ever-evolving and emerging world?

Options to improve focus include medication (well beyond the scope of our discussion), creating positive habits, rewards, magnifying awareness, willingness, and the desire to focus. We suggest that mindfully selecting music, creating patterns, and developing connections are other behaviors to include on this list.

How about rewards and punishments to help gain focus? Should parents and guardians reward the child with a song they like if the child focuses and exhibits behavior the parents and guardians are hoping for? Or should music or other motivating approaches lead to focus? What if the child doesn't achieve the expected behavior? Will music or other motivators be withheld?

Breathe deeply, look at me, pay attention.

The study by NCES opens many questions. We submit that the repetition of patterns through music will create focus for most students. Parents, guardians, and teachers need playlists that are personalized and customized. They need to share musical preferences, create combined playlists, and embrace techniques that connect to their children, each other, and to their students.

NOTES FROM THE CLASSROOM

Kathy Park, an NYC public school teacher at NEST +M (New Explorations in Science, Technology, and Mathematics), brings music into her classroom to enhance focus and engagement despite limited resources and musical expertise. Kathy shared that she is "not a musical person at all, but I admire music very much. I try to incorporate music as much as I can in my classroom, but there's a big part of me that wishes I could do it more organically."

Noting the limitations of her musical skills, Kathy expressed a strong desire to expand her use of music: "I feel limited in the way that I can use it in the classroom because I am not a naturally musical person." This sentiment may be common among educators who feel constrained by their musical abilities yet recognize the immense benefits music can bring.

Kathy observed the immediate positive impact of music on her students, stating, "When I put music on in the morning before the kids come in, just something soft and calm, I see an immediate effect compared to kids coming into a silent classroom." Calming music has been shown to reduce cortisol levels, the hormone associated with stress, creating a more peaceful, productive environment.[5]

As with our earlier story about George, setting the tone for the day in the classroom can be as simple as playing a piece of purposefully selected passive music. This is not music for active listening but rather music that creates a mood that positively impacts the students.

TAILORING MUSIC TO CLASS NEEDS

Kathy often tailors musical choices in the classroom to the specific needs and energy levels of the students. "There are times when I choose music depending on the feel of the class. If the class is already energized, I use a calm tune like 'Memories' by Maroon 5 to help calm their energy." Studies have also observed that rhythmic music, like Miley Cyrus's "Party in the USA," can be used to positively affect brain regions responsible for emotional regulation, making it an ideal tool for classroom dynamics.[6]

Kathy also took note of how her first graders responded differently to music than the older students. "There are years when kids would prefer chanting or the more PE aspects of things where it feels like an arcade game and they jump through things. It is definitely very independent to the class." Teachers can mindfully select the way in which they use music and mindful action in the classroom to best reach their students. Making it a collaborative experience ensures every student feels that connection to their classmates and the teacher.

Younger children benefit from rhythmic and interactive songs, preferring the structured beats of clapping games and the soothing, meditative sounds. Rhythmic songs with clear patterns are easier to react and understand, providing a sense of security and familiarity. This structure is easier for them to follow than the dancing and singing typically found in Kidz Bop movement breaks.

Strategically matching music to the desired emotional and cognitive outcomes allows teachers to manage classroom dynamics effectively. By adjusting music selections to suit the class's mood and developmental needs, teachers can create an engaging and supportive learning environment that promotes both focus and enjoyment.

We often stick with what we know, choosing songs or movements which are familiar, part of our implicit memory. What about students who listen to different music at home or who could benefit from a wider range of cultural musical? How about teachers, parents, guardians, or business leaders who want to expand what they sing to their children, what their children listen to, or curate what their employees hear during the day—but don't know where to start? The goal is to develop mindful listening skills, leverage the technology tools available to expand musical repertoire and discover new possibilities, so we can go from implicit to explicit (as explored in chapter 7).

MOVEMENT BREAKS AND ENGAGEMENT

While music helps set the tone for focus, it can also energize students throughout the day through movement breaks. Kathy utilizes these breaks to maintain focus. "That three minutes you spend giving them time to sing, be joyful, and move their bodies will save you ten minutes later on because you're not going to have to stop and remind them to sit still," she emphasized. These breaks help students release energy and refocus on their tasks.

During "Family Fridays," when parents and guardians visit the classroom, Kathy utilizes movement breaks even with adults present. Students regroup from the excitement of having an audience and for everyone to experience a shared collective bond through music.

One Friday, after a math lesson observed by the adults, the students' attention started to waver twenty minutes in. A familiar tune, Taylor Swift's "Anti-Hero," came on the speakers, accompanied by a large screen displaying dance moves for everyone to follow. As the verse began, the kids mumbled the lyrics while dutifully following the dance moves. The adults' smiles turned to laughter as the chorus started, and every student sang out, "Hi, it's me, I'm the problem, it's me."

This was more than a movement break; it was fun for everyone! A joyful experience for all present to collectively feel the music. Once the song was over, they were able to focus on the next task at hand. This worked because the incorporation of movement with music activates multiple brain regions, enhancing neural connectivity and supporting cognitive processes such as attention and memory.[7]

CREATIVITY AND MUSIC IN LEARNING

Kathy also used music as a tool for creativity during a poetry unit. "We exposed them to different ways of collecting ideas. One was listening to music." Students listened to songs like Jack Johnson's soundtrack for *Curious George*, then sketched what came to mind. "It was amazing to see their interpretations," she recalled. "One student drew a vibrant forest, while another imagined a bustling city."

This exercise evolved into a segment where the students wrote their own poems. The poems ranged from verses the kids sang to poems about trees, birds, or their first day of school. This lesson highlighted the importance of not judging, as all these responses reflected the unique experiences and perspectives each student brought when listening to the same piece of music.

Integrating music into the classroom can significantly enhance students' learning and focus. When students listen to music, their brains engage multiple regions that are crucial for cognitive development, including areas responsible for processing emotions, memories, and creativity.

OVERCOMING CHALLENGES AND FINDING RESOURCES

Despite the benefits, Kathy acknowledged the challenges of incorporating music into a busy curriculum. "Teachers really struggle with how we can fit all of our teaching and expectations and still incorporate all the fun and movement and music." Access to curated music resources designed to align with curriculum topics would be invaluable.

We imagine a library of interdisciplinary resources where music is woven into content areas such as history and language arts. However, our imagination goes well beyond those two subjects!

If music can enhance memory retention, improve cognitive skills, and increase student engagement through creating associations between melodies and information, then creating playlists of music written during historical periods they are studying could allow students to experience the mood and culture of the time. Composing songs based on the literature they are studying could deepen both their understanding of the material and their creative interaction with it.

There is unlimited potential for using music to enrich lessons and enhance content. Classrooms should have music not as an extra component but as an important part of learning, boosting students' understanding and engagement.

Creating interdisciplinary resources that integrate music with various subjects, teachers like Kathy can have ready-to-use tools at their disposal. This approach can provide a rich learning experience without overwhelming the curriculum, ultimately benefiting both educators and students. Integrating music not only supports academic growth but also helps students express emotions and connect with others, leading to a supportive classroom environment.

We searched online for "music for lessons on the Revolutionary War," looking for playlists that are "school appropriate" with no curse words, only PG content in the songs, and so on. We found that almost no playlists have been created to complement the curriculum.

There is a wide-open opportunity to create these playlists, combining the arts and lessons for students leading to more interdisciplinary curricula. A sampling of a variety of lessons for students ranging from pre-K to high school can be found at the end of this chapter.

THE AUTOPILOT EXPERIENCE

Allow us to detour into passive listening for a moment. How many times have you found yourself walking somewhere or driving down the road and suddenly wondering, "How did I even get here?" Or perhaps you've read a page of a book only to realize you have no clue what it's about? (Like the tired parent at bedtime who reads an entire story but mentally drifts off to another planet.) Countless times, we have all driven on autopilot, arriving safely but with no memory of the journey.

To be "on" and hyper-focused constantly is difficult and probably not desirable. Our brains need to relax. When we let our minds wander by engaging in passive listening, our brains rest, allowing for daydreaming and creative thinking, which can enhance problem-solving. We call this "purposeful passive listening." Just like our bodies need to rest from activity, our brains do too! We can think of purposeful passive listening as active listening's opposite. Teachers like Kathy intuitively understand these concepts. By incorporating active listening exercises into lessons, they can help students develop the skill of purposeful passive listening, encouraging focus while maintaining creativity. Together, they create a harmonious ecosystem to our well-being.

SOME THOUGHTS ABOUT ACTIVE AND PURPOSEFUL PASSIVE LISTENING

This is a lot to unpack. While we attempt to categorize the concepts that come from music and mindfulness, they are not always clear-cut. Just like we can't talk about focus without talking about the brain, we can't talk about purposeful passive listening without also talking about active listening (table 6.1).

Table 6.1. Listening with Purpose

	Active Listening	Purposeful Passive Listening
Engagement Level	Requires full attention and purposeful listening. Perhaps picking out a melody, beat, or simple pattern to listen to.	Involves listening while performing another task, like drawing, reading, or resting, with music enhancing the environment. Does not require full attention.
Cognitive Impact	Enhances critical thinking, memory, and problem-solving through focused engagement.	Supports relaxation and concentration in other tasks, improving mood and reducing stress.
Emotional and Social Skills	Fosters emotional awareness and empathy by encouraging deep emotional connections with the music.	Creates an ambient background that can stabilize emotions without active emotional engagement.
Creativity and Imagination	Stimulates creativity by encouraging exploration of purposeful listening.	Can inspire creativity indirectly by providing a calming or stimulating backdrop.

KIDS AND MUSIC AS A TOOL FOR FOCUS

Have you ever heard over one hundred children (babies included) and adults be absolutely silent? As a society, we often shy away from taking children to concerts, fearing they might be loud or bored. Boredom and mind-wandering, as we've just seen, are both paths to mental freedom, sparking creativity or giving our brains a much-needed rest. So listening to music, even in a purposeful passive listening state, helps us learn our thought patterns and become more active listeners.

To actively listen and reap the benefits of music and mindful action we have learned to create experiential learning moments that leave space for us to engage with the music actively and passively.

During a live interactive outdoor concert with Mozart for Munchkins at Hudson Yards in New York City, an almost instant transformative moment occurred when the audience was asked to "Breathe with Bach" in two different ways.

BREATHING WITH BACH: TWO APPROACHES

1. "Bach Cello Suite No. 1 in G Minor": The audience followed the sounds of the phrases, the swirling shapes from the bow of the cello, and breathed naturally. For the children too young to understand, we asked the parents and guardians to help them sway to the music, to feel the breath. Silence. Magic. Over two hundred people collectively lowered their stress levels by breathing with Bach. That number includes babies, kids of all ages, teenagers, and adults.
2. "Prelude and Fugue in C Major BWV 846": A conductor on stage led the audience in measured breaths with the music. Think of this as a runner taking measured breaths to the cadence of their feet, the double Dutch jumper watching the ropes before they jump in, the surgeon taking focused breaths while scrubbing in, the deliberate breath after a long day. This exercise had a different impact on the audience when we asked for feedback. Some loved having a beat to breathe to, others felt frantic and overwhelmed by not being able to follow their body's natural rhythms.

This feedback is incredibly valuable to better see the obvious: that everyone reacts differently and needs different stimuli to perform, breathe, and *be* our best. Our suggested playlists are just that, merely a starting point to find what works best for you.

Music is for everyone. By engaging both children and adults in purposeful active listening exercises, we can use music not only as a source of enjoyment but also as a powerful tool for focus. We can practice switching between our active listening and purposeful passive listening modes.

FROM AUTOMATIC TO PURPOSEFUL: STORIES OF CONNECTION

How do we encourage our minds to intentionally wander through music? Easier said than done! Think back to a time when your mind wandered—where were you? Was it a vibrant place filled with swirls of colors, or was it a blank canvas? Allowing our minds to wander through music can be a powerful tool.

During a professional development day at the United Federation of Teachers, everyone in the room was provided crayons and markers. Miles Davis's "Blue in Green" and Debussy's "Clair de Lune" were played, and the educators were asked to draw what they heard. These vivid titles, one evoking colors and the other "moonlight," might suggest a "right" and "wrong" way to interpret them. However, when it comes to letting your mind wander, there is no correct way—it's all about exploring possibilities.

As the educators responded, some eagerly grabbed their chosen colors, drawing in big swooping swirls, while others were hesitant at first, unsure of what to do. After the first few minutes, there was a collective release. The room felt lighter. Pages filled with colors, all unique in design, showing that everyone's mind had journeyed somewhere else.

By engaging with music and allowing our minds to wander, we develop a state of creativity and mental rest. There's no single way to experience music and the act of listening and interpreting without judgment for ourselves or others can be deeply personal and liberating.

OBSERVATIONS AND EXPERIENCES

These types of mindful actions through music and other similar creative activities not only helps in reducing stress but also enhances our ability to focus and be present when needed. Finding the balance between structured thought and the freedom to let our minds explore *is* a mindful action.

By integrating such practices into our daily routines, especially in educational settings, we start to create environments where both children and adults can benefit. Engaging in purposefully letting go of the constraints of what we believe focus is supposed to be may be exhilarating.

TOOLS FOR FOCUS AND RELAXATION

During a teachers' professional learning workshop, the twentieth-century minimalist composer Philip Glass was played. Activities were left open-ended for the teachers to breathe, write, draw, or engage in another mindful task while actively listening.

An eighth-grade teacher named Leanne mentioned that her mind kept wandering. Initially, she was frustrated by her inability to stay present in her writing. She eventually decided to follow her thought patterns without judgment, instead of forcing herself to "pay attention." Allowing herself the freedom to listen and not judge her wandering thoughts led her to feel present, grounded, and eventually less anxious while alone with her thoughts, supported by the music.

Tools should be and could be available to help us achieve focus. Many teachers use a sound or a simple piece of music to signal, "Time to sit down and work!" Music ignites the implicit memory as a cue for the student and the whole class . . . maybe even school-wide. A parent or guardian may use musical signals to let the family know it's time to get out the door. The stock market rings a bell to begin and start the day. How about walking into what may be a stressful meeting to a soothing, relaxing tune?

We know the possibilities are endless. Through intentional action and mindful use of music, we can create awareness of the benefits of both active and purposeful passive listening, turning these into positive habits.

PRACTICAL STRATEGIES

Here are some strategies for success in the classroom:

- Involve students in choosing music for the classroom to ensure it resonates with their preferences and enhances engagement.
- Use music to facilitate movement breaks that allow students to release energy and refocus on their tasks.
- Integrate music into lessons on history, culture, and other subjects to create a richer, more engaging learning experience.
- Employ familiar tunes and rhythms to create routines and signals that help students understand transitions and expectations.
- Help students to get creative with projects using music. Encourage students to express their interpretations of music through art or writing, using music as an inspiration for creativity and exploration.

For home:

- Utilize music as a tool for focus: Create playlists for different activities to enhance focus and relaxation, using music as a signal for transitions between tasks.
- Active listening exercises: Engage in family activities that involve focused listening, like "Breathing with Bach," where family members follow musical phrases and breathe in rhythm with the music.
- Purposeful passive listening: Encourage activities such as "Drawing with Debussy," where family members listen to music while drawing or doodling, allowing the music to enhance creativity without requiring full attention.
- Journaling with music: Use music as a background for journaling, allowing family members to reflect and express themselves creatively, whether through writing or drawing.
- Purposeful background music: Music can be used to set the tone and create a mood, even if used as ambient background. Pick music to reflect the mood and energy you want to bring into the home.

Mindful Breathing with Music

What You Need: A quiet space, a selection of calm, instrumental music, and a timer.

- *Activity:* Combine deep breathing exercises with music. Start by setting a timer for five to ten minutes. Play soft, instrumental music in the background as you focus on your breath, inhaling deeply for a count of four, holding for a count of four, and exhaling for a count of four. Allow the music to guide the rhythm of your breathing.
- *Tip:* Use this practice as a way to reset during stressful moments. Regularly practicing mindful breathing with music can enhance emotional regulation, reduce anxiety, and build cognitive resilience by improving focus and mental clarity.

SAMPLE CURRICULUMS

Jazz and the Harlem Renaissance

- Objective: Understand the cultural and historical impact of jazz music during the Harlem Renaissance.
- Activities:
    - Play pieces by Duke Ellington, Louis Armstrong, and Ella Fitzgerald to introduce students to jazz music's distinctive features.

- Study the Harlem Renaissance, focusing on its significance as a cultural and artistic movement for African Americans in the 1920s and 1930s.
- Have students write a short story or poem inspired by jazz music and the themes of the Harlem Renaissance, such as identity, empowerment, and cultural pride.
- Explore how jazz influenced other art forms and societal changes during this period.
- Subjects Integrated: music, social studies, and language arts.

Environmental Awareness through Music

- Objective: Explore how modern music addresses environmental issues and promotes sustainability.
- Activities:
  - Listen to songs like "Earth Song" by Michael Jackson and "Big Yellow Taxi" by Joni Mitchell. Discuss the environmental messages and how they inspire action.
  - Research current environmental challenges and discuss how music can raise awareness and influence public opinion.
  - Create a multimedia presentation or music video advocating for an environmental cause, using music to convey the message.
  - Subjects Integrated: science, social studies, and music.

Classical Music and Scientific Discovery

- Objective: Explore the relationship between classical music and scientific advancements during the Enlightenment.
- Activities:
  - Introduce students to works by Wolfgang Amadeus Mozart and discuss the precision and clarity of his compositions.
  - Examine key scientific figures and discoveries of the Enlightenment, such as Isaac Newton and his laws of motion.
  - Conduct a simple science experiment (like making a paper airplane) while listening to classical music, encouraging students to think about the relationship between structure and creativity.
  - Discuss how the principles of order and rationality in both music and science reflect the Enlightenment's intellectual ideals.
  - Subjects Integrated: music, science, and history.

NOTES

1. Mark Twain, *A Connecticut Yankee in King Arthur's Court*, ed. M. Thomas Inge (Oxford University Press, 2006), 97.
2. Willoughby Britton, "Can Mindfulness Be Too Much of a Good Thing? The Value of Moderation in Mindfulness Practice," *Current Opinion in Psychology* 28 (2020): 159–165, https://doi.org/10.1016/j.copsyc.2018.12.011.
3. NeuroArts Blueprint, "NeuroArts Blueprint: Advancing the Science of Arts, Health, and Wellbeing. International Arts + Mind Lab," *NeuroArts Blueprint Report*, Johns Hopkins University, 2022, https://neuroartsblueprint.org/blueprint-report/, 46.
4. "About One-Quarter of Public Schools Reported That Lack of Focus or Inattention From Students Had a Severe Negative Impact on Learning in 2023–24," National Center for Education Statistics, last modified July 18, 2024.
5. Myriam V. Thoma, Roberto La Marca, Rebecca Brönnimann, Linda Finkel, Ulrike Ehlert, and Urs M. Nater, "The Effect of Music on the Human Stress Response," *Psychoneuroendocrinology* 38, no. 1 (2013): 133–141.
6. Susan Hallam, John Price, and Georgia Katsarou, "The Effects of Background Music on Primary School Pupils' Task Performance," *Educational Studies* 28, no. 2 (2010): 111–122, https://doi.org/10.1080/03055690220124551.
7. Robert J. Zatorre and Valorie N. Salimpoor, "From Perception to Pleasure: Music and its Neural Substrates," *Proceedings of the National Academy of Sciences* 110, no. 2 (2013): 10430–10437, https://doi.org/10.1073/pnas.1301228110.

Chapter 7

Legato

Understanding the Long Arc of Mindful Actions

The brain is more than an assemblage of autonomous modules, each crucial for a specific mental function. Every one of these functionally specialized areas must interact with dozens or hundreds of others, their total integration creating something like a vastly complicated orchestra with thousands of instruments, an orchestra that conducts itself, with an ever-changing score and repertoire.—Oliver Sacks[1]

THREADS

- The arc of life is connected through music through melodies and lyrics.
- Connections can be created and recreated through mindful actions.
- Stevie Wonder: "Songs in the Key of Life."

THE LONG ARC OF MUSIC

Dancers are poised backstage, taking that mindful breath before stepping into the spotlight. That moment of anticipation, of tuning into the music that will carry them, mirrors so many moments in life. Think about it: We pause before a big presentation to gather our thoughts, a parent takes a deep breath before helping with homework, a teacher centers themselves before walking into the classroom. These small, mindful pauses are what ground us in the present. They create a ripple effect of calm that extends beyond us, influencing everyone we interact with (figure 7.1).

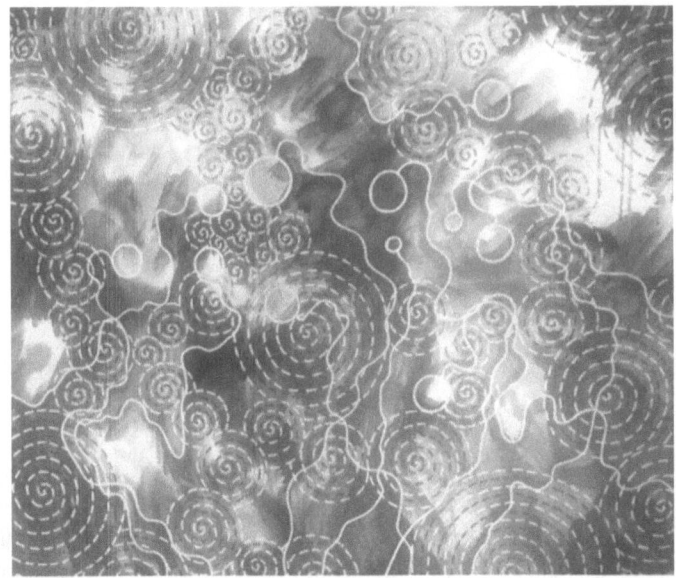

Figure 7.1. *Octopus Garden. Original art courtesy of the Paul Goldstein collection.*

How wonderful our lives would be if this grounding habit became second nature. What about if this could be applied to how we curate and listen to music? Of course, most of us actively select music we like for the moment and the mood. These transactional moments can become the sparks that ignite the music of life.

Go beyond your usual playlist. Step out of the comfort of familiar songs to enhance your personal connection to music, and open doors for building community, fostering connection, and creating deliberate cultural outreach.

It's easy to stick to what's familiar. Maybe hearing Stevie Wonder brings you back to a joyful moment, or listening to Lionel Richie makes you want to dance. What if we asked, who else and what other kinds of music could bring us that same joy? What untapped emotional landscapes could we explore?

This is where music and memory intertwine so beautifully. Our awareness of thought patterns and emotional connections to music can be used to create positive habits. Every time we revisit a song, we are actively reinforcing a memory, and each new experience we have while listening becomes part of our emotional history. This self-understanding naturally leads to more mindful behaviors, as we become aware of how music can be a tool for memory, focus, and even motivation.

A scene: The lights dim, and an entire crowd of strangers is transported into collective silence. The screen shows a countdown, as if we're about to be launched into outer space. Everyone counts down together, and then—darkness. The drums hit, and the audience erupts in a deafening cheer. On this thirtieth anniversary of a band's most famous album, there is singing and dancing as strangers share the moment, united by the music.

Thirty years ago, we first heard these songs. The memories flood in—old friends, awkward middle school fights, riding bikes in the suburbs, singing these very lyrics. The music and the memories are inseparable, each song triggering a feeling or a story from our past.

The magic of music is that it doesn't just live in the background; it has the power to shape our emotional landscape, to evoke memories, and even to create new ones. When we listen with intention, music becomes more than sound—it becomes a bridge to memory, an anchor to the present, and a pathway to mindful action.

Beyond the emotions, we can make positive, purposeful associations with songs to create habits. This powerful connection to the purposeful creation of new musical attachments, turning listening into a habit, supports our emotional and mental well-being.

By actively integrating music into our daily routines—whether for focus, relaxation, or pure joy—these small moments turn into meaningful, mindful experiences. And as we do, we build habits that stay with us, guiding us through the long arc of life, with music as our companion.

"SONGS IN THE KEY OF LIFE"

"You Are My Sunshine"—a song so familiar that it has become a part of our collective DNA. A lullaby, family favorite, first dance, a preschool staple. First recorded in 1939, and still going strong in our hearts today, the music is fresh for each generation. Reinvented by bluegrass, jazz, classical, folk, and even hip-hop, the memories of the song make us feel. We smile when we hear it, hum it without thinking, and carry the tune with us. How many versions of this song have we heard? Countless. We know the words. We feel the memories tied to it.

What comes to mind for you? Comfort? Nostalgia? Maybe a grandparent sang it to you, or you've passed it on to your own children. Music connects our brains, hearts, and histories in ways that go beyond words. It's that magic—one simple song reaching across generations, emotions, and time.

But what is happening in our brain when a song like "You Are My Sunshine" sparks these feelings? Well, the brain's implicit and explicit memory systems work together to bring up these emotions and memories.

Implicit memory involves unconscious recall and is responsible for automatically bringing up elements like the melody and lyrics of a song, which you might recognize without conscious effort.

Explicit memory, on the other hand, is related to conscious recall, and it would indeed evoke the personal associations tied to the song—like specific moments, people, or places.

Music doesn't just bring up memories—it activates our executive functioning skills too, such as planning, decision-making, and problem-solving. These neural pathways are engaged when we listen to music, making it a tool for both cognitive and emotional resilience. Think of a tune you hum to stay focused or the playlist you rely on to get through a difficult task.

So many of us already do this each and every day. What's your "pump it up" song? What music do you like to listen to when you need to focus?

We submit that we are underutilizing music in this way.

Not only does creating these associations and habits energize and inspire, it also helps us establish positive routines, reinforcing motivation and habit formation. By understanding these connections, we can use music strategically to boost cognitive performance and emotional well-being.

Music moves us in powerful ways—lifting us to emotional heights, pulling us from the depths, persuading us to buy something, or reminding us of our first date. It gets us dancing or helps us escape sadness when nothing else can. Music occupies more areas of our brain than language itself. We humans are a musical species.

Like "You Are My Sunshine," our childhood memories are often intertwined with music. From the "Clean Up Song" to the songs at our first school dances, these melodies live in our implicit memory, shaping our emotional and cognitive associations with the world around us. They latch onto our "phonological loops," those earworms we memorize without even realizing it, creating powerful associations with memories, holidays, smells, and movements.

What's the first memory or association these tunes bring to mind:

- "The Addams Family" theme song
- The teacher's clap
- "Happy Birthday"
- *Jaws* theme / "Baby Shark"
- "Jingle Bells"

Do these songs bring up one memory or several? Perhaps none? If they don't, think of the last song that got stuck in your head. Can you recall where you were when it happened? How it might have annoyed you? Did you hum it out loud or try to replace it with another tune?

Music, through these associations and memories, shapes our experiences and connects us across generations. These melodies and moments enhance our lives, becoming internalized and triggering automatic reactions within us.

What are your songs? What tunes have been passed down through your family? Will they continue to be passed down, or will they evolve with the constant shifts in musical preferences?

WHAT'S IMPLICIT MEMORY GOT TO DO WITH IT?

Implicit memory is the kind of memory that operates without us even thinking about it. It's behind all the tasks we perform automatically—those everyday things that don't require conscious effort. When we ride a bike, brush our teeth, or even hum a tune without realizing it, that's implicit memory at work. These tasks are deeply embedded in our brains, relying on regions like the basal ganglia, cerebellum, and motor cortex, all crucial for motor control and coordination.[2]

Examples of implicit memory in action include:

- riding a bike,
- boiling water,
- singing a song without thinking of the lyrics,
- brushing your teeth,
- swinging a baseball bat, and
- walking around the block.

These are things we've practiced so much they've become second nature. Our brain puts them on autopilot, freeing up mental space for more complex things. Implicit memory runs the show here, guided by the cerebral cortex, though the hippocampus plays a role early on when we're first learning a new skill. Once it's locked into our motor memory, it happens without much thought at all.[3] We don't consciously think about buttoning our shirts or how our feet need to press down on the pedal to ride a bike. Once these behaviors are learned, they become subconscious over time.

While we usually think mindfulness is all about being present and aware, implicit memory may seem like the opposite of mindfulness, implicit memory can actually complement mindfulness. When we become aware of these deep-seated, automatic reactions, we can use them to our advantage. Imagine using music to build automatic reactions—certain songs that help us focus, calm down, or energize, without even thinking about it. That's the power of turning music into a habit.

For example, when we pair a specific song with relaxation, the song itself becomes a cue for the body to relax over time (explicit memory). Each time we experience the calming effects of the song, our brain reinforces the behavior, making it more likely to happen automatically the next time we hear the music (implicit memory). Suddenly, you've created a powerful, mindful tool to carry with you.

Musically engaging in our memory systems helps create a "legato" arc—a seamless flow—between music, memory, and action that can guide you through life's rhythms. This reciprocal learning helps our mindful action in the use of music, moving us closer to the point where what was once an explicit and deliberate action becomes ingrained as a pattern, an implicit approach to decision-making.

HOW DOES THIS WORK?

The list of songs Sara's children ask Alexa to play is both wide-ranging and a bit repetitive. One minute it's Katy Perry's "Firework," the next it's Yo-Yo Ma's renditions of J. S. Bach's "Cello Suite No. 1 in G Major," followed by the "Pokémon Theme Song" or "There's a Cat Flushing the Toilet." It's safe to say their musical tastes cover a lot of ground!

But over time, certain songs have taken on specific meanings. Bach, for example, has become a cue for quiet time, whether that's reading, drawing, or simply winding down. On the flip side, when the household energy dips into grumble mode, a quick dose of "I Like to Move It" can get everyone dancing and releasing oxytocin together.

For years, Sara has used Bach's "Cello Suites" by Yo-Yo Ma, a famous cellist, to focus while working or writing. It's the soundtrack that signals her brain: time to focus. When she tried switching things up to Joshua Bell's arrangements, the unfamiliar phrasing was distracting—her groove was thrown off, breaking her concentration. This is a clear reminder that Bach had become more than just background music; it was now a learned behavior, a mental cue to sit down, focus, and get to work. Implicit memory was in play supporting this routine!

Even Sara's son has picked up on this. When he needs some downtime or isn't feeling the loud popular music, he asks Alexa to play Bach. It's a proud moment for Sara—watching her son recognize his need for calm and using music to guide him there.

Enabling explicit memory involves conscious recall—it's how we remember everyday details like what we had for breakfast or who we spoke to. This type of memory is essential for retaining information, and we can strengthen it through regular practice of music through mindful action.

When we intentionally use music, we create strong memory attachments. Picking intentional songs for specific moments help you later recall the emotional and cognitive impact, which further strengthens memory retention. Over time, these positive emotional connections reinforce both your mindfulness and your explicit memory.

When you first learned to ride a bike, do you remember that wobbly feeling as someone—maybe a parent or sibling—ran behind you, holding on until they let go? At first, it took practice and focus, but eventually, it became second nature. That learned behavior shifted into your implicit memory, allowing you to ride without thinking about it. Music works the same way.

We can use music intentionally to create an environment for focus or relaxation. By associating specific songs with certain activities, we can harness its power to shape our daily routines and well-being. This applies beyond family into settings such as classrooms.

In the last chapter, we discussed how teachers might use music to signal transitions. A specific song could mean quiet time or focus time, while another could signal an activity change. Over time, the students won't need to be told what to do; they'll hear the song and automatically know. The music will trigger their behavior, thanks to the habit-forming power of implicit memory.

Through repetition, this process becomes automatic. Suddenly, the music no longer needs to be actively processed—it triggers the desired behavior all on its own. When students hear that calming piece, they instinctively quiet down and focus because the association is now ingrained their minds have made the shift from conscious effort to automatic response, but through intentional, deliberate practice (figure 7.2).

MUSIC ACTIVATES THE BRAIN

By cultivating both implicit and explicit memory in our lives and classrooms, we build not only our cognitive and emotional well-being but also a lasting connection between music and mindfulness. We can guide ourselves through the long arc of life's rhythms, just as learning to ride a bike becomes second nature.

The nub of the discussion about implicit and explicit memory is how to bridge the two, over time, to create life patterns, habits, through music. Our goal has always been to breathe life into academic understandings born out of scientific research, to offer a path that is not accidental but deliberate and focused (figure 7.3).

Chapter 7

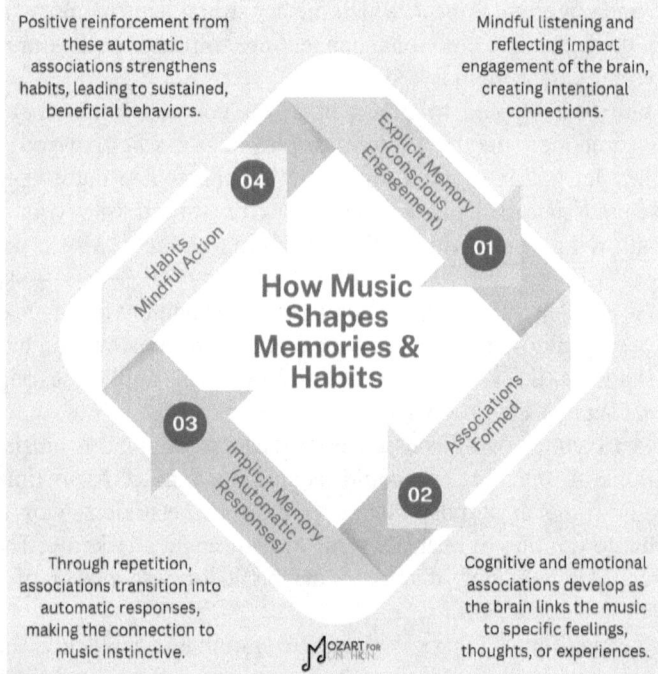

Figure 7.2. Music and memory associations. *Created by Sara Sherman.*

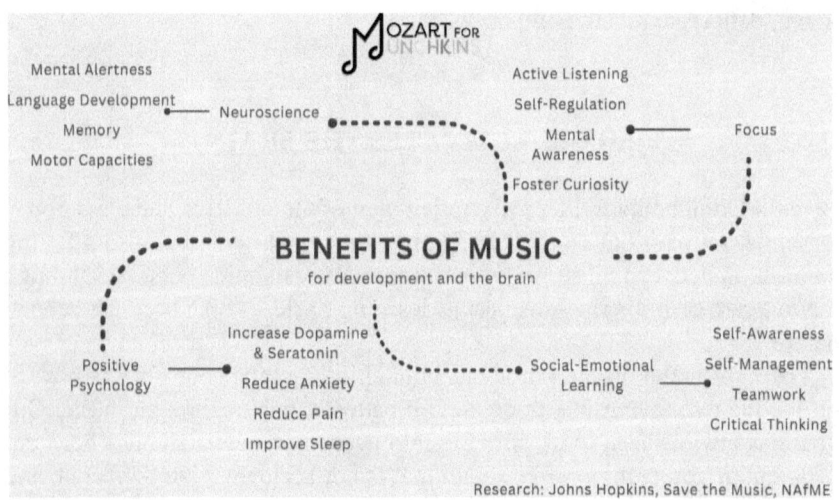

Figure 7.3. Chart of benefits of music. *Created by Sara Sherman.*

PRACTICAL APPLICATIONS AND ACTIVITIES

- Curating a life soundtrack: Reflect on key moments in your life (childhood, teenage years, adulthood). Create a playlist that captures the essence of each stage, paying attention to how these songs make you feel now. What emotions, memories, or stories do they bring up?
  Tip: Revisit this playlist during different moments of your life, and note whether the songs bring up different memories or associations as you grow older.
- Expanding your musical horizons: Pick one new artist or genre each week. Listen mindfully, paying attention to how it affects your mood, energy, and focus. Reflect on how these new sounds compare to your usual choices.
  Tip: While listening to unfamiliar music, practice deep breathing or mindful listening techniques. Notice how the experience feels compared to listening to a song you already know by heart.
- Music as a memory tool: Choose a song that reminds you of a positive memory (a family gathering, a trip, a meaningful conversation). Close your eyes and listen to the song, reflecting on the emotions and details of the memory. Use this song as a tool to boost your mood when needed.
  Tip: Keep a journal to document how specific songs connect to different memories. Over time, you'll have a personal emotional "music map" that helps guide you through different moods and stages of life.
- Creating positive associations with music: Select a simple song that you can connect to a daily activity, like "You Are My Sunshine." Play it during moments of quiet or relaxation, reinforcing a sense of calm and mindfulness.
  Tip: Pair the song with a calming activity (like yoga or journaling) to create a positive emotional association. Over time, just hearing the song will help you shift into a calm, mindful state.
- Strengthening memory through music: Choose a song that you associate with a specific event or person. Listen to it while reflecting on the details of that memory. Over time, this can strengthen your ability to recall important information.
  Tip: Use a song as a memory tool for studying or learning. Pair the song with the material you're reviewing, and play it during moments of relaxation to help solidify the information in your memory.
- Engaging in positive habits with implicit memory: Select a song that you enjoy and play it at the same time every day, pairing it with a mindful

activity like deep breathing, stretching, or meditating. Over time, the song will become a cue for relaxation and mindfulness.

Tip: Track your progress by noting how quickly you begin to relax or focus when the song plays. As it becomes part of your implicit memory, the association will become automatic.

- Music in the workplace: In your work environment, select specific songs to signal the beginning or end of tasks (e.g., quiet work time, group discussions, or breaks). Use repetition so the song becomes an automatic cue for those transitions.

Tip: Explain the connection between the music and the specific transition. After a few weeks of repetition, notice how the transitions happen automatically when the music begins.

- Turning music into a daily mindfulness tool: Choose a song or playlist that you associate with relaxation or focus. Play it daily during specific activities (like writing, exercising, or meditating). Over time, this practice will turn into a habit, helping you achieve a mindful state effortlessly.

Tip: Evaluate your progress after a month. Have these songs become part of your automatic routine? Do they trigger calm, focus, or joy without needing conscious effort?

NOTES

1. Sacks, *Gratitude*, 14.
2. Larry R. Squire and Andrew J. O. Dede, "Conscious and Unconscious Memory Systems," *Cold Spring Harbor Perspectives in Biology* 7, no. 3 (2015), https://doi.org/10.1101/cshperspect.a021667.
3. Julien Doyon and Habib Benali, "Reorganization and Plasticity in the Adult Brain during Learning of Motor Skills," *Current Opinion in Neurobiology* 15, no. 2 (2005): 161–167, https://doi.org/10.1016/j.conb.2005.03.004.

Chapter 8

Counterpoint

Executive Function

USING SKILLS TO TAKE MINDFUL ACTION

Music enhances the education of our children by helping them to make connections and broadening the depth with which they think and feel.
—Yo-Yo Ma[1]

THREADS

- Intentional, deliberate, mindful use of skills help us focus, make decisions.
- Executive functions provide a path to creating habits, threads of life through music.

Monday. Nyssa's alarm buzzes sharply. She flinches before stumbling out of bed. Her feet thud on the floor, matching the staccato of the hissing coffee brewing. Next comes the hurried zipping of backpacks, tapping of texts and emails, packing of school lunches, and kids out the door. On to the next task.

Standing in the kitchen, she pauses. Realizing that things feel chaotic, she remembers that music helps her melt the frenzies away. "Alexa, play my calming playlist that we created last night." As the music starts, she takes a deep breath, and starts to feel the release of stress. Time to regroup her thoughts. She grabs her coffee, inhales the rich scent, and instead of rushing through her to-do list, she mentally rearranges the morning, slowing the tempo so she can start to think about the transition between activities. Today will be legato— a day where each action will flow purposefully and smoothly into the next.

Much like a symphony, life has its own sections—some fast and intense, others slow and reflective. With practice we can learn to transition smoothly, using our executive function skills to connect the dots. As Nyssa drives to work, she's no longer just checking boxes; she's conducting her day with intention, letting life's rhythms guide her, just as she practices each day.

USING EXECUTIVE FUNCTION SKILLS

The idea of legato—smoothly connected, flowing notes—wonderfully captures our optimism about music, intentionally helping to develop a positive long arc of life. Just as legato playing requires smooth transitions between notes, we navigate life with greater flow when we intentionally guide our actions. As we grow, evolve in our careers, and face challenges, we become the conductors of the playlists of our lives.

In the prelude, we touched on the concept of a mental spark—a moment of clarity or realization. We considered how, in the same family, one sibling might be drawn to music while another takes a completely different path. Igniting a mental spark, a mindful moment, a pause, an "aha" through musical mindful action can happen at any moment in life's journey. Through emotional appeal, movement, and connections with others, those moments happen. Music can make those moments happen.

To fan the flame, to become aware of the possibilities of music, and to be deliberate about decisions made, use of executive functions kicks in.

The ongoing, reciprocal nature of learning and living establishes the habits of our lives. Those habits are discussed in the next chapter (figure 8.1).

In this chapter, Ellen Galinsky provides a wonderful perspective and understanding of executive function and music. One of her most inspiring experiences was working on the set of *Mister Rogers' Neighborhood*, where she observed firsthand how Fred Rogers intentionally used music, routines, and emotional appeal to teach children important life lessons. Through their work together, music and media ignited a "mental spark" in children, creating emotional growth and enhancing their executive function skills. Ellen is also the author of *The Breakthrough Years* and *Mind in the Making*, and was previously the Chief Science Officer for the Bezos Family Foundation. She is a lead thinker in the use of executive function, working with the AASA (The School Superintendents Association) to better understand how to go from theory to action.

Executive function skills—cognitive flexibility, working memory, and self-control—allow all of us to navigate life's complexities with purpose. These skills, as Ellen Galinsky's research shows, help us transition from one moment to the next, making deliberate decisions rather than letting the day carry us away.

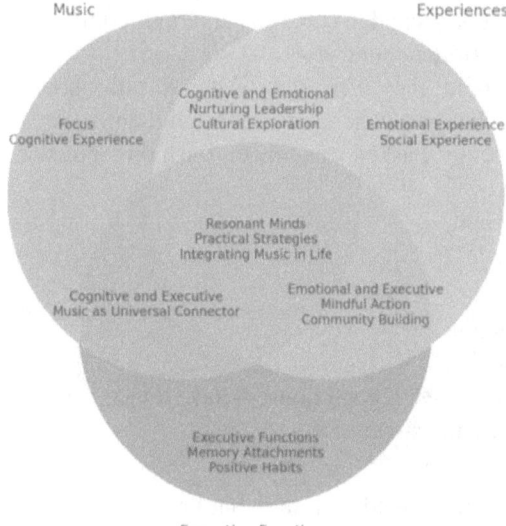

Figure 8.1. Impact of music on focus, cognitive, emotional, and social experiences. *Created by Morton Sherman.*

HOW I DISCOVERED THE IMPORTANCE OF EXECUTIVE FUNCTION SKILLS AND THEIR CONNECTION TO MUSIC

Written by Ellen Galinsky

If you'd told me twenty-five years ago that I'd be studying executive function (EF) skills, I wouldn't have believed you. But I am.

This journey began with an unexpected turn. In 1999, my team and I were conducting a series of studies on how nationally representative groups of middle schoolers and high schoolers saw the burning issues in their lives—how they felt about working parents, their dreams for their futures, and how violence and school shootings were affecting them.

The next in our series was to be on learning. As a practitioner of civic science, I always begin by asking the people I will be studying what they want to know, then co-creating studies with their input. So, there I was doing focus groups of fifth through twelfth graders, asking them to talk about learning: "Tell me about a time when you learned something. It could be something that you set out to learn or not. It could be in school, at home, in your community, or anywhere."

In response, there was silence, fidgeting, pretty expressionless faces. This didn't just happen with one group, it happened with all of them. It didn't just happen in cities, it happened in suburban and rural communities, on the coasts and in the middle of the country.

On the other hand, they were very eager to talk about "not learning"—about a math teacher or a coach who ridiculed them.

In the focus groups, I asked students to finish this sentence: "It is important to learn so I can . . ."

Far too many said:

- Get good grades.
- Go to good schools.
- Get a good job.
- Support myself—have a good house—have a nice car.
- Not be a bum on the street.

These are all good reasons for learning, but I am sure you can see the problem right away, like I did.

These reasons are largely extrinsic. Learning was for the future, not for now. Their engagement in learning was low.

That became the moment when I began to change course—this was something I needed to address.

The studies on school engagement seemed to confirm what I was hearing. One of the best at the time—a regular survey conducted by Indiana University—asked, among other questions: "Why do you go to school?"[2] The most frequent answers had learning on the sidelines, like:

- getting a degree and going to college (73%)
- being with other kids (68%)
- because it's the law (58%)
- only 39 percent responded because of what they learn in classes and only 34 percent that they enjoyed being in school.

Young people are born learning. Their eyes are on fire. They want to see, to touch, to taste, to experience everything.

In contrast, the eyes of far too many of the older students I was interviewing had dimmed. They weren't just dropping out of school, they were dropping out of learning!

My question became: How can we keep the fire for learning burning in the eyes of children?

So I pivoted to find out more. I knew I needed to begin with research on our youngest learners—to look at what helped them learn and thrive.

In the end, I've had an opportunity few others will ever have—I could cross academic borders, looking at neuroscience, psychological development, and the development of literacy, and numeracy and to document what I found.

Whenever I turned, I could see that the category of young children most likely to be learning and thriving were developing a set of crucial skills. Take the research conducted by Alison Gopnik of the University of California, Berkeley. She and her colleagues found that very young children begin to learn that others have different beliefs, desires, and intentions from their own.

We filmed a study where the experimenter put a bowl of Goldfish crackers and broccoli in front of very young children.[3] The experimenter would taste the raw broccoli or the crackers and randomly say "yum" to one snack, and "ugh" to the other. They would then ask the children to "give me what I like."

Children around fourteen months old would dig into the crackers, enjoying them and giving crackers to the experimenter without discrimination for their preference. The older children in the experiment, about eighteen months old, would hand the experimenter what the experimenter had indicated they liked.

There was one child we observed named Nathan. His face registered disgust when the experimenter (in this case, Gopnik herself) said she loved raw broccoli. When she then asked Nathan to give her what she liked, he dumped the whole bowl of raw broccoli into her hands.

Besides being very funny to watch, I was amazed at the skill that this takes. Nathan had to use his working memory to remember what the experimenter liked. He had to think flexibly—she likes broccoli and I don't like it. He had to pause before reacting and then use self-control not to give her the crackers (although, he had already eaten most of them himself).

Nathan's skill wasn't simply a matter of maturation. Ross Thompson of the University of California, Davis, and his colleagues have found that if parents talk about other people's thinking and feelings, children are more adept at perspective taking.

Furthermore, perspective taking matters because it helps children make sense of the social world they live in. Studies show that children who can understand others' perspectives do better in kindergarten because they're better able to understand what their teachers want and expect. Later in life, business leaders thrive or fail depending on their ability to understand the perspectives of their potential customers.

Researchers in different disciplines called these skills by various names, but the most frequent term is executive function skills.

WHAT ARE EXECUTIVE FUNCTION SKILLS?

A colleague of mine at the time said, "Executive function! That sounds like an executive in a pinstripe suit bossing you around in your head." She wasn't that far off. The Harvard Center on the Developing Child uses the analogy of an air traffic controller, while Jennifer Silvers of UCLA talks about an orchestra conductor. The analogy of an air traffic control managing all of the incoming and outgoing flights at an airport or a conductor directing the individual players in the orchestra to work together to create a piece of music work because we use these "top-down neurocognitive processes" to manage and coordinate our emotions, thoughts, and behavior to achieve goals.[4]

Philip David Zelazo of the University of Minnesota says that executive function skills are best seen as a "broad umbrella concept" because they're defined behaviorally in terms of what people do: "Executive function skills provide a foundation for learning deliberately and for adapting to life's challenges. Whenever we want to do something deliberately—we want to pursue a goal—we need to rely on these attention regulation skills."

Zelazo and others have learned that these skills are foundational to success in learning and thriving. And that's the reason that I've spent the last twenty-five years on executive function skills.

WHAT'S UNDER THE "UMBRELLA"? THE FOUR COMPONENTS OF FOUNDATIONAL EXECUTIVE FUNCTION SKILLS

If I continue with Zelazo's analogy, the umbrella itself would be focus because executive function skills are attention-regulation skills. When we're trying to achieve a goal or solve a problem, we need to focus attention on it, just as when we're out in a storm and the umbrella has to be open to keep us dry.

Under the umbrella are four component skills: cognitive flexibility, working memory, inhibitory control, and reflection. These skills enable us to:

- Think flexibly: Consider alternative perspectives and think flexibly in response to changing circumstances (cognitive flexibility).
- Use what we know: Keep information in mind so it can be used (working memory).

- Use self-control: Resist automatic and impulsive behaviors (inhibitory control) so we can engage in goal-directed reasoning and problem-solving and persist in reaching goals.
- Reflect: Notice challenges, pause, step back, consider options, and put things into context before responding (reflection).

I am going to "pause" for a moment to discuss reflection. While this skill is not usually included as an executive function skill because it takes place in the default network of the brain, not the cognitive control network where the other three skills are centered, the use of these EF skills depends on reflection as we monitor and think about the goals we want to achieve. For this reason, I think it is essential to include it under the umbrella of EF skills.

These four component skills become the building blocks for other life and learning skills, such as perspective taking. Remember how Nathan had to use his working memory to remember what the experimenter liked; he had to think flexibly—"she likes broccoli and I don't"; he had to pause before reacting; and then use self-control not to give her the crackers. Those skills together enabled him to take the perspective of others.

In addition to perspective taking, my years of both doing and reviewing research have led me to identify four other skills that build on foundational EF skills and that I see as essential: (1) setting goals, (2) communicating and collaborating, (3) problem-solving (including creative thinking and critical thinking), and (4) taking on challenges.

WHY ARE EXECUTIVE FUNCTION SKILLS SO IMPORTANT?

There are countless studies that show that executive function skills help children—and adults—succeed now and in the future. The best syntheses of this research are two review articles by Adele Diamond and Daphne Ling of the University of British Columbia.[5] In the first of these articles, they only included studies that . . .

- Were published in a peer-reviewed journal in English.
- Showed causal effects. Causality is a big deliverable. For example, if a study simply compares two groups of students—let's say, those who were in orchestras and those who weren't—and concludes that students in orchestras have better executive function skills, that's a correlational finding, not a causal one. You wouldn't know from this finding whether the orchestra students in this study just happened to have more "get-up-and-go"

(to quote neuroscientist Michael Gazzaniga) or whether something about being in orchestra actually improved their cognitive skills.
- Included a comparison or control group. To show causal effects, you need to show that an intervention creates an improvement over time. You do this by presenting evidence that a comparable population, one that at best was randomly assigned to a group without the intervention, does not change.
- Examined longer-term effects—that is, the improvement lasts for a measurable amount of time and not just immediately after (e.g., an hour after the intervention).
- Demonstrated far transfer—that is, shows effects beyond improvements on the immediate task. Diamond and Ling write: "We were interested in . . . improvement in a basic cognitive ability that generalized at least to similar tasks."[6]

They found 84 interventions meeting these criteria in 2016, and in 2020 they included 179 studies from 193 papers. Here—in their words—is a summary of the findings:

> EFs are predictive of achievement, health, wealth, and quality of life throughout life, often more so than IQ or socioeconomic status. They are more critical for school readiness than IQ or entry-level reading or math. They are predictive of success throughout the school years from preschool through university (often more so than IQ).
>
> The importance of strong EFs does not stop in childhood. There is abundant evidence that EFs are crucial for success in getting and keeping a job as well as career advancement, making and keeping friends, marital harmony, staying out of jail and resisting substance abuse. Adults with better EFs also report they are happier and have a better quality of life.[7]

EARLY CHILDHOOD AND ADOLESCENCE ARE PRIME TIMES FOR THE DEVELOPMENT OF EF SKILLS

As I've said, children aren't born with executive function skills, but they are born with the capacity to learn them. As the Harvard Center on the Developing Child says, "genes provide blueprints, but the environments children are in leave lasting signatures on those blueprints."[8]

Executive function skills grow rapidly in early childhood and adolescent years. The Harvard Center points out that the development of EF skills corresponds to the development of the prefrontal cortex. In the early years, this development is formative, "as relevant circuits emerge, mature, and forge critical interconnections." In adolescence and early adulthood, these "circuits are then refined and made more efficient."[9]

Two major changes in the brain during the adolescent years explain why adolescence is such a prime time for the development of these skills. First, the prefrontal regions—regions central to executive function—develop significantly. Second, there's improved connectivity within and between the outer cortical regions (areas linked to cognitive control) and inner cortical regions (areas linked to emotional responses, rewards, and learning).

Executive function skills improve rapidly in adolescence, and on emotionally "sunny" days, according to Jennifer Silvers at UCLA, adolescents can use these skills as well as adults or even outperform them. But on emotionally "stormy" days, it can be a different story. Silvers compares the developing connections between the prefrontal and subcortical regions to newly paved roads. When a storm of strong emotion comes in, the cement can get wet and things can get messy.

Notice that I use the word "can." In fact, adolescence is a critical time for gaining these skills, which can buffer adolescents against difficulties throughout their lives.

WHAT EF SKILLS ARE *NOT*

Over the past two decades, I have spoken to many different groups about EF skills and I often ask people if they've heard about them—and many haven't.

If they have heard about them, I ask them what EF skills are. Here are the most common confusions.

To begin, EF skills are not non-cognitive or soft skills. That's probably said because they differ from learning academic content, like English or math or science. EF skills are mostly centered in the cognitive control parts of the brain, including the prefrontal cortex. It's better to think of them as neurocognitive skills that pull together our cognitive, social, and emotional capacities to achieve goals.

Second, executive function skills are not just compliance skills (be quiet, sit still, listen to the teacher) or study skills (prioritizing homework and creating tabs on your notebook). In a 2016 report for the Department of Education, Zelazo, Clancy Blair of New York University, and Michael Willoughby of the Research Triangle Institute write, "Executive function (EF) skills are the attention-regulation skills that make it possible to sustain attention, keep goals and information in mind, refrain from responding immediately, resist distraction, tolerate frustration, consider the consequences of different behaviors, reflect on past experiences, and plan for the future."[10]

You can see that these skills are central to learning in school and learning in life. They do matter when we are trying to sit still and listen (sustaining attention, resisting distractions, tolerating frustration), and when we are studying. But they are so much more. For example, think about keeping goals and information in our minds, refraining from responding immediately, considering the consequences of different behaviors, reflecting on past experiences, and planning for the future.

Finally, these skills are not just for people who have executive function challenges, like ADHD or autism. They are critically important for these children and adults, but they are also important for all of us.

EF SKILLS AND MUSIC

When I was becoming immersed in EF skills, one of the researchers I interviewed was Clancy Blair, now retired from NYU.

Like me, he didn't expect to study EF skills—until he made a discovery in the longitudinal study he was conducting. He found that children's ability to pay attention, as well as to shift their attention, were the best predictors of their cognitive function at ages six, ten, and twelve.

One of the ways he began to assess EF skills in preschoolers was through what he fondly called the "glorious peg-tapping task." He told me, "In the peg-tapping task, you sit down with the child and you hand them the peg [a wooden stick] and say, 'Can you tap this?' And children usually don't have any trouble with that—[they] tap away. And we say, 'Okay, we're going to play a tapping game, now that we know you can tap.'"

In this task, the child is asked to tap once when the experimenter taps twice, and tap twice when the experimenter taps once. In other words, the rules of the game keep changing, and the children need to focus and pay attention to follow what's going on in order to do the opposite of what they see the experimenter doing. Blair continued, "This exercise measures children's ability to remember the rule (working memory) and to overcome their automatic response of copying what they see the experimenter doing (inhibitory control). That's why the peg-tapping task is a good measure of the executive functions of the brain."

I was really struck by this. The peg-tapping task was very similar to the exercises my son practiced as a drummer. Today, my grown son is a percussionist-ethnomusicologist, and he still uses exercises like this to continue to learn and to teach others. That observation made me wonder.

DOES LEARNING MUSIC HELP DEVELOP EXECUTIVE FUNCTION SKILLS?

The research results are, in fact, mixed—some meta-analyses say music training is not causally linked to better executive function skills, while others say it is, especially in promoting inhibitory control and, to a lesser extent, working memory and cognitive flexibility.

One of the more comprehensive studies, still in process after ten years, is being conducted by Assal Habibi of the University of Southern California and her colleagues. It began with children aged six to seven years old. All of the seventy-five children originally enrolled in the study were from low-income communities and all were given extensive tests of their cognitive abilities at the study's outset so the researchers could be assured as much as possible that there were no pre-existing differences among these children.

Over the years, the researchers have compared the development of three groups of these children: (1) some who participated in the Los Angeles Philharmonic Youth Orchestra Program (YOLA) six to seven hours weekly; (2) some who participated in community soccer or swimming programs several times a week and on weekends; and (3) some who initially didn't participate in any systematic after-school activities—the control group. Although it's a small sample, that's not atypical of studies that include expensive brain scans.

Habibi, trained as a classical pianist as well as a neuroscientist, launched these studies because she saw schools cutting back on music education. Because children today are growing up in a stressful world—climate change, wars, violence, pandemics, to name a few—she feels strongly that adults should give children a tool box to help them succeed in school and life. Music, she says, is one of these important tools in the tool box.

After two years, Habibi and her colleagues found that children in the music group showed a different rate of cortical thickness maturation between the right and left posterior superior temporal gyrus, and more connections among superior frontal, sensory, and motor regions. These findings led the researchers to conclude that music training induced macro and microstructural brain changes in school-age children, and that these changes were not attributable to pre-existing neural differences.

Beginning after three years, behavioral assessments of executive function showed that children with music training were better at a delayed gratification task than the control group. When given a choice between a larger reward later and a small reward now, they were more likely to use self-control to wait for the larger reward. In addition, after three to four years of training, the children in the music group had better attentional skills than those in the sports group and the control group. On the other hand, the researchers found that after four years, some of the differences in brain development they had observed two years earlier in the musically trained group had disappeared, suggesting that these children had matured earlier and the other children had caught up. Their overall conclusion to date is that four years of training leads to modest gains in inhibitory skills.

Additionally, according to parents, children in the music group are less aggressive, less hyperactive, more compassionate, and better able to understand others than the other groups. As the musically trained children enter high school, Habibi expects to find that these social, emotional, and EF skills will affect their decision-making and to see less negative risky behavior.

AM I SURPRISED THAT THE GAINS ARE MODEST?

No. A persistent challenge in the research on executive function has been the lack of far transfer of skills from training programs to other activities. Adele Diamond and Daphne Ling addressed this challenge directly in their comprehensive review of EF interventions. In fact, their 2016 review is titled "Conclusions about interventions, programs, and approaches for improving executive functions that appear justified and those that, despite much hype, do not."[11]

For this reason, Phil Zelazo and I recently reviewed the research to identify where far transfer of EF skills does take place. In the future, we think that interventions will be more successful if they:

- Include opportunities for children to engage in prospective and retrospective processing on the skills they are gaining. Prospective reflection is important because it interrupts automatic processing, allowing for consideration of goals and top-down control in light of them. Retrospective reflection on what has been learned is also important because it can help individuals understand how and when to apply their trained skills in new situations. The addition of a metacognitive component to EF training has been shown to produce far transfer.
- Are given opportunities to practice the skills in different places. Studies find that skills practiced in just one setting are harder to generalize. To promote far transfer, EF skills need to be practiced in a variety of settings, including real-world settings.
- Are learned in the context of life and learning skills. Children need to see the connections between the core EF skills (like inhibitory control and cognitive flexibility) and life and learning skills, like problem-solving and taking on challenges.

THE TIME TO ACT IS NOW

I have been feeling for years that we need to act on this knowledge, and that conviction is even stronger post-pandemic.

This isn't just educators' perceptions. Parents have come to similar conclusions. In a longitudinal, population-based study in the state of Massachusetts conducted by researchers at Harvard University, of close to 3,000 children, parents, and teachers, parents reported that their children's externalizing and internalizing and dysregulated behaviors increased after the pandemic shutdown, while children's adaptive behaviors declined.

And it isn't just perception. Analyses of children's executive function skills—measured behaviorally—are underway in the Harvard study and show that executive function skills declined considerably during the pandemic and have not rebounded two years later.

In addition, these are the skills that employers are looking for in new hires. In its annual survey, year after year, The National Association of Colleges and Employers found that employers are less likely to look at the grade point averages of potential hires. Instead, they are more likely to seek people with skills like the ability to work in teams, problem-solve, communicate, and think analytically.

We know that executive function skills are essential to school success, job success, and life success. We now know how to promote them. There is typically a lag between research (what we know) and action (what we do). We must interrupt this lag and act now to help children learn and thrive, and to keep the fire for learning burning in their eyes.

Children, their teachers, and their parents can't wait!

NOTES

1. Laurence Vittes, "Exclusive Interview with Yo Yo Ma on the Spirituality of Music," *Huffpost: The Blog*, last modified September 30, 2012, https://www.huffpost.com/entry/yo-yo-ma_b_1920286.

2. Ethan Yazzi-Mintz, "Voices of Students on Engagement: A Report on the 2006 High School Survey of Student Engagement," *Center for Evaluation and Education Policy, Indiana University*, 2006, https://eric.ed.gov/?id=ED495758.

3. Betty M. Repacholi and Alison Gopnik, "Early Reasoning about Desires: Evidence from 14- and 18-Month-Olds," *Developmental Psychology* 33, no. 1 (1997): 12–21, https://doi.org/10.1037/0012-1649.33.1.12.

4. Philip David Zelazo and Stephanie M. Carlson, "Hot and Cool Executive Function in Childhood and Adolescence: Development and Plasticity," *Child Development Perspectives* 6, no. 4 (2012): 354–360, https://doi.org/10.1111/j.1750-8606.2012.00246.x.

5. Adele Diamond and Daphne S. Ling, "Conclusions about Interventions, Programs, and Approaches for Improving Executive Functions That Appear Justified and Those That, Despite Much Hype, Do Not," *Developmental Cognitive Neuroscience* 18 (2016): 35, https://doi.org/10.1016/j.dcn.2015.11.005.

6. Diamond and Ling, "Conclusions about Interventions," 35.

7. Ibid.

8. National Scientific Council on the Developing Child, "Building the Brain's 'Air Traffic Control' System: How Early Experiences Shape the Development of Executive Function," Working Paper No. 11, Center on the Developing Child at Harvard University, last modified February 2011, https://developingchild.harvard.edu/resources/building-the-brains-air-traffic-control-system-how-early-experiences-shape-the-development-of-executive-function/.

9. Ibid., 4.

10. Philip David Zelazo, Clancy B. Blair, and Michael T. Willoughby, *Executive Function: Implications for Education* 6. NCER 2017–2000. *National Center for Education Research, Institute of Education Sciences*, U.S. Department of Education, 2016.

11. Diamond and Ling, "Conclusions about Interventions."

Chapter 9

Ostinato

Developing Mindful Habits for Life

Resilience is more available to people who are curious about their own line of thinking and behaving. —Brené Brown [1]

THREADS

- Habits of mind are habits of life.
- Those habits become the threads to which we hold true throughout our lives.
- Emerging technologies offer remarkable opportunities for mindful behavior.

In this chapter, we are fortunate to feature a thoughtful piece by Bena Kallick and Art Costa, whose lifelong dedication to the creation of Habits of the Mind is well-known. Their insights help us explore the powerful intersection of music and mindful behavior. Additionally, we had a chance to connect with and interview Shara Senderoff, an innovator in creative technologies who exemplifies the transformative potential of imagination and presence. Their contributions bring a distinct perspective to this exploration of mindful habits.

One of the most important lessons Mort learned as a young school administrator was when Bena advised, "Don't just do something; stand there!" Quiet yourself and listen. Be an anthropologist. Look at yourself and those around you. Focus, focus, focus! Listen, and then act.

Awe-inspiring figures like Bena Kallick and Art Costa have consistently influenced how we think about mindful action. Whether thinking about thinking (metacognition) or listening with empathy and understanding—two of the sixteen habits of the

mind—generations have been influenced by the habits of learning through life as a feedback spiral.

Walking into a presentation and discussion with Art and Bena has always been immediately uplifting. Music welcomed participants. Not just a random playlist, but songs such as "I Hope You Dance" by Lee Ann Womack reminded us not to lose our sense of wonder and awe.

Music is a lever helping to shape and reinforce dispositions that lead to meaningful actions and growth. This feedback spiral is a path through the habits of mind to a life filled with music, respect, care, and thought. Their decades of work provide perspective and optimism that we can move from implicit to explicit and then on to life habits, using music as a powerful lever and motivator.

The concept of "habits of life" or "habits" as a guiding force in human behavior has been explored for centuries across various disciplines, including philosophy, religion, and literature. Exploring these long-standing discussions, particularly through the lens of mindful development, is a key part of how we approach change and action. Habits shape our choices and growth, creating a framework for personal development that is rooted in intentional, mindful practices.

The long arc of history and thought about habits includes Aristotle's *Nicomachean Ethics,* written in the fourth century B.C. He discusses the role of habits in developing virtue and goes on to argue that virtues are not innate; rather, they are acquired through habitual practice: "We are what we repeatedly do. Excellence, then, is not an act, but a habit." Aristotle emphasized that the formation of good habits is essential for achieving eudaimonia (flourishing or happiness), which is the ultimate goal of human life.

Confucius's *The Analects*, written in the fifth century B.C., referred to the importance of cultivating good habits and moral behavior through ritual and continuous practice. Saint Augustine's *Confessions,* written in the fourth century CE, explored the idea of habits in the context of spiritual life, particularly in his struggle with sinful habits and the transformation through divine grace.

Habits, like biting your fingernails, are very different from what Kallick and Costa describe as the "Habits of Mind." We embrace their point of view that the habits of life are the dispositions of successful, creative, and effective thinkers.

Their practice and research wonderfully connect to the long arc of life, where positive dispositions, practiced and repeated over time, lead to lasting growth and fulfillment

We appreciate Bena and Art reflecting on mindfulness, music, and the Habits of Mind.

MUSIC AND MINDFULNESS: HOW MUSIC SPEAKS TO US

Written by Art Costa and Bena Kallick

Music is often ambient noise in stores, restaurants, or while on hold during a phone call—we don't attend with any depth. But what happens when we intentionally immerse ourselves in music we love, when we really *listen*? Whether a song or a full concert, music finds its way into our bodies, minds, hearts, and souls. We listen in the gym as we move to the rhythm and beat; we share and feel a sense of community in the crowd as we listen at a concert; we listen to energize our creative spirit as we dance, paint, compose; we listen to calm the chatter in our brains as we meditate, and sometimes we even listen to inspire new ways of thinking.

THE NEUROSCIENCE RESEARCH

Why do we find music so rewarding? Research in neuroscience suggests that music activates the brain's reward system triggering the release of the neurotransmitter, dopamine. Dopamine is responsible for many cognitive and neurological functions in the body including pleasure, reward, joy, focus, and motivation. Dopamine can even alter our mood.

This may explain why listening to music has been shown to enhance well-being and reduce stress. It's also known to affect a number of areas in the brain, including regions involved in emotion, cognition, sensation, and movement. Music moves us and soothes our overtaxed minds. Do you recall being brought to tears over a tender and beautifully performed piece of music or wanting to get up and dance to a particularly happy or energizing song?

MINDFUL LISTENING WITH HABITS OF MIND

Regardless of what draws us to listen to music, or the particular genres of music we prefer, we can enhance our enjoyment of music by bringing mindful awareness to our listening sessions. Mindfully listening to music can help us to slow down, to fully engage with the present moment, and to more deeply appreciate the gift of music in our lives.

Based on our work, we chose four Habits of Mind that describe the dispositions of successful, creative, and effective thinkers in order to explore and highlight the connections between mindfulness and music. When we lend ourselves to being present in the musical experience we are responding with wonder and awe.

Keltner and Haidt include music as one of eight awe-generating wonders of life. Their research suggests that when we are engaged and in awe with the music, we may stimulate feelings of vastness and mysteries that cannot be explained. As we listen, we are restraining our brain from being over-analytical. We may find ourselves asking questions: *What is life? What is love? What are we all doing here, anyway?*

Experiencing awe often puts us in a self-transcendent mental state where we focus less on ourselves and feel more like a part of a larger whole. Studies have shown that awe is often accompanied by feelings that increase awareness and connectedness with other people. So, what might be going on in your own mind as you engage with music could strengthen your disposition for including music more intentionally in your life.

LISTENING WITH UNDERSTANDING AND EMPATHY

When listening to music, we are putting aside the habits we have developed in our experiences using spoken and written language. We are asked to put aside the skills that are captured in the syntax of language—subjects, objects, verbs, and thinking in more linear terms about time. Rather, when freed from those constraints, we experience music more holistically and intuitively, and our thoughts give rise to life patterns or possible truths about living.

Listening to music has been shown to enhance well-being and reduce stress. Langer says that when in this aesthetic emotional state, there is "no counterpart in any vocabulary. Music is a tonal analogue of emotive life."[2] As we attend to the music, we listen with our bodies as well as our ears, minds, and hearts. It can evoke emotions, memories, and epiphanies. We can become lost in the moment as we soothe our weary minds and hearts.

When we identify ourselves with what the composer might have imagined, we become empathic listeners. We are able to give ourselves over to the thinking, feeling, and choreography of the performers.

THINKING INTERDEPENDENTLY

Many of our musical experiences are ones that are shared. All sorts of musical events, such as concerts, are attracting increasingly larger crowds. People come together in their homes, churches, and schools to play music. Even when individual people listen on their own, they are also sharing their playlists, seeking out online communities, and commenting on their response to what they hear.

Classical music, always considered to be exclusively in the concert hall—and therefore inaccessible to those who could not afford a ticket—can now be heard in the subway station, on the street, in the park, or in one's social media feed. Similarly, genres like heavy metal, rap, and country, maligned by the uninitiated for decades for being vulgar or plebeian art forms, can now be found in the Top 40 playlists on radio stations, on many of the highest-grossing concert tours, and in the curricula of music history courses at some of the world's most prestigious universities. The beauty of thinking interdependently is that we are able to be part of a larger community and can be influenced by the thinking and experiences of others. Cross-pollinating with others, and even learning about different perspectives through music, enhances the sense of meaning and mystery.

REMAINING OPEN TO CONTINUOUS LEARNING

As we expand our universe of musical experiences, we learn more about other ways of thinking and being. If we remain in an echo chamber in which we limit ourselves to what we know and take comfort in, we will miss the beauty of being exposed to other cultures, new sounds, and innovative experiences.

When we open our minds to learning, we are often motivated by our relationships with others. For example, we hear music from the perspective of someone much younger than we are, and it is as if we are hearing it for the first time. Our love of music can open us to hear one another in more ways than we ever imagined.

IDEAS FOR MINDFUL LISTENING INTERDEPENDENTLY

Get ready for a good listen!

- Find someone with whom you want to share the experience and agree on the music you would like to listen to together.
- Turn off your cell phones and any other sounds or technologies that might distract or interrupt you. (Or if you're using the device to play music, put it on airplane mode or "do not disturb.")
- Get comfortable. Immerse yourselves in the experience of just listening.

After it is over:

- Share anything you might have noticed, such as the pace of the music, the sounds of and predominance of different instruments, the volume, the melody, or the rhythm. What parts of your body were you aware of as you listened?
- Share any thoughts or feelings that may have been evoked—a memory, a movie, a book, a place, or even a relationship you visited.
- Now, take a moment to reflect at the conclusion of your listening session. Attend to the overall quality and condition of your body, mind, and heart now you have, having just completed your mindful music listening session. Describe your feelings to your partner.
    - Are you more excited or relaxed?
    - More enthused, or calmer, or more energized?
    - Was the music a good fit? Why or why not?
    - What might you look for in another piece for your next mindful music listening session?

THE THREAD OF HABITS AND IMAGINATION

Bena and Art set the tone beautifully through the four habits they discussed, ending their section with thoughtful questions. This approach to opening our imaginations also happens when we see the possibilities in advancing technologies. We look at this next with Shara Senderoff, co-founder and president of Rise Entertainment and co-founder of the generative AI platform Jen.

Tapping a beat on the table, you might feel like Ringo Star. You might even imagine the sounds as the rest of the band joining into your groove. You pause, hit record, and upload that beat into an AI program. Within moments, an entire song is created around it—bass, vocals, and harmonies—all while staying true to the feeling originally intended. What was once a solo practice is now a collaboration, and all that was needed was the spark of your imagination and the help of technology.

This is a reality Shara Senderoff is helping to build now.

Merging human imagination with cutting-edge advancements, Shara Senderoff, is a visionary in the fields of technology and creativity. Shara's work is driven by a passion for the potential of the human mind and spirit. Shara's mission is "building technology to enable imagination and creative collaboration."[3]

Being present, developing habits, and opening imaginations are at the foundation of Shara's work. She reminds us that being truly here in the moment isn't just about mindfulness in the traditional sense. Releasing our imaginations and letting technology help us access creative possibilities are connected. Technology tools, like AI, aren't taking away from what we can create. They give us new ways to imagine, new ways to connect, and new ways to share. As with music, it's not the technology that defines the experience—it's the human spirit behind it.

She believes that the importance of being present must become a priority. "You can't see the world if you're not present." This idea of presence isn't just central to mindfulness—it's at the very core of music and creativity.

To find that singular space where you're fully engaged and aware is what drew her to generative AI.

Shara grew up listening to artists like Stevie Ray Vaughan, Chuck Berry, Patsy Cline, and others in the blues genre. When she listens, something happens in her soul. She pointed out, "We can point to the skill set scientifically but can't really point to the soul magic."

Her attitude five years ago was that computers could never create what a human artist can create. But now her larger mission in life has become to get people to open their minds. "I build all these technologies because I believe that the way you can be the most present is if you can open your imagination. The way we historically detailed our way of opening our imagination was watching something, someone telling us what our imagination should think, whether that was a Disney movie or a show or whatever. We were an audience member and an observer of someone else's imagination."

As with Terry Thoren, and others who have pushed the question of imagination and being present, Shara wondered how we bring adults back to childhood? Technologies are coming soon that would provide the opportunity to open our imaginations by asking AI to create a song. We may feel like we created the song, although what we really did is open our minds to possibilities, take mindful action to develop parameters of a song, and then let the technology create it for us, including the opportunity to edit.

Some people worry that technology like this is killing artistry.

Shara's response? "It's really about mindfulness. In the end, it's not really about technology.

"With generative AI companies, we're enabling people to create playlists together of music that they create and generate. We're building an entire, sort of, community-driven approach by creating a path where people can go in and work with a group of people—could be five, could be 5,000—making a playlist that they would curate together.

"Then let's take the sonics of that playlist and tell AI to just keep generating on that sound. An infinite playlist can be created. Once we give the power back to the individual to decide that they want to curate a sound experience, then generative AI can come in and make that experience infinite, and you won't run out of songs.

"The imagination component of generative AI is allowing us to open our minds, prompt whatever you want, what is in your imagination, because everyone is so unique."

When we think about the future, Shara says it's not just about opening minds and helping people to express what's on their minds. "We've invented something that when you put in a prompt—a happy song for a beach day with friends, tropical dance music, or whatever you put in—[it] goes into a language model that's encoding it to say, okay, these things would sonically sound like 'blank.' But how do we get the emotion out of it that the individual intended but didn't have the words to explain?"

This journey, then, is about more than just technology. "It's about cultivating the kind of leadership that is heart and mind centric, with the heart leading the way. I believe we can do more. We can do better."

Figure 9.1. *The Thread. Original art by Debra Sherman.*

The thread of life, the long arc of legato, is captured beautifully in the first two lines of William Stafford's poem, "The Way It Is":

> There's a thread you follow. It goes among
> things that change. But it doesn't change.[4]

We appreciate Bena, Art, and Shara's weaving of the threads of intentionally using habits, much like the steady flow of legato, weaving together our changing experiences, holding us together. As Stafford's words remind us, even in times of flux, this thread persists, guiding us through the music of our lives and into deeper connection with ourselves and others. It is this constant—a thread we can always hold onto—that brings both mindfulness and music into harmony.

NOTES

1. Brené Brown, *Rising Strong* (Random House, 2015), 8.
2. Susanne Langer, quoted in Dacher Keltner, *Awe: The New Science of Everyday Wonder and How It Can Transform Your Life* (Penguin Press, 2023), 155.
3. Shara Senderoff, "Biography," *Shara W. Senderoff*, accessed September, 18, 2024, https://www.sharawsenderoff.com/bio.
4. William Stafford, "The Way It Is," in *The Way It Is: New and Selected Poems* (Graywolf Press, 1998).

Chapter 10

Tutti

Putting It All Together: Community, Emotions, and Connections

Alone, we can do so little; together, we can do so much. —Helen Keller[1]

Mindfulness is the practice of purposely focusing your attention on the present moment—and accepting it without judgment.—Jon Kabat-Zinn[2]

THREADS

- Community building through music.
- Music to help focus in the classroom.
- What does any of this have to do with mindfulness? How can becoming more deliberate and focused on the associations between music and emotions impact your mindful actions?
- How can we use music or nonverbal cues to help others feel safe to communicate?
- How can you create your musical threads just as a conductor creates a program?
- Spirituality, music, and mindful awareness.

THE POWER OF MUSIC IN BUILDING COMMUNITY: FROM NEANDERTHALS TO MODERN GROOVES

The summer of 2020 was a tumultuous and transformative time. That May, the murder of George Floyd ignited a wave of anger, passion, and a desperate need to be heard. Sara and her family joined the marches, advocating for George Floyd, Black lives, and those too fearful or unable to march themselves. The rhythmic chants of "No justice, no peace!" became a powerful form of music, unifying thousands in their call for justice. Throughout history, music and chants have unified movements, from the 1960s' "We Shall Overcome" to MLK's sonorous "I Have a Dream."

But the power of communal sound-making that summer wasn't limited to protest. Music was also a source of comfort and connection in a pandemic that had just begun. In New York City, field hospitals stood in Central Park, the wearing of masks was nearly universal, many people wiped down grocery packages, and we tried to maintain six feet of separation from one another in public.

Every evening at 7 p.m. New Yorkers would open their windows, and the city would erupt in a chorus of claps, pots, and pans, thanking healthcare workers. This nightly ritual became a lifeline, linking people together in ways that echoed the communal chants and songs that have brought people together since the time of the Neanderthals.

As the clapping and banging started to recede, Broadway star Brian Stokes Mitchell, recovering from COVID-19, would belt out "The Impossible Dream" from his window, adding another layer of shared emotional experience to these moments.

Together, people leaned out their windows singing "My Girl," "Yellow Submarine," and so many more. These are everyday songs that are familiar and make us feel good.

Across the ocean in London, Bonaventura 'Bon' Bottone sang "Nessun Dorma" from his front garden, while in Italy, Illinois-based opera singer and teacher Courtney Mills sang "Time to Say Goodbye" from her balcony as a neighbor filmed her.[3]

Suzy Perelman, a Broadway violinist from Phantom of the Opera and many others, serenaded her neighbors with a mix of classical, broadway, and more. Kids leaned close to the rail separating the performers from the street, and people filled up half a city block just to listen, to be a part of the music. In other parts, jazz bands found themselves outdoors, playing swing and other music to get people dancing—older couples, parents with babies, and kids dancing together. It was where strangers become friends, with joyous, desperate music to feel connected.

These rituals of sound were not just acts of gratitude; they were a form of communal resilience, a way for people to feel connected and supported in a time of isolation. Just as early humans might have used flutes made from vulture bones to express themselves and bond with others, these pandemic-era soundscapes served as a reminder of our deep-seated need for connection through music and rhythm.

During the uncertain months that followed, New Yorkers sought ways to feel connected while staying safe. By spring 2021, Central Park became a refuge for families seeking normalcy amidst the pandemic. Mozart for Munchkins hosted outdoor pop-up concerts, drawing large crowds who lingered on picnic blankets, still wary of the virus. Central Park, often likened to the Wild West during these years, became a hub for countless baby and kid music classes, with multiple a day occurring all over the park. Concerts ranged from jazz to classical to bluegrass. We tried our best to be inclusive, but often asked, "what does that really mean?"

One spring afternoon, lingering on a checkered picnic blanket after a jazz concert led by the unparalleled Alphonso Horne, Sara's kids running around, Sara and Alphonso got to talking—about the world, the unrest, and the power of music.

Sara knew she had a loyal audience in her series with outdoor concerts in Central Park becoming more popular. The previous month, they hosted a Black Lives Matter concert for children and their families in partnership with the Brooklyn Chamber Orchestra. But naturally, it didn't feel like enough—it never felt like enough.

Sara broached the subject with Alphonso. "I really want to put on a Juneteenth event since it's the first time it will be recognized as a federal holiday. But I'm a white Jewish girl living on the Upper West Side . . . is this absurd? Can we do this?" She knew the sensitivity of the topic and the need for genuine representation.

They immediately began figuring out how to make the event a reality. Alphonso took charge of curating the show, while Sara coordinated with various organizations—Greenwich House Music School, Soapbox Presents, Ars Nova, and The Door—to co-produce a large-scale event, their first since the pandemic began.

That June, they closed down Jones Street in the West Village to create a multi-generational Juneteenth Jubilee. This event featured artists like Grammy-winner Samara Joy, poet Mikah Michele, drag queen Janae Sais-Quoi, pianist Jon Thomas, drummer Norman Edwards, and more. The event included a puppeteer, crafts, pottery, and even a van for COVID-19 testing and free masks.

In such a world of chaos, this collaboration merged music with education with community. A sense of hope as people danced through the streets of the West Village.

MINDFUL ACTION, MUSIC, AND COMMUNITY BUILDING: AN EVOLUTIONARY PERSPECTIVE

What's that one piece of music that makes you feel something? Maybe you go back to it time and time again, or you save it for that day when you're sad and need a pick-me-up.

Music makes us feel.

Music helps us connect.

While these stories often focus on challenging times, it's equally important to think of the moments of joy that music brings into our lives—weddings, baptisms, confirmations, bar mitzvahs, spontaneous dance parties, concerts, or even the simple act of singing "Happy Birthday" together. These shared musical experiences are more than just entertainment; they are the threads that weave us together as a community.

Humans have been creating music for longer than we've been farming or painting. It is not just an art form but a fundamental part of our evolutionary history, playing a crucial role in our survival and social cohesion. If we better understand music's role in human development, we could integrate it more effectively into our lives. This need for connection through music is ancient, dating back tens of thousands of years, even to the time of the Neanderthals.

Imagine yourself in a cave, surrounded by beings that you might not be able to communicate with through words. What would you do? You might gesture, clap, or even invent a simple instrument to connect and share your emotions.

In the Aurignacian culture in Southwest Germany, dating back 40,000 years, early humans created flutes from vulture bones and mammoth ivory.[4] These instruments, crafted with skilled handiwork, were likely used for self-expression, communication, and social bonding. Why, in a time of chasing food and avoiding predators, would early humans spend time making instruments? Because, just like during the pandemic, music served as a tool for connection and resilience.

These ancient flutes were perhaps the precursor to the elementary school recorder—an instrument many children first learn to play as part of an ensemble. The Neanderthals, in their own way, were engaging in a form of mindful action, using music to build community and express emotions, much like the communal clapping and singing discussed earlier.

Music, along with dance, played a crucial role in the formation of large social groups among early humans. Unlike the practice of physical grooming, or cleaning, which is limited to small groups due to its need for physical contact, music and dance allowed early humans to bond in larger groups. This bonding was likely reinforced by the release of endorphins and other pleasure-related chemicals in the brain during these activities.

When we listen to music, the responses that occur in our brains are automatic. Our brains are wired to react to sounds without conscious effort. But what we can control are the songs we choose—those that help us connect with our emotions and strengthen community bonds.

PUTTING IT ALL TOGETHER

Dancing and grooves synchronize our brains, harmonies and melodies evoke emotions, and together they create connections. The science is solidly emerging behind the groovy links of music, emotions, and community, bringing it all together.

So what does it mean for us when we become more deliberate and more focused on these associations?

We are deeply connected to our emotions, and the soundtracks we choose can shape how we feel. Our neurological synapses respond to music in ways that influence our emotional state. The history and the science behind this connection are clear. So how do we intentionally encourage this innate power? You can actively shape your emotional responses rather than simply reacting. Pick music for the mood you want to create, the community you want to build, the comfort you seek, and the groove you want.

Understanding the historical and philosophical contexts of music's emotional impact enriches our appreciation of its role in our lives. As we continue to explore the intricate relationship between music, communities, and emotion, the power of music to enhance our well-being, connect us with others, and navigate the complexities of the human experience becomes increasingly evident.

Throughout human history, music and rhythmic expression can be found as a source for emotional connection and community building. Dating back to our earliest ancestors with limited language capabilities, we know they relied on sounds, gestures, and rhythms to convey emotions and build social bonds. As philosopher Susanne Langer noted, "The most highly developed type of such purely connotational semantic is music."[5] The emotional meaning conveyed through music predates the development of complex language, which shows that music is a foundation in human communication.

If we think of the first "instrument" as the human voice, it becomes clear how integral music has been in expressing a wide range of emotions and facilitating social cohesion. From the rhythmic heartbeat that a fetus hears in the womb to the communal clapping and drumming of early human societies, music has always been a tool for connection. Langer emphasized that voices, being more versatile than drums, quickly became integral to communal celebrations through the creation of primitive songs.[6] Spoken language and music likely evolved from a proto-language, or "musi-language," used by Neanderthals.[7] This proto-language was emotional and musical, further underlining the role of music as a primary form of emotional communication.

THE SCIENCE OF GROOVE: SYNCHRONIZING HEARTS AND MINDS

"Groove to the beat!" or "Groovy sounds" are phrases we've all heard, evoking images of Woodstock and carefree dancing. But groove is more than just a feeling—it's a scientific phenomenon that describes our irresistible urge to tap our toes or move to a beat.

Groove is recognized in cultures worldwide: the Brazilian "balanço," the Swiss-German "lüpfig," the Japanese "nori," the Swedish "svängig," and in jazz music, "swing." These terms all capture the universal experience of rhythmic connection.

On a warm summer evening in 2023, Jones Street in NYC's West Village came alive with the sounds of Ingoma Nshya, Rwanda's first all-female drumming group. Formed as a beacon of healing and empowerment after the 1994 genocide against the Tutsi, these women defied cultural norms that once forbade them from drumming.

Dressed in vibrant colors and radiating joy, the eight performers gathered in the middle of the street. Their drumming began softly, drawing in a crowd of curious children, adults, and passersby. The rhythmic groove was magnetic, rooting people to the spot, unable to resist the call of the beat.

Their performance was more than just drumming; it was a dance, a chant, a cultural revival. The intricate rhythms and movements of these women created a spellbinding display of connection and cultural pride.

The power that groove and rhythm have to bring together language and culture, creating a powerful, shared human experience is astounding. Through music, we connect, heal, and celebrate.

Newborns have been shown to discern different beats and the lack of beats. The Music Cognition Group performed an experiment with newborns "playing drum rhythms, occasionally omitting a beat, and observing the newborns' responses. Astonishingly, these tiny participants displayed an anticipation of the missing beat, as their brains exhibited a distinct spike, signaling a violation of their expectations when a note was omitted."[8]

Those grooving babies were not just a neat party trick; they revealed that groove and rhythm are fundamental to our brains. When we listen to music with a strong groove, especially in a group, our brainwaves can actually synchronize.

According to Weineck et al, this most commonly happens when:

- We listen to music that is 60–120 beats per minute (this is similar to a walking pace and most Western pop pieces. For this study, people gravitated toward Western pop music);
- There are changes in the melody; or
- There is a strong beat.[9]

When our brainwaves sync up with those around us, it's correlated with increased social connection and cooperative behavior. The groove creates a shared experience, a common ground for communal cohesion, making us feel connected to others.

Being in the groove isn't just about music. It's about what music does for us as social beings. The pleasurable sensation of moving to a beat—the way our bodies and brains sync up with those around us—strengthens our bonds with others.

The social aspect of groove has been explored by several musicologists and ethnomusicologists, like Berliner[10] and Monson,[11] who highlight how groove furthers cohesion among musicians and audiences. Witek et al. (2017) also observed that experiencing groove can enhance group synchronization, making people more likely to feel connected and in sync with one another.

The ability to synchronize body movements to a beat, a key component of experiencing groove, is seen in very few species outside humans. While some animals like cockatoos and rats have shown the ability to move to music, this spontaneous synchronization is primarily a human trait. This ability likely played a critical role in the development of social cohesion and cooperation in human societies, making groove a fundamental part of our social evolution.

Groove is a powerful, shared human experience that links us to one another, strengthens our social bonds, and taps into something deep within our evolutionary history. Whether we're swaying to the rhythms of Ingoma Nshya on a New York street or nodding our heads to a favorite song, groove is a reminder that music is one of the most powerful ways we connect, heal, and celebrate our shared humanity.

DRUM IT OUT: THE POWER OF THE BEAT

Growing up, we had table beats. During meals, someone would start drumming on the table, then another would add a rhythm until all five of us had a collective groove going. This usually ended in giggles and cacophony. A beat band!

During assemblies and professional development days, Mozart for Munchkins always brings out a drum circle. It's a simple way to connect as a direct result of the rhythmic beating on the kitchen table.

Often, in the middle of the program, when folks might be getting antsy, everyone gets up. Grammy-nominated percussionist Norman Edwards Jr. then takes his snare and walks into the audience. If the audience is able, he gets everyone up in a circle. Dancing back and forth to his own beat, he calls out, "Repeat after me!" To which the audience dutifully claps the rhythm back. As the practice continues, the rhythms get more complicated in a call-and-response pattern. A sort of trance takes over the room as everyone rhythmically claps back, creating a groove as we all sync together.

Norman doesn't continue to lead the rhythm the whole time. While continuing to play, he encourages people to be the heartbeat of the drum circle, leading the "call" while everyone else continues to "respond." The longer the drum circle goes on, the more comfortable participants seem to be to lead their own rhythm, their own beats. Even if they're a math teacher, a store owner, or a stay at home parent, it's their rhythm, and the collective clap back continues that sense of unity.

Not only does this synchronize everyone, which leads to connection and cooperation, but it also practices active listening. We can't passively listen in a drum circle and expect to be on time with anyone. We're purposefully listening and connecting, together.

While some of the oldest drums date back to China around 5500 BCE, drumming became more common during the African diaspora. Rhythms from the Middle East, Europe, India, and Asia were later spread widely through the Silk Road trading routes. Drumming seems to have had a place in every ancient culture. It was a way to communicate between villages, to signal the time to march during war, and for Native American tribes to gather for spiritual celebrations.

This paints just a tiny picture of the deep roots of drumming. Beyond the beats, drum circles were used to tell stories, pass down traditions, and bring communities together. At home or at school, it makes sense to get in the groove! It might feel unnatural to get started, but children love it, and grown-ups do too, once we forget about judging ourselves and others, and simply connect.

THE DANCE OF COMMUNITY: MOVEMENT, MUSIC, AND THE MAGIC OF CONNECTION

In the heart of New York City, where the pace of life rarely slows, a group of people found themselves gathering in a quiet studio. Some were young,

Figure 10.1. Grooving. *Courtesy of PJ Library.*

others older, but all were there for the same reason: to move, to connect, and to feel something that words could not easily express.

David Leventhal, founder of Dance for PD at Mark Morris Dance Studio, knows the importance of these moments. As he looked around the room, he could see the anticipation in the faces of the participants—some eager, others a bit hesitant. He understood the power of that moment before movement begins, a time when the room falls into a hushed expectation. "It's a moment of instant mindfulness," David explained. "A heightened awareness of your body, the space around you, and your connection to others."

David knew the quiet moment was crucial. It was here, in the stillness before the dance, that something special would begin to happen. As the music started, a swell of emotion filled the room, and with it, the dancers began to move. Their movements were not just exercises or routines—they were expressions of something deeper, something that connected each person to the others in the room.

"When we move together, it's like we're all breathing in sync," David said. "That rhythm, that connection—it's not just in our minds. It's in our bodies. It's oxytocin; it's dopamine; it's the chemicals that make us feel connected, bonded, like we belong."

This sense of belonging is something that's often missing in our fast-paced, disconnected world. But in this studio, with music guiding their movements, the participants found a sense of community. Movement and rhythmic synchronization—like the kind found in group dancing—releases oxytocin, the "bonding hormone," which plays a key role in social bonding and trust. Dopamine, another neurochemical released during rhythmic activities, enhances mood and reinforces the pleasure of social connection.

David's approach to teaching was deliberate. He chose music with care, selecting pieces that not only had strong rhythms but also carried emotional depth. He knew that the music needed to resonate with the dancers, to pull them into the movement and into the community they were building together. "Music isn't just background noise," he said. "It's a guide, a partner in the dance. It helps us to focus, to feel, and to connect."

Curious to learn more about how David uses music to build this sense of connection, we caught up with him between classes. As he explained his methods, he emphasized that even when participants were initially hesitant or resistant, the music often moved them—both literally and emotionally. "We have participants who initially come in thinking they can't do this, that they're not dancers," David explained. "But by the end, they're moving with everyone else, feeling that same connection, that same joy."

This kind of community building isn't just important in dance studios—it's vital in all aspects of life. Whether in schools, workplaces, or neighborhoods, creating spaces where people can move together, feel together, and connect on a deeper level can positively change how we interact with each other. Group activities like dance not only improve mental health but also create a sense of community and social support, which are crucial for overall well-being.

For those looking to bring this kind of mindful movement into their own lives, David offered some practical advice. "Start small," he suggested. "Even a simple routine of stretching or moving to music in the morning can set the tone for the day. Get your family involved—have a dance break after dinner or start the day with a little movement. It doesn't have to be complicated. What's important is that you're moving together, creating those connections."

In a world that often feels fragmented and isolated, the power of movement and music to bring us together is more important than ever. As David reflected on the work he does, he noted, "We're not just dancing. We're building something. We're building a community."

WE LIKE TO MOVE IT: THE POWER OF MUSIC AND MOVEMENT

Movement doesn't have to be confined to a dance studio or a formal class. It can be as simple as clapping along to a beat during a concert, tapping your foot under the table, or swaying your hips when no one is looking. Movement is inherent to human nature and deeply intertwined with our history, from the rhythmic stomps of our ancestors to the synchronized cheers at a sports game.

Think of the "boom, boom, clap" at a sports game, the synchronized clap for an encore, or even something as simple as a morning stretch. These moments are already in our lives everyday, but we are working on bringing them to our consciousness, becoming aware of our movements through music and bringing intent behind them to strengthen how we use music in our everyday lives.

When we move to music—whether through dancing, running, or even clapping—our brain releases dopamine, the "feel-good" chemical that promotes a sense of pleasure and reward. Dopamine is crucial for reinforcing behaviors that are essential for survival, such as eating and, in this case, moving rhythmically.

Simply putting on music by ourselves or with others, and listening or dancing will release dopamine. Shared musical experiences tend to have a greater impact.

The act of moving together to music can be seen as a form of nonverbal communication, transcending language barriers and bringing people together. This is why communal dances and group exercises are so effective in building community—they create a sense of unity and shared purpose.

PRACTICAL APPLICATION: MOVEMENT AND COMMUNITY BUILDING THROUGH MUSIC

Let's Move It!

- Morning Stretch and Song
  What You Need: A morning song to set the mood and room to move.
  Activity: Start your day with a stretch while listening to your favorite upbeat song. This can set a positive tone for the rest of the day.
  Tip: The same song can be used every day to create a positive association with stretching and starting the day. Morning stretches accompanied by music can enhance mood and increase energy.

- Work/Home/School Break Groove
  What You Need: Music, space to move.
  Activity: During breaks at work, take a few minutes to move to a rhythm.
  Tip: Whether it's a quick dance or a walk around the block with music, this can boost your mood and productivity. This is something that can be done alone or collectively. Together, it boosts community morale, but alone, it still releases the positive effects of dopamine, which enable us to focus better when we get back to work/class/listening to others.
- Dance Party
  What You Need: Family, friends, classmates, colleagues—the list is endless! An open mind and a nonjudgmental perspective for yourself or others.
  Activity: Make movement a fun activity with others. Have a spontaneous dance party in the living room to your favorite tunes. This can work at home, at school, or in the office. Whenever you need to relieve stress—move it out!
  Tip: It's a great way to bond and relieve stress together. Dancing together can enhance social bonding and reduce stress, thanks to the release of endorphins and oxytocin.
- Rhythmic Exercise
  What You Need: A device to create a personalized playlist for yourself or others.
  Activity: If you're into walking, running, cycling, and so on, create a playlist that matches the pace you want to maintain. The rhythm will help keep you motivated and consistent.
  Tip: Beyond keeping a steady pace, the music can help control steady breath. Try breathing to the beat or find your own pattern of controlled breathing (in two, out two). Rhythmic music has been shown to improve exercise performance and adherence by enhancing motivation and regulating breathing patterns.
- Create a Drum Circle
  What You Need: Anything that can be used as a percussion instrument—pots, pans, wooden spoons, or even a tabletop.
  Activity: Start with a simple beat that everyone can follow. Gradually add complexity by introducing different rhythms. Encourage each person to take turns leading the rhythm. This not only strengthens coordination and listening skills but also brings a sense of unity and cooperation.
  Tip: Make it a weekly ritual. Over time, you can explore different styles, such as African drumming, Brazilian samba, or even create your own unique family groove. Regular drum circles have been shown to reduce stress and build social connections, enhancing the release of oxytocin and lowering cortisol levels.

- Mindful Listening and Sound Exploration
What You Need: A quiet space and an open mind.
Activity: Play different types of music and focus on how each piece makes you feel. Notice the instruments, rhythms, and melodies. Discuss with family members or friends how certain sounds resonate with you emotionally. This practice enhances emotional awareness and can deepen your connection with others.
Tip: Explore sounds from nature, such as birds chirping or rain falling, and see how they can be incorporated into your musical explorations. This can also be a relaxing way to wind down the day. Engaging in mindful listening has been linked to reduced anxiety and improved emotional regulation.

REFLECTIVE JOURNALING

1. Reflect on a time when music brought a group of people together. What was the event, and how did music enhance the sense of community?
2. How do you already use music to help focus in the classroom or at home? Is it before an exam, after recess to help the students transition back for the rest of the day, or mid-morning to refocus as a group?
3. How can we use music or nonverbal cues to help others feel safe to communicate? Consider a situation where someone is struggling to express their emotions. How might you use music to create a safe space for them?
4. How can you create your musical threads just as a conductor creates a program? Think about the different elements that make up your daily life. How can you weave music into these moments to enhance your experience and well-being?
5. Reflect on a time when music brought a group of people together. What was the event, and how did music enhance the sense of community?
6. What does any of this have to do with mindful action? How can becoming more deliberate and focused on the associations between music and emotions impact your mindfulness practice?

NOTES

1. Linda Peterson, John Brereton, Joseph Bizup, Anne Fernald, and Melissa Goldthwaite, eds., *The Norton Anthology 13th Edition* (W.W. Norton & Company, 2011), 58.

2. Jon Kabat-Zinn, *Wherever You Go, There You Are: Mindfulness Meditation in Everyday Life* (Hatchette, 2005), 4.

3. "Soprano in Lockdown Passionately Sings 'Time to Say Goodbye' over Italy's Rooftops," ClassicFM, last modified March 23, 2020, https://www.classicfm.com/discover-music/periods-genres/opera/soprano-lockdown-viral-time-to-say-goodbye/.

4. Nicholas J. Conard, Maria Malina, and Susanne C. Münzel, "New Flutes Document the Earliest Musical Tradition in Southwest Germany," *Nature* 460 (2009): 737–740, https://doi.org/10.1038/nature08169.

5. Susanne Langer, *Philosophy in a New Key* (Harvard University Press, 1951), 93.

6. Langer, *Philosophy in a New Key*, 93.

7. Steven Mithen, *The Singing Neanderthals: The Origins of Music, Language, Mind, and Body* (Weidenfeld and Nicholson, 2005).

8. "It Turns Out We Were Born to Groove," Scientific American, last modified January 10, 2024, https://www.scientificamerican.com/article/it-turns-out-we-were-born-to-groove/.

9. Kristin Weineck, Olivia Xin Wen, and Molly J. Henry, "Neural Synchronization is Strongest to the Spectral Flux of Slow Music and Depends on Familiarity and Beat Salience," *Elife* (2009), https://doi.org/10.7554/eLife.75515.

10. Paul F. Berliner, *Thinking in Jazz: The Infinite Art of Improvisation* (University of Chicago Press, 1994).

11. Ingrid Monson, *Saying Something: Jazz Improvisation and Interaction* (University of Chicago Press, 1996).

Chapter 11

Espressivo

Playing with Expression

The greatness of a community is most accurately measured by the compassionate actions of its members. —Coretta Scott King[1]

THREADS

- How can sounds influence our feelings?
- What does any of this have to do with mindful action?
- How can we use music to change or impact our mood?
- How can you create your musical threads just as a conductor creates a program?
- Community building through music.
- Spirituality, music, and mindfulness.

THE UNIVERSAL LANGUAGE

Turning in their seats, talking with friends, and waving to others across the room. the students kept buzzing even as the teachers hushed them. It was time for the morning assembly! As the principal began to introduce the band, the musicians were still nowhere in sight (figure 11.1).

Then, from the hallway, a trumpet blares, announcing, "Here we are!" The room quiets. As the rest of the band joins the trumpeter, the musicians parade down the aisles, playing as they go. The students, eyes wide reach out to touch the instruments and performers like devoted fans devoted fans at a rock concert.

Picture 11.1. Juneteenth celebration, West Village 2021. *Courtesy of ©2025 Juan Patino Photography.*

The next concert, same music, same purposeful program to introduce music as a vehicle for mindful action to students. Only this time the room is full of neurodivergent students. Some are nonverbal and some in wheelchairs. In one part of this session, students come up on stage, select an instrument, and choose an emotion they want to express. The musician then plays a piece that reflects that emotion. The students often clap, smile, and point at the instrument.

One young boy, who had been quietly observing, suddenly points to "happy" on his communication device and shows it to the French horn player. Without hesitation the skilled musician Peter DelGrosso, Creative Director of Mozart for Munchkins, plays a joyful, bouncy tune. The boy's eyes light up, and he begins to smile and sway to the music. The room fills with laughter—a shared joy of creating something beautiful together.

This story vividly illustrates how music, as a nonverbal form of communication, can transcend typical barriers and connect us on a deeply emotional level. Whether in a classroom, at home, a concert hall, or in a therapy session, music creates a shared language of connection, understanding, and emotional well-being.

Through the music, the students and teachers were fully present and aware. They are open to deeper connections, not just with others, but with themselves. Those amazing moments of interaction without words between students and musicians built connections, touched hearts, and perhaps ignited a mindful spark of possibilities for the teachers, assistants, and administrators.

THE EMOTIONAL LANGUAGE OF MUSIC

Musicians recognize how certain sounds stir specific emotions. For some, a melancholic minor key might bring a deep sense of calm and beauty, while an upbeat tune might stir frustration rather than joy. The listeners' emotional responses are highly individual, shaped by personal experiences, cultural background, and neurological differences.

Music seems to be a form of communication that predates language, but if each listener's emotional responses vary greatly, how does it connect us to others? How does this work?

In concerts, the musicians are usually on stage and the audience responds differently depending on the type of event. Classical concert halls are usually silent. A bluegrass jam is usually filled with clapping and singing. Rap, pop, and hip-hop concerts are energetic, with fans cheering and singing along, almost no silence!

What if we broke that fourth wall during concerts to connect the musicians with the audience? Even when words feel impossible, music speaks.

KIDS FEEL IT: UNDERSTANDING MUSIC AND EMOTION THROUGH A CHILD'S PERSPECTIVE

We put this to the test with a breakfast interview, asking Sara's five- and seven-year-olds how music makes them feel. Granted, these are kids who are exposed to music through lessons, dance, at home, and at school. The conversation was fairly open-ended to capture their raw and genuine responses.

Eva, the oldest, responded first, saying, "If you feel angry or distressed or sad, music will actually just help you calm down and make you feel better." Her younger brother, Marlowe, chimed in with his own take: "If you're sad, if you get angry about something that I did, sometimes I can actually go and do some music. And that made me feel better. I was on my mom's piano. I played some music, and I felt better."

Marlowe's response highlights a natural, intuitive use of music to self-regulate emotions. Playing an instrument or simply engaging in music-making can significantly reduce stress and enhance emotional well-being. Engaging in musical activities, whether playing an instrument or listening, can activate brain regions involved in emotion regulation, reducing stress and improving mood.[2] When Marlowe feels overwhelmed, he often retreats to the piano, hides under it for a moment, then emerges to play, finding calm in the sounds surrounding him.

When asked why he started doing this, Marlowe simply replied, "Feel better." Don't we all want to feel better? As simple as that answer is, there is such clarity in his words.

To expand beyond playing, Eva added, "Sometimes I like to play a sound machine or calming music of a waterfall. It really helps when I fall asleep, when I get stressed out, or [if I'm] getting really tired. Then I don't feel stressed out, and . . . I can have some nice sleep. It feels really calming to me. It feels like I just get better when I start getting angry, stressed out, or even sad."

The idea that music helps her "just get better" reflects the universal experience of using music for emotional regulation, which is backed by numerous studies highlighting the calming effects of music. Listening to relaxing music before a stressful event has been shown to significantly reduce cortisol levels, helping individuals to recover more quickly from stress.[3]

As a family, we often listen to the same songs on repeat. Wanting to explore this further, we asked, "What happens if we play a song that you don't know?"

Marlowe, raising his hand enthusiastically, said, "You should listen to it first. See if you like it or not. And if you don't, then you can listen a little bit more if you want to try the whole song. Or if you don't, you don't have to."

This approach, listening without judgment, aligns with principles of mindful listening, where the focus is on being open to the experience of the music without preconceived notions. Engaging in mindful action and music in a nonjudgmental, open way can enhance emotional awareness and lead to more positive emotional experiences.

During the school year, Eva's class often danced for movement breaks, following prescribed dance moves from programs like Kidz Bop or GoNoodle. She would bring these dance moves home, asking for the same songs. But what happened when she forgot the moves?

"If I remember, I just do that move. The moves I remember. And then when I can't remember, even though I get frustrated, I just try to feel calm and relaxed and just do moves that I like. Like doing splits, which is my favorite thing. I'm great."

Eva's ability to adapt and create her own movements when she can't remember the prescribed ones illustrates how movement, especially when paired with music, can serve as a powerful tool for self-expression and emotional regulation. Dance and movement, particularly when synchronized with music, can enhance emotional regulation, improve mood, and create a sense of self-efficacy in children.[4]

These children come from a home, among many like it, that inspired *Resonant Minds*. Why does this work for them? Why do they like to work or read to certain music? As mentioned earlier, Bach's "Cello Suites" has linked to their implicit memory over the years, creating an automatic response of calm, focus, and work.

Eva said, "I like to have it in the background because it makes me feel better if I get frustrated, [like when] I can't figure out the answer. Or if I just get stressed out that I'm so angry that I don't even know what the answer is. It helps me, and it makes me feel like it's fine."

Fine is not better. When we're "stressed out" or "frustrated," music can help move us to "fine," we'll take it. From "fine" we can become "better," and hopefully even "good."

This is an amazing sense of presence in kids. It's hard to be in touch with emotions and to know what might help us. We wanted to explore this a bit more, so we asked Eva for more details.

"When I get the answer right, I feel encouraged. And sometimes when I can't do it, it makes me feel discouraged, but I just put up all my strength and try [to] remember how it makes me feel better. I say, 'I can do this. I got this.' Those are great in my mind, and it feels real. And then I get braver, and I just feel like I can do anything I want."

This dialogue underscores the profound impact that music and movement can have on emotional regulation and well-being. Their insights lend lived experience to the growing research behind the therapeutic benefits of music, particularly in how it helps individuals process emotions, reduce stress, and create a community.

So many of us already have these patterns in life.

Why do we pick certain songs for our friends to listen to? We want to entertain them and we want to share with them something important and personal. What do the songs trigger? Love, affection, concern. From an intentionally chosen song, we share emotions. Remember that graduation playlist? Songs were added to elicit the remembered emotions, not just the memory itself.

Music doesn't just bring back memories, it revives the emotions attached to the memories. Different parts of the brain work together, connecting music and mindful action for emotional regulation, cognitive functions, and stress reduction. By understanding and applying this knowledge, we enhance the benefits of both practices, promoting greater emotional balance, cognitive resilience, and overall mental health. Integrating music into mindfulness practices offers a powerful, accessible way to engage the brain's natural abilities for healing and growth.

EMOTIONAL BALANCE AND COGNITIVE RESILIENCE

Music's role in emotional balance and cognitive resilience can be extremely profound. The purposeful use of music to influence emotions isn't just something that happens passively; it can be a tool intentionally used to regulate emotional states. For educators, parents, and individuals alike, this means that music can be a practical tool for managing emotions in both everyday life and challenging situations.

Cognitive resilience gives us the mental strength for:

- adaptability,
- stress management,
- emotional regulation,
- social support, and
- neuroplasticity.

Cognitive resilience refers to the brain's ability to adapt to stress, adversity, or trauma while maintaining cognitive function. Engaging with music, particularly through active participation such as playing an instrument or singing, can enhance cognitive resilience by stimulating brain regions involved in memory, attention, and emotional regulation.[5]

Participating in musical activities can enhance social bonding and create a sense of belonging, which is crucial for emotional health and resilience.[6]

CONTINUING THE THREAD THROUGH TIME

Music has always played a vital role in bringing people together. From the sacred echoes of Gregorian chants to the lively madrigals, operas, and soirees that punctuated social gatherings throughout history, music has served as a universal language. This connection between religion, politics, history, and music is profound and multifaceted, weaving through centuries and across cultures. While we can't cover every aspect of this rich tapestry, we can focus on the simple link of music and emotions.

René Descartes, the seventeenth-century philosopher, proposed that music has the power to stir and influence human emotions through six basic affects:

1. *admiration* (admiration),
2. *amour* (love),
3. *haine* (hatred),
4. *désir* (desire),

5. *joie* (joy), and
6. *tristesse* (sorrow).[7]

These emotional responses can be evoked through certain scales, intervals, and sounds. Over time, additional emotions like sadness, anger, and jealousy have also been associated with specific musical elements. Even today, we instinctively associate certain sounds with specific feelings. A minor key might evoke a sense of sadness, while a major key can uplift our mood. This isn't just an historical observation—it's a deeply relevant aspect of our modern lives. Music's ability to influence emotions is not only evident anecdotally.

Juslin and Västfjäll's research provides scientific evidence that different musical elements can significantly alter mood and emotional states.[8] They have observed the various mechanisms through which music induces emotions, including brain stem reflexes (automatic responses to sounds), rhythmic entrainment (synchronization of the body's rhythms with the music), and evaluative conditioning (associating certain music with specific events or feelings).

In our everyday experiences, we observe how we instinctively react to these musical elements. A tense movie scene with high-pitched dissonant strings can stir anxiety, while a serene landscape accompanied by slow, melodic piano music might bring feelings of peace.

Would a horror scene be as scary without the music leading up to it?

This emotional influence of music can be a double-edged sword. When feeling down, listening to sad music might intensify those feelings, leading to a deeper emotional experience. On the other hand, it's almost impossible to remain upset while singing "Sweet Caroline" in a stadium surrounded by thousands of "friends" for the night.

The collective joy and energy of such a moment showcases our ability to create a shared emotional experience through music. Similarly, when you're overly excited, it's challenging to maintain that heightened state if you start listening to slow, soothing music.

The cyclical relationship between music and emotion is fascinating—music evokes emotions, and in turn, emotions can be enhanced or altered by the music we listen to. Let that resonate for a moment. We can pick music to bring on certain emotions, or we can pick music to alternate the current emotion we are feeling.

Imagine a song that reminds you of an ex-partner. Every time you hear it, you may be flooded with sadness, joy, or nostalgia. The emotional connection to that song is so strong because of the attachment to your implicit memory. In fact, you might avoid the song altogether to prevent revisiting those feelings. As we learned about in chapter 7, with enough repetition and new habit formations to this song, we can create new emotional attachments.

This interplay between music and emotion is so intrinsic that even the word "emotion" itself contains the root "motion," reminding us that movement—both physical and emotional—is central to our experience of music.

Music, unlike language, is a "language of feeling."[9] Rhythms mirror the patterns of life, with tensions, resolutions, crescendos, and silences that evoke complex emotional responses. Eliciting measurable physiological changes, music creates variations in heart rate or hormonal levels, corresponding to the emotions being expressed or experienced.[10]

EXPLORING THE CONNECTION BETWEEN MUSIC AND SPIRITUALITY

Music and spirituality are deeply intertwined through their shared capacity to tap into and amplify emotions. Music can stir emotions in ways that words alone often cannot.

The relationship between music and spirituality is intricate and deeply personal. Spirituality, broadly defined, refers to a sense of connection to something greater than oneself, which can involve religious beliefs, but also broader notions of purpose, meaning, and inner peace. This sense of connection is often facilitated by music, which can lead to an array of emotional responses.

In a recent conversation on this topic, we were told, "I don't think I'm a spiritual person. I'm not sure I believe in spirituality or that higher place through religion." This perspective is not uncommon; nearly all of us go through this questioning. What about when children are sung to sleep by their mother? Is that spiritual? Or the same mother, now with grandchildren, repeats the tune of "Puff the Magic Dragon" (remember that one?!) or makes a simple repetitive sound such as "sha, sha, baby" while stroking their backs. Are these repetitive sounds spiritual, meditative, mindful moments in their own rights?

Music that elicits emotions is well-documented. Listening to music can trigger the release of oxytocin, which is linked to feelings of connection and trust. Those connections of shared songs while putting a child to sleep, the intimacy of singing together, and that inner peace connects us to whatever we might believe. These biochemical responses help explain why music is so often intertwined with spiritual practices—it creates an emotional experience that feels transcendent, elevating the listener beyond their ordinary state of being.

The simple act of singing a lullaby to a child not only soothes the child but also strengthens the emotional bond between parent and child through the shared experience of music. Similarly, communal singing in religious settings can create a deep sense of inner peace and collective unity, connecting individuals to their spiritual beliefs through the power of music. These shared songs link that inner peace connecting us to whatever we might believe in.

Spirituality can be the moment someone plays music in a hospice room; it can be connecting to a parent with dementia through a shared song that, even though they don't know who you are anymore, may resurface the remembered lyrics of the song they sang to you when you were growing up.

Spirituality through music is seen in the gospel music of churches, where repetitive chants and words create their own kind of music. The haunting strands of *Kol Nidre* during Yom Kippur, with stories of a single melody dating back to the Spanish Inquisition. Perhaps it's in *qawwali*, with its repetitive rhythms and melodies, that helps Sufis transcend ordinary consciousness. Spirituality can be found in something as simple as the familiar strands of "Jingle Bells" and shouting "Hey!" together on a cold evening.

Can we be spiritual without music? Sure. Does it have the same impact? Music connects us, no matter what we believe.

When talking with Gregory Hutchings, he mentioned gospel music on his own, and it was impossible to ignore his draw to this type of music. "When I heard gospel music growing up, it was always in church, [and] I always felt a sense of peace. That's how I get my peace. It gives me a better understanding about what I need to do. Whether it's a decision I have to make in regards to my life, or a professional decision."

Gospel music has such deep roots, both historically and familial. Greg remarked that he "got introduced to gospel music through my great-grandmother, Nanny Hutchings. She was in Newtown, Pennsylvania, in the country. In my household, though, we didn't go to church every Sunday. That wasn't a thing that I did growing up."

Greg now goes to church every day. What about the music? What if there wasn't gospel music or any type of music as part of the experience? The answer was clear, "The sermons are good too, but I couldn't see myself just going to listen to a sermon without any music. We moved throughout my life, [but] even now with our family, they had to have a good choir. So that was a part of the . . . deal breaker. If they didn't have a good choir and some good music, as well as a good sermon, then I wasn't going to be a part of that."

Music's role in spiritual experiences highlights its ability to go beyond the ordinary, to connect us with the sacred, the divine, or the deeply personal. Whether through the soaring harmonies of a gospel choir, the meditative chants of a Sufi dervish, or the quiet contemplation of a classical symphony, music provides a gateway to the spiritual, making it an essential part of human experience.

Spirituality is music. And music is spiritual. We seek a connection—a deep bond and awareness with oneself that can include others or remain a personal experience—and spirituality through music can be how it resonates within us.

THE HARMONIOUS POWER OF MUSIC

Music is more than just sounds strung together—it's a vital thread woven into the fabric of our lives. We've explored how music transcends the ordinary, acting as a bridge between our emotions, spirituality, and cognitive resilience. Whether in a crowded school auditorium, a quiet moment at home, or a gathering of friends, music is there, guiding us through life's highs and lows.

Music is that universal language we all speak, regardless of the words we use or the culture we come from. It connects us on a deeply emotional level, whether we're sharing a laugh with thousands of strangers at a concert or finding solace in a song that understands our pain. It's not just about the melody or the rhythm—it's about the emotions that are stirred, the memories that are sparked, and the sense of community that is created.

Music helps us heal. It helps us connect. It helps us feel. And in those moments of feeling—whether it's joy, sorrow, or something in between—music offers us a way to understand and express what might otherwise be inexpressible. It helps us find balance in a chaotic world, offering a steady rhythm to cling to when everything else seems out of sync.

Music's power doesn't stop there—it's also a tool for building tenacity. In those moments when life gets tough, when the challenges seem too great, music can be the anchor that holds us steady. It allows us to process emotions, to find strength in vulnerability, and to connect with something greater than ourselves. Whether it's the spiritual lift of a gospel choir or the calming influence of a favorite tune, music provides the emotional and cognitive support we need to keep going.

As you move forward, think about how you can intentionally use music in your life. Play that song that makes you feel invincible when you need a boost. Turn to the melodies that soothe you when you're feeling overwhelmed. And don't hesitate to share music with those around you—because in sharing, we create connections that go beyond words.

Hans Christian Andersen once said, "Where words fail, music speaks." Let music continue to speak to you, for you, and through you, guiding you through the complex harmonies of life.

EMOTIONAL RESET WITH MUSIC

What You Need: A pair of headphones or speakers and an open mind to intentionally select a playlist. The playlist can include any tune that impacts your mood—whether it's fast, upbeat, calming, or soothing. It's an opportunity to explore what resonates with you for a mental and emotional reset.

Activity: Whenever you or those you are leading feel overwhelmed or stressed, take a five-minute break to listen to a favorite song or piece of music. Focus on the rhythm, melody, and how the music makes you feel. Use this moment to let the music guide you through the emotions and help you transition from one state of mind to another.

Tip: Create specific playlists for different emotional needs—calm for stress, upbeat for low energy, and so on. This practice becomes more effective and accessible when needed most. To encourage a greater sense of community, discuss with those around you how your mood might have changed from the start of the song to the end. This heightens emotional awareness and strengthens emotional resilience as you learn to manage and regulate your emotional states through music.

Family Music Time

What You Need: A variety of instruments (they don't have to be professional—pots, pans, or even clapping hands work) and an open space.

Activity: Set aside time each week for a family music session. Let each family member choose an instrument or a rhythm and create a spontaneous family band. Rotate leaders so everyone gets a chance to direct the music.

Tip: Make this a ritual, and consider recording your sessions. Over time, you'll see how everyone becomes more attuned to each other, and it's a great way to bond and create groove.

Music and Emotional Awareness Workshop

What You Need: A selection of music spanning different genres and emotional tones, a comfortable seating arrangement, and a journal.

Activity: Organize a workshop where participants listen to different pieces of music and journal their emotional responses. After listening to each piece, participants can share how the music influenced their mood and reflect on any memories or emotions that surfaced. Discuss how music can be used to navigate emotional challenges and build resilience.

Tip: Encourage participants to create their own "emotional toolkit" of music—songs or pieces that help them manage specific emotions, such as stress, sadness, or anger. This toolkit can be a powerful resource.

Personal Mindfulness with Music

What You Need: A quiet space, a comfortable seat, and a selection of instrumental or ambient music.

Activity: Set aside ten minutes each day to practice mindful listening. Sit comfortably, close your eyes, and focus entirely on the music. Notice the details—different instruments, changes in rhythm, and how the music flows.

Tip: Use this practice to start or end your day, helping to center your thoughts and emotions. Over time, you'll find it easier to tap into this calm state during more stressful moments.

Cognitive Resilience Building

What You Need: A musical instrument (or an app that simulates one) and a basic tutorial.

Activity: Challenge yourself or your students to learn a new instrument. Start with simple melodies and gradually increase the complexity. Focus on the process, not just the outcome—learning an instrument strengthens cognitive flexibility and resilience.

Tip: Don't rush the learning process. Celebrate small milestones, and encourage reflection on how learning music impacts your mood and cognitive abilities.

More practical applications:

1. Think about a time when a specific sound or piece of music changed your mood. What was it, and how did it make you feel?
2. Reflect on a piece of music that evokes strong emotions for you. Why do you think it has such an impact?
3. Have you ever used music to change how you feel? What type of music do you listen to when you need to calm down, focus, or cheer up?
4. How can becoming more deliberate and focused on the associations between music and emotions impact your mindfulness practice?
5. Think about the songs you turn to when you're feeling different emotions. Why do these particular songs resonate with you?
6. Reflect on how you might use music intentionally to shift your mood or emotional state throughout the day.

7. Consider a situation where someone is struggling to express their emotions. How might you use music to create a safe space for them?
8. Think about the different elements that make up your daily life. How can you weave music into these moments to enhance your experience and well-being?
9. For fun, generate a poem by AI:
   In the stillness of a mindful breath,
   Where spirit whispers, soft as death,
   Music flows, a sacred stream,
   Uniting hearts in a shared dream.

   Notes that dance on air so light,
   Echo through the silent night,
   Melodies that touch the soul,
   Filling empty spaces, making whole.

   Mindfulness, a gentle guide,
   In the quiet, thoughts reside,
   Listening with an open heart,
   Each moment a work of art.

   Spiritual paths entwine with sound,
   In this harmony, we're unbound,
   A deeper sense of self we find,
   In music, spirit, intertwined.

   Strings that pluck the chords of grace,
   Voices lifting, finding place,
   Rhythms beating with the earth,
   A symphony of sacred birth.

   In mindful practice, we align,
   With the divine, the pure, the kind,
   Breathing in and out with ease,
   Feeling spirit in the breeze.

   Songs of old and new collide,
   In this space where truths abide,
   Echoes of a higher plane,
   Where soul and music share domain.

Chants and hymns, a sacred prayer,
Lifting spirits, laying bare,
The essence of our inner light,
Guiding us through darkest night.

In this blend of sound and still,
We find our purpose, feel the thrill,
Of unity with all that is,
A sacred, mindful, musical bliss.

So let the music soothe your mind,
In mindful moments, peace you'll find,
Embrace the spiritual song within,
And let the sacred dance begin.

NOTES

1. Coretta Scott King, *My Life, My Love, My Legacy* (Henry Holt and Company, 2017), 217.
2. Daisy Fancourt and Saoirse Finn, "What Is the Evidence on the Role of the Arts in Improving Health and Well-being? A Scoping Review," *World Health Organization,* Regional Office for Europe, Health Evidence Network synthesis report, no. 67, 2019, https://www.ncbi.nlm.nih.gov/books/NBK553773/.
3. Thoma et al., "The Effect of Music on the Human Stress Response," 133–141.
4. Kimberley D. Lakes and William T. Hoyt, "Promoting Self-Regulation through School-Based Martial Arts Training," *Journal of Applied Developmental Psychology* 25, no. 3 (2004): 283–302, https://doi.org/10.1016/j.appdev.2004.04.002.
5. Thoma et al., "The Effect of Music on the Human Stress Response," 133–141.
6. Stefan Koelsch, "Towards a Neural Basis of Music-Evoked Emotions," *Trends in Cognitive Sciences* 14, no. 3 (2010): 131–137, https://doi:10.1016/j.tics.2010.01.002.
7. René Descartes, *Les Passions de l'âme* (Henry Le Gras, 1649).
8. Patrick N. Juslin and Daniel Västfjäll, "Emotional Responses to Music: The Need to Consider Underlying Mechanisms," *Behavioral and Brain Sciences* 31, no. 5 (2008): 559–621, https://doi:10.1017/S0140525X08005293.
9. Langer, *Philosophy in a New Key,* 199.
10. Juslin and Västfjäll, "Emotional Responses to Music: The Need to Consider Underlying Mechanisms," 559–621.

Chapter 12

Conducting

Leading through Resonance

Empathy is an essential leadership quality. It allows leaders to understand and connect with their team's concerns and struggles, inspiring them to work together towards a shared goal.

—Doris Kearns Goodwin[1]

THREADS

- How does mindfulness become part of a culture, and what is our role as leaders?
- What if we don't know much about music or mindfulness?
- Using music as a tool for leadership and motivation.
- Explanation of mindfulness and its benefits for creative problem-solving.
- Connection between mindfulness and enhanced leadership qualities.

ALL ABOUT NURTURING

The Bear was one of 2024's most popular streaming shows. In one episode, a wise and seasoned chef talks to a chef completing his first day. The gentle tone and clear definition of the seasoned chef's purpose serves well as a guide to leadership for all of us. Reflecting on his twenty-three years in the role, he remarks that being a chef is not just about the food. It's about nurturing and connecting with people (figure 12.1).

Figure 12.1. Conductor. *Original art by Debra Sherman.*

His simple yet powerful advice is to come to work each day and aim to be just a little better than the day before. Over time, he advises, this consistent effort—combined with education, training, and skill-building—creates a path to mastery.

We love his guidance, which was to come to work every day and just try to do a little better than the day before. Just a little better. Over the years that will build. The path will be filled with education, training, and skills.

Nurture yourself. Nurture the team for whom you are cooking. Nurture those you serve. And remember they are nurturing the farmers, fishermen, foragers, gardeners . . . all who brought the ingredients.

It's all about nurturing.

Thank you, Chef.

While we use chefs as our analogy in this chapter, this can be replaced with a first grade teacher, chairman of the board, or any other leadership role you wish to substitute.

WE ARE ALL LEADERS

Each of us make decisions—about ourselves, our families, our friends. When we use the terms leaders and leadership we often think of a CEO or another formal head of an organization. Over many years of case studies, research, and reflection about leaders and leadership, we've come to better understand the leadership potential within each of us.

Doris Kearns Goodwin, in *Team of Rivals: The Political Genius of Abraham Lincoln*, highlights the critical role empathy played in Lincoln's leadership, particularly his "extraordinary ability to put himself in the shoes of others, to see the world from their perspective."[2] This quality allowed him to connect deeply with both friends and foes, building trust even in the most divisive of circumstances. Lincoln's empathetic understanding of the "motives and desires of others" was not just a personal trait but a leadership tool.

Here is another excellent quote about leadership, written by Simon Sinek: "Leadership is not about being in charge. It is about taking care of those in your charge."[3]

These comments resonate with us.

We do not think that it's such a huge leap from the chef or home cook in a kitchen who nurtures, to a president who puts themselves in the shoes of others. Both have empathy for those around them.

Leadership is the ability to guide, influence, or inspire individuals, groups, or organizations toward the achievement of specific goals or a shared vision. Effective leadership involves a combination of qualities, skills, and actions, such as:

- vision and strategy,
- communication,
- motivation,
- decision-making,
- adaptability,
- empathy, and
- integrity.

We the people make the difference as leaders and as shapers of the culture around us. For our vision of a movement focused on music and mindful action, leadership is so important. Just as we believe that each of us can be conductors of the music that shapes our lives and communities, we recognize that we all have the potential to be leaders—both of ourselves and for others.

It starts small. We open the windows of our minds and take the first step in mindful use of music to be the leaders of our empathetic, caring lives.

At the beginning of this book, in Forte, we wrote about the need to include music in the curriculum and workplace, not as an adjunct, but as a core tool toward understanding one another. Who should take the first step in making this empathetic, more complete view of life take place? We could wait for policymakers, educators, business leaders, or administrators to include music in English literature or social studies curriculum . . . or we could all take initiative and become leaders in our own right by intentionally including music in our learning and living.

This does not diminish the responsibility of "formal" leaders to set the tone, use music, and build connections. We know there is shared responsibility.

Our alignment of music with mindful action is the moment we take that breath, think a moment about what we're doing, and dream how we might make our lives a little bit better each day, just as the seasoned chef advised. That moment of calm reflection is the moment to open our minds and hearts.

We know that music is not the whole answer to resonant leadership. However, we do know that the use of music as mindful action, coupled with executive function skills, will lead to the habits of successful and effective leadership.

NOTES FROM THE KITCHEN

In the demanding and high-pressure environment of a professional kitchen, where precision, speed, and coordination are paramount, Chef Jessica Masanotti has found that music plays a critical role in creating a productive and harmonious workspace. Her approach to leadership, deeply intertwined with the strategic use of music, offers valuable lessons on how to cultivate mindfulness, enhance focus, and build a strong sense of community among team members.

In organizations around the world, the tone and culture are essential. Anyone entering a company, team, or even a meeting can immediately sense the energy from the environment. Everything from the way communication flows, to the speed at which decisions are made, to the underlying values signals the type of experience that employees, partners, and clients are about to have.

Just as chefs use music to create the right atmosphere in the kitchen, leaders use their influence to cultivate a positive, productive, and inclusive environment. This involves being mindful of the "beat" of the organization—whether it's the pace of work, the flow of communication, or the rhythm of teamwork. Just as different musical genres can inspire various moods and energies in a restaurant, different leadership styles can evoke varying responses in a team.

Jessica's experience in the kitchen can be seen as a microcosm of leadership at large. "It's a stage, and these chefs aren't just cooking food. They're performing, and everybody has their part," she tells us during an interview. This reflects how leaders must also recognize that every team member has a role to play in the larger organizational "performance." By orchestrating these roles with intention—much like a conductor guiding an orchestra—leaders can ensure that their teams work in harmony, achieving greater outcomes together than they could individually.

In this analogy, every movement—whether it's cutting vegetables, sautéing, or plating a dish—is a part of a larger, choreographed dance. "Every single movement that you're doing, from cutting to cooking to mixing together in a bowl and putting it on a plate, all of that is being orchestrated along with the vibe and the beat of the music."

This orchestration is key to ensuring that the kitchen operates smoothly, with each team member moving in sync, avoiding collisions, and maintaining the flow of service. Music, in this context, acts as the conductor of this culinary orchestra, setting the tempo and ensuring that all the chefs are working in harmony.

BUILDING FOCUS AND REDUCING STRESS

In a high-stress environment like a busy kitchen, where the stakes are high and the pace is relentless, maintaining focus is crucial. Jessica has found that music helps her and her team stay centered and avoid the kind of spiraling thoughts that can lead to mistakes or heightened anxiety. She thought back to her first week in a high-paced NYC kitchen several years ago. "If it was silent, I would have been a wreck. I would have been in my head spiraling these thoughts of, 'you're not good enough. You're not gonna get it. You're never gonna get it.'" This is akin to George's story in the classroom, alone with his thoughts without the guidance of music to latch onto.

The presence of music, particularly the right kind of music, shifts the atmosphere, making the kitchen or workspace feel less like a pressure cooker and more like a space where creativity and efficiency can flourish. Sometimes, the absence of this music can have detrimental effects. Jessica notes that on days when the kitchen's speaker isn't working, the energy and productivity dip noticeably. "There were times where the speaker in the kitchen wasn't working. It drastically changed the vibe in the kitchen because it just felt slower and lower and just not as energetic." This highlights the importance of maintaining a positive and engaging atmosphere in any setting. Without it, the motivation and cohesion that drive success can quickly dissipate.

MUSIC AS A TOOL FOR BUILDING COMMUNITY

Beyond improving focus and reducing stress, music in Jessica's kitchen also serves as a powerful tool for building community. "Chefs are moving around each other. No one's bumping into each other, and there could be so many opportunities for crashes and cuts and burns, but generally, when everybody's focused and performing at their highest and best potential, it's this beautiful dance."

A shared experience—whether through music, shared goals, or collaborative projects—is a place where leaders can create an environment for everyone to feel connected and motivated to contribute.

Jessica's approach to leadership extends beyond the kitchen. "My job as a leader is to make our people feel like we know them, we see them, and that they have a purpose," she says.

This philosophy is universal. Whether in a kitchen, an office, a classroom, or on a project site, leaders are responsible for nurturing their teams, ensuring that each person feels valued, understood, and motivated to do their best work. By being intentional about the environment they create—much like Jessica is with her music selections—leaders can set the stage for success, not just for individual tasks but for the overall harmony and productivity of the entire organization.

Jessica's use of music to build community aligns with the idea that shared musical experiences can enhance social bonding and create a sense of belonging. In the high-stress environment of a kitchen, where teamwork is essential, music serves as a unifying force that helps to maintain a positive and collaborative atmosphere.

The key is intentionality. Just as a chef selects music to enhance the kitchen's atmosphere and performance, leaders must carefully choose their actions, words, and strategies to shape the organizational culture. By doing so, they create an environment where everyone can thrive, contribute, and feel a part of something greater.

SHINING EYES

Benjamin Zander inspires us with the concept of "shining eyes" as a measure of success and connection in leadership, education, and life. In his TED Talk and book, *The Art of Possibility*, co-authored with Rosamund Stone Zander, he shares transformative insights on leadership, music, and the power of perspective.

At the heart of the "shining eyes" concept is the belief that true leadership and teaching should inspire and ignite passion and enthusiasm in others. It should nurture that inner spark by encouraging others to see their potential and embrace learning with excitement. When people's eyes shine, it's a signal of a deep connection to, understanding of, and appreciation for the experience they're a part of.

Zander encourages leaders and educators to approach interactions with the belief that everyone is an "A" student. This perspective creates an environment of trust, respect, and high expectations. When individuals are treated as though they are already successful, they are more likely to see their potential and strive for excellence, resulting in "shining eyes" filled with excitement, confidence, and enthusiasm for learning and growth.

In the *Art of Possibility*, Zander emphasizes the importance of shifting from a mindset of scarcity and competition. Instead, he champions the mindset of abundance and possibility—one that prioritizes opportunities, creativity, and collaboration. He believes that leaders can inspire others to see new possibilities, embrace challenges, and approach situations with optimism, leading to "shining eyes" filled with hope, curiosity, and new possibilities.

Zander believes in the power of connection, empathy, and understanding in leadership and education. By listening actively, understanding others' perspectives, and showing genuine care and support, leaders and educators can build trust and nurture meaningful relationships. Creating a supportive and inclusive environment where individuals feel valued and heard, they are more likely to respond with passion and engagement, bringing "shining eyes" to all they do.

HOW DO YOU KNOW IT'S WORKING?

One cold wintry evening, an orchestra had just finished performing Beethoven's Fifth Symphony in front of a packed concert hall. As the final notes echoed through the air, the audience sat in rapt silence, their eyes wide. That moment of quiet, the space between the notes, meant the performance went beyond mere technical mastery; it connected with each person in a way that moved their hearts and minds. This is how you know it's working.

The Cleveland Orchestra is one of the most renowned orchestras in the world, celebrated not just for its exceptional artistry in musicianship but also for its ability to resonate deeply with audiences. The measure of success for the Cleveland Orchestra extends beyond technical proficiency and critical acclaim; it encompasses a broader vision of impact, relevance, and contribution to society. Their goals may come from the perspective of an orchestra, but with just a bit of tweaking, the goals can apply to just about any field. We can learn from their success indicators how to help view our own success and that of our communities.

Indicators include:

- Quality: reflecting in artistic precision, interpretive styles, and inspiring performances that resonate with audiences, critics, and musicians.
- Community and Engagement: developing a love and appreciation for music.
- Innovation: expanding the boundaries of traditional orchestral repertoire and presentation to explore new ways to connect with audiences.

In leadership, this concept of resonance is equally important. Emerging leadership research indicates three trends: resilience, nimbleness, and resonance. AASA, The School Superintendents Association, and Hanover Research explored the concept of resonant leadership, emphasizing its importance in positive relationships, building trust, and creating a supportive and collaborative work environment.

RESONANCE IN LEADERSHIP

We love the word "resonance." Beyond using it as a leadership attribute, it's a descriptor in music, business, physics, astronomy, chemistry, and love. Resonance occurs when one vibrating object causes another object to vibrate at a higher amplitude, suggesting a lasting powerful connection. "To resonate" typically suggests that a single lasting sound is produced.

Resonant leaders exhibit empathy, actively listen to their team members' concerns and perspectives, and showing genuine care for their well-being. By doing so, they create a supportive and inclusive culture where individuals feel valued, heard, and empowered to contribute their unique skills and insights.

Leading by example, showing integrity, transparency, and authenticity are the hallmarks of a resonant leader. Similar to the open hearts and open minds discussed in previous chapters, this intentional mindset encourages communication, innovation, and diversity of thought.

Just as a skilled conductor brings together individual musicians to create a symphony, a resonant leader brings together diverse individuals, collaborating to achieve shared goals. Like a well-composed piece of music, resonant leadership creates a sense of unity, cohesion, and inspiration, encouraging team members to contribute their best work together toward a common vision.

Many leaders struggle with the balance between being a sage on a stage and an inclusive collaborator. Some teachers were told as they started their careers not to let the students smile until Christmas. Parents often fall back to, "Because I told you so," in answer to a child's questions about why something has to be done. Administrators in many kinds of organizations, business and schools, were trained to be the lead goose where all would follow in tight formation, under the guise of fidelity.

Patterns have changed. Leaders now work hard trying to keep everyone going in the same direction even as their place at the point of the flock continues to evolve.

The conductor still leads. The parents are still the adults. The business supervisor is still in charge. However, how each of us goes about our roles has a greater chance of success if we find balance, using the metaphor and the practice of music mindfully.

Rhythm and tempo in music are similar to the flexibility, pacing, and adaptability of leadership. A skilled leader knows when to accelerate the pace to drive progress and when to slow down to reflect, adapt, and support team members. By maintaining a harmonious balance and rhythm, resonant leaders create a supportive and inclusive culture where individuals feel valued, motivated, and empowered to contribute their talents and insights, much like the various instruments in an orchestra coming together to create a beautiful and cohesive piece of music.

MUSIC AS A TOOL FOR LEADERSHIP AND MOTIVATIONAL STRATEGIES

As we saw with Chef Jessica's kitchen, leaders who effectively integrate music into their leadership approach can leverage its psychological benefits to motivate and inspire their teams. For example, playing background music during work hours can create a more pleasant work environment and help reduce feelings of anxiety and pressure. Music can also serve as a nonverbal form of communication that can reinforce a leader's message and vision.

The strategic use of music in leadership can be seen in various organizational rituals, such as team-building exercises, corporate events, and even during critical project meetings. Music can set the tone for the event, drive engagement, and help to align the team's mood and energy with the goals of the meeting.

Music's role in motivation is particularly significant. Certain types of music can energize the team, while others can help individuals focus or unwind, depending on the needs of the moment. As we saw in Jessica's kitchen, leading can be a dance, and we can set the tone that helps us not step on each other's toes. Leaders who understand and utilize the emotional and physiological effects of music can enhance their motivational strategies, ultimately leading to improved team performance and cohesion.

MINDFULNESS AND LEADERSHIP QUALITIES

Music and mindful action share a unique relationship that can significantly enhance leadership capabilities. Music, by its very nature, encourages individuals to be present and engaged, resonating deeply with the principles of mindfulness. For leaders, integrating music into daily routines or organizational practices can act as a catalyst to create an atmosphere that promotes focus and presence.

In chapter 6, we introduced the use of how different types of music can help us focus. This practice enhances cognitive flexibility, allowing leaders to better adapt to changing situations and to thinking more creatively about problem-solving. The emotional resonance of music aids in regulating mood can be particularly effective in managing stress, a common challenge in leadership roles.

LEADERS WHO USE MUSIC IN THEIR LEADERSHIP PRACTICES

Starting a meeting with guided meditation aided by background music helps to center the group, reduce distractions, and build a collective focus, enabling more productive discussions and creative outcomes.

In politics, leaders often use music at rallies and events to evoke emotions, unify crowds, and communicate messages at a deeper emotional level. When politicians engage with music mindfully, they can more effectively harness its power to inspire and mobilize supporters.

In the arts, directors and conductors exemplify leadership that seamlessly integrates music and mindful action. By deeply understanding the emotional landscape of the music they work with, these leaders guide their performers not just technically but emotionally, enhancing the overall impact of the performance. Their leadership goes beyond mere direction, embracing an empathetic and mindful approach that elevates the collective artistic expression.

The integration of leadership, music, and mindfulness is essential for leaders seeking to navigate the complexities of the modern world. Current and aspiring leaders should consider how they can incorporate these elements into their leadership practices.

RAISING THE BATON

An image that resonates with us is that of a conductor raising their hands in a moment of pause and silence.

The goal is to find mindful, quiet moments so that music can help move us to centering, quiet focus and deliberate action. In order to achieve this, here are the key points of practical applications mentioned throughout this chapter:

1. Start Meetings with music or mindfulness exercises.
2. Create team playlists.
3. Use music to reinforce a message or theme.
4. Take mindful music breaks.
5. Build emotional connection through resonance.
6. Personalize musical experiences.
7. Orchestrate collaborative "team performances."
8. Encourage flow states with music.
9. Use music for stress management.
10. Create a culture of resonant leadership.
11. Use music to enhance creativity and innovation.

NOTES

1. History.com editors, "Doris Kearns Goodwin on Empathy," *History*, accessed September 18, 2024, https://www.history.com/topics/us-presidents/doris-kearns-goodwin-on-empathy-video.
2. Doris Kearns Goodwin, *Team of Rivals: The Political Genius of Abraham Lincoln* (Simon & Schuster, 2005), 145.
3. Simon Sinek, *Leaders Eat Last: Why Some Teams Pull Together and Others Don't* (Penguin Publishing Group, 2014).

Chapter 13

Harmony

Transcending Barriers; Creating Opportunities

Music has to be recognized as an agent of social development in the highest sense because it transmits the highest values—solidarity, harmony, and mutual compassion. —*El Sistema* founder José Antonio Abreu[1]

THREADS

- Music, often referred to as a universal language, plays a vital role in connecting people across different socioeconomic backgrounds and neurodivergent communities.
- Terms like universal are used with full realization that cultural and economic differences shape our personal and collective cultures.
- Music's ability to cross cultural, linguistic, and economic boundaries is one of its most powerful attributes.

Music is often called a universal language, bridging people from different socioeconomic and neurodivergent communities. But while we embrace the term "universal," it's important to acknowledge that personal and collective cultures, shaped by both cultural and economic differences, influence how we experience music. Still, one of music's most powerful traits is its ability to transcend these boundaries. Through mindful action, executive function skills, and deliberate connections, music becomes a bridge—accessible and engaging for everyone (figure 13.1).

Figure 13.1. Music and Mindful Action for All. *Photograph by Rachel Strasburg.*

WHAT IS YOUR BOOK ABOUT, MOMMY?

One morning, Sara's daughter crawled into bed with her and asked, "What's your book about anyway, Mom?"

Oh, what a great question! Sara's daughter, Eva, was the inspiration for Mozart for Munchkins and has been immersed in live and recorded music every day of her life since she was in the womb. That musical spark has passed down through their family.

Sara explained to Eva, that the book is about helping people use music to focus, experience joy, think creatively, and feel part of something bigger. Eva snuggled in close and asked, "But what about people who don't have Alexa?"

This was another insightful question. What about people who don't have access to Alexa, or even to electricity? "How would those people living in remote areas or on restricted means interact with music in the ways discussed in this book?" These are important considerations, and the question goes beyond technology—it's about accessibility and inclusion.

MUSIC AND SOCIOECONOMIC BARRIERS: A HISTORICAL PERSPECTIVE

Music, often considered a universal language, has historically created socioeconomic barriers that persist today. For centuries, the ability to access and enjoy music has been closely tied to wealth and social status. For example, Prince Nikolaus Esterházy employed Joseph Haydn as an in-house composer, allowing the Esterházy family exclusive access to new symphonies and sonatas—a luxury that highlighted the cultural divide between the aristocracy and the common people.

Fast forward to the early twentieth century, and the introduction of radios and record players changed the way we experience music. These devices were luxury items that not every household could afford, creating a significant divide between those who could regularly access a variety of music and those who could not. Radio became a tool for shaping public taste but also reinforced existing social inequalities by limiting access to diverse music to only those who could afford the technology.

TECHNOLOGICAL SHIFTS AND FINANCIAL BURDENS

From the 1940s to the 2000s, music technology advanced rapidly, from records to tapes to CDs. Each new format promised better sound quality and more convenience, but it also came with a price. Constantly needing to update and upgrade music collections was an ongoing expense that some simply could not afford. While these technologies democratized music to an extent, making it more widely available, they also created cycles of obsolescence that disproportionately affected lower-income households.

MUSIC EDUCATION AND WESTERN BIAS

Barriers exist in music education, particularly in the way Western classical music has been upheld as the gold standard, often to the exclusion of other traditions. This bias reinforces cultural hegemony and marginalizes non-Western musical practices, making it more difficult for students from diverse backgrounds to see their cultures represented in formal music education.

Diverse musical traditions enhance cognitive development and allow for greater cultural understanding among students. Yet, access to such diverse musical education is often limited by socioeconomic factors. Schools in wealthier areas are more likely to offer comprehensive music programs that include a wide range of musical genres, while schools in lower-income areas may have limited or no music education options at all.

THE MODERN DIGITAL DIVIDE

Today, the rise of digital music platforms like Spotify, Apple Music, and Amazon Alexa offer vast music libraries accessible to millions. But this access isn't universal. The digital divide—between those who have access to technology and those who don't—remains a real barrier. Without reliable internet or money for subscriptions, accessing a broad range of music is still a challenge.

On top of that, the algorithms used by these platforms often favor more popular artists and genres, which can further marginalize less commercially viable music, often linked to non-Western or independent artists. So, while music is more accessible, it's also less diverse, reinforcing existing socioeconomic and cultural inequalities.

NOW WHAT?

So we don't all have Alexas. But most of us do use streaming services, many of which are free with ads. We all consume music differently, as individuals and as societies. Even with economic divides, globally, we trend toward streaming devices, with radio in second place. This shows that we don't pay for our music listening in the same way we did ten years ago, let alone a century ago (figure 13.2).

The point stands that music is for everyone. In recognizing the socioeconomic divide, we can look at how communities use music to connect with each other without needing technology or an in-house composer.

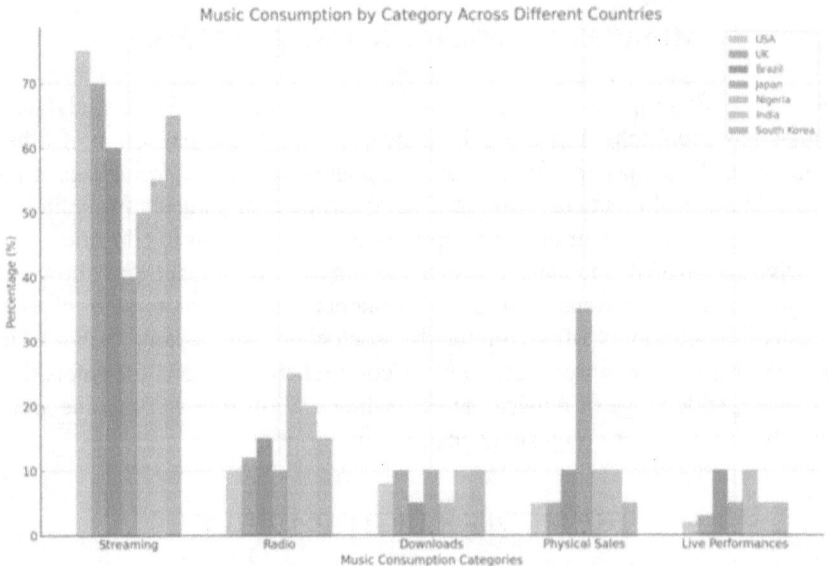

Figure 13.2. Music consumption by category across different countries. *Created by Sara Sherman.*

Music is for everyone. Yes, we know we said that already. Making music with our bodies by singing, clapping, stomping, and dancing is free and universal. While there is a privilege in being able to buy concert tickets—like the cheapest Taylor Swift concert ticket in 2024 starting at $450 and reaching up to $2000,[2] or the average price of tickets to the New York Philharmonic or Broadway hovering around $100—music itself doesn't have to be elite or exclusive.[3] In its most essential form, music transcends economic barriers and can bring joy, comfort, and connection to people everywhere.

THE MODERN MINDFULNESS DIVIDE

Mindfulness has the potential to benefit everyone, regardless of socioeconomic background, but the reality is that current practices are often more accessible to those with higher socioeconomic status. To truly bridge this gap, we need intentional efforts to make mindfulness more affordable, relatable, and available to a broader range of people, especially those in lower-income communities.

Several factors contribute to this socioeconomic divide in mindfulness practices:

- Access to resources: cost.
- Cultural perceptions and acceptance: seen as a niche or luxury.
- Time and flexibility: work-life balance.
- Education and awareness: accessible opportunities.
- Social support and community: limited sites or communities.
- Health disparities: limited access to healthcare.

Studies such as those by Brown, Ryan, and Creswell (2007) in *Social Cognitive and Affective Neuroscience* have pointed out that mindfulness interventions are more likely to be accessed by individuals with higher socioeconomic status.[4] Socioeconomic factors shape the accessibility and overall effectiveness of these practices. Addressing these disparities is essential to ensure that mindfulness, like music, can truly be for everyone.

THE UNIVERSAL LANGUAGE OF MUSIC: ACCESSIBILITY BEYOND ECONOMIC BARRIERS

While we often talk of playlists and curating music, using music for focus can be as simple as creating a call and response like we talked about in chapter

10. Perhaps it's singing a folk tune together, such as "Down by the Bay," and changing the rhyme each time for some laughs and active listening.

But there is a larger problem with accessibility to programming. Several global foundations work to address this, such as The Harmony Project, El Sistema, and the Little Mozart Foundation. These programs aim to provide musical education to underserved communities. However, finding these programs isn't always easy, and even when they are available, they might not resonate with everyone, particularly when trying to cater to diverse communities and musical preferences.

MUSIC IN DIVERSE SOCIOECONOMIC COMMUNITIES

In Brazil, Capoeira—a martial art that incorporates elements of dance, acrobatics, and music—is a powerful example of accessible art form. The music, played on simple, hand-crafted instruments like the berimbau, pandeiro, and atabaque, guides the rhythm and energy of the movements, creating a communal and immersive experience. Capoeira was designed to be accessible in any environment, whether rural or urban, indoors or outdoors, demonstrating how music and movement can be for everyone, regardless of economic status.

Similarly, the Griots of West Africa—storytellers, historians, and musicians—preserve oral traditions and culture through music and poetry. Often, only string instruments or drums are used, making electricity unnecessary. Music plays an essential role in ceremonies such as weddings, births, and funerals, and it is key to maintaining social cohesion and cultural identity.

In the Appalachian region of the United States, folk music traditions continue to thrive, particularly bluegrass and old-time music. These musical styles are rooted in the rural, working-class communities of the region and are often performed on acoustic instruments like the banjo, fiddle, and guitar. Folk music in Appalachia is traditionally performed in homes, churches, and community gatherings, with little need for amplification or electricity. It is a genre deeply connected to storytelling, communal values, and shared cultural heritage, making it accessible and relevant to people across different economic backgrounds.

Shift to the 1970s in the Bronx, NYC, where hip-hop is born out of the struggles and resilience of the community. A warm summer evening block party sees DJs, using turntables and portable generators, create a new sound that pulses with the energy of rebellion and hope. Children are running around dancing, and adults are talking while the beats, the rhymes, and the breakdancers thrum around them—each element of hip-hop is a response to the environment, a powerful voice for the marginalized, and a tool for social change. Even today, hip-hop continues to resonate, proving that music can be powerful for both personal expression and collective action.

Across the globe, people continue to connect through music in diverse ways—whether it's the soothing strum of a ukulele in Hawaii, the gong ensembles, or the infectious rhythm of samba in Latin America. These musical traditions, often passed down through generations, remind us that music is not just an art form, but a vital thread that weaves communities together, regardless of socioeconomic status or geographic location.

On a cold, wet Monday morning in December in NYC at St. Paul and St. Andrew's Church, a special concert was held for migrant families. This wasn't just any concert; donations of clothes, holiday presents, strollers, diapers, and a warm meal had been prepared for the families. Upon arrival and the opening of the church, a family was discovered sleeping outside on the church steps instead of in their shelter, fearful they would miss the opportunity to receive holiday presents.

The hard-working volunteers at St. Paul and St. Andrew's are warm-hearted, incredible people doing amazing work for all communities. As the team set up, it was noticeable that the audience was primarily adults with only a handful of children. The concert featured a husband-and-wife duo, Jesse Elder on keys and Blanca Gonzalez on violin and vocals, who run Musiquita, a bilingual music experience. This particular concert was titled "Jazzy Nutcracker," complete with tap dancing instead of a ballerina.

Blanca, originally from Venezuela, engaged with the crowd effortlessly. She sang in Spanish, conversed with the audience, and got everyone up and moving.

Mid-performance, the tap dancer was joined by a guest soloist—a three-year-old girl! One of the few children in the audience, she brought infectious energy that got everyone up, dancing, singing, and cheering.

This concert was more than just a performance; it was a celebration of community, resilience, and the universal language of music, bringing joy and warmth on a chilly day.

MUSIC IN NEURODIVERGENT CLASSROOMS: A TOOL FOR FOCUS AND CONNECTION

The universal language of music extends beyond cultural boundaries and into classrooms, where it serves as a vital tool for connection, especially for neurodivergent students.

Rachel Strasburg, a brilliant special education teacher, starts her mornings with music in the car with her fifteen-year-old son. She often uses that time to call to check in with her parents and her sisters, but sometimes Rachel knows that Ethan needs quiet time. On occasion, she plays music for the two of them. If it's a really good day, Ethan will sing, filling the car with his beautiful voice.

For Ethan, who faces neurodiverse challenges, music has become a lifeline. It replaced sports and helped him find focus, mastering the art of reading music, memorizing songs, and excelling in choir and theater. On days when they are choosing music for both of them, they carefully curate their playlist, and on others, they let randomness take the lead—singing loudly together, sharing moments of joy and connection.

Rachel arrives at school before the buses. Walking through the hallways, she hears the energy of different classrooms—some blasting lively music, others opting for a more subdued tone, but rarely calm. Teachers set the stage for the day with music and lighting, creating an environment where anything seems possible.

As students start to arrive, Rachel stands outside waiting for her class. She dances and sings to the music playing on the school speakers. Her students get off the bus, smile at her, and say, "Miss Strasburg . . ." They pretend they don't love seeing their teacher and teaching assistants singing, dancing, and smiling.

Never quite sure what music the administration has put on the school's playlist for that day, Rachel doesn't think much about the choice of songs. She just moves and sings. Most of her students navigate the morning halls alone with minimal supervision. They wait for one another and enter the school independently, supporting one another.

Class then begins with music. Each year, they start differently depending on the needs of the students. Some years, morning meetings are filled with songs about the days and months of the year. Students sing along from memory, while others act out the scenes from the large touchscreen. Occasionally, the whole class sings together, though that's rare; not every student participates in the same way.

Other days, the co-teacher plays instrumental music in the background with calming scenes on her Promethean board. A few students are animated, while others fall silent, but the music always signals the start of their day. Rachel plays familiar songs, whether streaming or recommended by friends and colleagues. These first few minutes help the students settle into their routines.

Rachel and her assistants work constantly to find what works for each student and then reflect and adapt.

Many of Rachel's students, including those on the autism spectrum, respond strongly to music. Throughout the day, she integrates calming sounds—ocean waves, forest murmurs—designed specifically for sensory-relaxing environments. Transitions are easier with music, and although the administrators select the mixes, Rachel often wonders what it would sound like if the students were the DJs of their own day. She also reflects on how many homes have music woven into daily routines, as it is in her classroom.

Rachel dreams of personalized playlists for each student—songs to match transitions, fire drills, or even their individual moods. It would help her shape the classroom's energy, offering something unique to each child. She also imagines a playlist for teachers, knowing that moments of joy and release are rare for them during the day. Sometimes, when things feel chaotic, she finds herself saying, "Just dance!" It's not often during the day that Rachel and her teaching assistants get a moment for themselves.

Music remains central to the students' routine, particularly after lunch, when calming sounds fill the room as they prepare for quiet activities like reading or drawing. Rachel often sings to them—nursery rhymes or simple songs like "If You're Happy and You Know It." She even uses music as a way to get them ready for lunch, singing their names to alert each student to the change.

Most days do not include a school-wide band or choral concert, but when they do, Rachel's students are always invited. For the most part, they're wonderful audience members, with some needing a little extra assistance. Noise-canceling headphones, fidget boards, or small whiteboards are often used to help them focus and follow the program. Their ability to enjoy these concerts often depends on whom they sit next to, but regardless of seating arrangements, they love interactive concerts—those where they can sing, clap, and dance along.

"I belong in music!" is a wonderful phrase her students have exclaimed in a promotional video for the United Sound program. This program creates opportunities for neurodivergent students to make music alongside their neurotypical peers. The initiative began at Rachel's school during the first year of COVID-19 when the band director approached her with the idea. Rachel eagerly said yes. After a year spent organizing and securing funding, the program was ready to launch.

United Sound is built on inclusion, with a ratio of three neurotypical students to one neurodivergent student. Together, they make music, proving that the ability to create sound knows no boundaries. A unique space is held where everyone, regardless of neurodiversity, can experience the joy and empowerment that music brings. United Sound carefully selects music to ensure it is accessible for all participants.

Music, as we've seen, has the extraordinary ability to bridge divides—not just across cultures and socioeconomic boundaries, but also across neurological differences. For neurodivergent students, programs like United Sound offer more than an opportunity to participate in music; they offer a space where every voice can be heard, every rhythm can be felt, and every student is valued for who they are.

At the heart of this inclusive approach are educators like Rachel, whose patience, brilliance, and ability to think on her feet ensure that every child feels welcomed and understood.

Their role requires constant attentiveness—shifting approaches and creating strategies that meet students where they are. It is this tireless dedication, combined with an open-hearted belief in the potential of every student, that makes their classrooms a space where all students, neurodivergent and neurotypical alike, can thrive.

When we approach education with open minds and open hearts, we invite the richness of diversity into our classrooms and communities. Neurodivergent students, who often face barriers to inclusion, find that music—like them—doesn't fit neatly into boxes. It flows, adapts, and invites creativity, and, in doing so, it provides a space where everyone can connect and grow together.

By allowing neurodivergent students to make music and experience the same sense of belonging as their neurotypical peers, we aren't just teaching them about notes and rhythms. We're showing them—and ourselves—that when we embrace differences, we create something far greater than the sum of its parts. The benefits of this open-hearted approach extend not just to the students, but to everyone involved.

RESONANCE IN OPEN DOORS

This connection between music and inclusion is not limited to neurodivergent classrooms. It extends to broader communities, as seen in the work of Rachel Black, the director of Greenwich House Music School in New York City.

As Rachel walks down the bustling streets of NYC, she isn't just greeted by the usual city sounds—the blare of taxi horns or the constant hum of voices. When she steps onto the street where her school stands, the gentle sound of music drifts through the windows of the historic 150-year-old building. It's as if the building itself, steeped in history, breathes music.

Rachel's mission, much like Strasburg's, centers on the idea that music can transcend all barriers—socioeconomic, cultural, and neurological. "There's something about this place," Rachel muses. "People can't help but stop when they hear the music. It pulls them in, makes them pause—even in a city that never stops."

It's not just about the building or the music itself. It's about creating a space where people feel connected, welcomed, and present. As Rachel explains, "It's my job to make sure that this feeling of resonance, this sense of place, is something that everyone who walks through our doors experiences."

Rachel's leadership aligns with the idea that music creates social cohesion and community. Studies have shown how group music-making can enhance social bonds by creating trust and cooperation among participants.[5] Rachel's vision embodies this, as she strives to build a community through the power of music.

The music school Rachel leads isn't a traditional conservatory. Its mission is rooted in making music accessible, particularly for those from immigrant communities who once lived in nearby tenements. "We weren't founded to produce the next great soloist at Carnegie Hall," she says with a smile. "We were created to make music accessible to everyone, to help people play music in their homes, to make them better humans, better citizens."

This idea goes beyond traditional music education and aims to break down socioeconomic barriers, ensuring music is not reserved for the elite but available to everyone. Music, when accessible, has significant benefits for cognitive development, emotional well-being, and social skills. Access to music can help individuals, regardless of background, achieve academic success and greater civic engagement.

Rachel's deep connection to the community is central to the school's identity. "We try to be as welcoming and immersed in our neighbors' lives as possible," she explains. "Our registrar has been here for over fifty years. She knows the students, their parents, sometimes even their grandparents. That deep connection to our community is something you can't replicate."

This intentional connection between the school and its neighborhood is cultivated over time. "You can feel the history, the resonance of over a century of creation and music-making," Rachel mentions. "This isn't just about teaching notes and rhythms; it's about nurturing a space where people—whether they're students, parents, or just passersby—can experience a sense of belonging through music."

Rachel's leadership, rooted in empathy and commitment to inclusion, ensures that the magic of music reaches everyone, regardless of background or financial status. "We're not about rigid rules or traditions," Rachel says firmly. "We're about creating a space where everyone feels welcome and can share in the joy of making music together. That's what it means to be a leader in this community."

Inclusivity and accessibility are essential to the arts. Studies have shown that when the arts are accessible to diverse communities, it enriches not only those communities but also strengthen the arts themselves by innovation and cultural exchange.[6]

"This place hasn't changed much," Rachel adds, "and that's a good thing. Because what we're doing here, it's timeless." She understands the challenges that often block access to music, particularly for those from marginalized communities. "Music is so powerful, so universal, but a lot of things can get in the way. My job is to clear the way."

Rachel ensures that the school's mission to break socioeconomic barriers through music thrives. Her leadership goes beyond managing a program—it's about creating spaces where music transcends social divides and touches the lives of all who enter, bringing them together in a shared experience.

Clearing the way to build community, nurture relationships, and create spaces where everyone can feel connected serves as a reminder that leadership in the arts isn't just about managing programs—it's about creating environments where the magic of music can touch lives and impact communities.

BREAKING BARRIERS THROUGH MUSIC AND MINDFULNESS

As we've explored throughout this chapter, music has an incredible ability to cross boundaries—cultural, socioeconomic, and even neurological. Yet, despite its power as a universal language, access to music and mindfulness remains uneven, shaped by deep-rooted socioeconomic divides.

Historically, technology, education, and even cultural biases have restricted who can fully engage with music, whether for learning, enjoyment, or personal growth. Today, while modern platforms like streaming services offer wider access to music, the digital divide still excludes many from experiencing its full benefits. Mindfulness, too, though universally beneficial, is often more accessible to those with higher socioeconomic status.

Yet, the message remains clear: both music and mindfulness have the potential to connect us in powerful ways—whether through communal traditions like Capoeira, folk music in Appalachia, or hip-hop's origins in the Bronx.

By making both music and mindfulness more accessible, we can break down the barriers that have historically limited access and instead build bridges—bridges to connection, growth, and understanding. Ultimately, when we take deliberate, mindful action through music, we create opportunities not just for ourselves but for entire communities.

Music, in its purest form, is for everyone. So is the practice of being present, of cultivating mindfulness. Together, they create a pathway—one that transcends barriers and opens doors to new possibilities, creating a world where everyone can experience the joy, connection, and growth they bring.

PRACTICAL APPLICATIONS

- Collaborate on playlists: Engage others by sharing playlists and exploring new songs together. Be open to different styles and genres.
- Meeting people where they are: Choose music that resonates with someone's emotional or cognitive state. Rather than categorizing music as for adults or for children, focus on how the music effectively communicates or connects with listeners regardless of age.
- Incorporate music for routines: Create a routine and create habits for daily activities based on practical applications from earlier chapters. Repeating certain songs or musical activities can strengthen positive associations, making routines more enjoyable and reinforcing the habits we've been discussing.
- Use music to incorporate emotions: Choose an emotion and express it through a song, whether it's by singing, drumming, or another method, such as using technology like JenAI.
- Let the music resonate with the moment and convey the feeling you want to share.

NOTES

1. Tricia Tunstall, *Changing Lives: Gustavo Dudamel, El Sistema, and the Transformative Power of Music* (W.W. Norton & Company, 2012).

2. Emily Dozier, "Taylor Swift Eras Tour 2024 Dates for U.S. Return: Ticket Prices, Cost, Full Schedule and More," *The Sporting News,* last modified May 23, 2024, https://www.sportingnews.com/us/nfl/news/taylor-swift-tour-2024-tickets-prices-us-schedule-dates/612e97acae959d6de55ea896.

3. TicketSmarter, "New York Philharmonic Tickets," *TicketSmarter,* accessed September 19, 2024, https://www.ticketsmarter.com/p/new-york-philharmonic-tickets.

4. Kirk Warren Brown, Richard M. Ryan, and J. David Creswell, "Mindfulness: Theoretical Foundations and Evidence for its Salutary Effects," *Psychological Inquiry* 18, no. 4 (2007): 211–237, https://doi.org/10.1080/10478400701598298.

5. Koelsch, "Towards a Neural Basis of Music-Evoked Emotions," 131–137.

6. Nick Rabkin and Eric C. Hedberg, *Arts Education in America: What the Declines Mean for Arts Participation* (National Endowment for the Arts, 2011).

Chapter 14

Coda

Now What, So What?

> Never doubt that a small group of thoughtful, committed citizens can change the world; indeed, it's the only thing that ever has. —Margaret Mead

THREADS

- Mindful use of music should be a purposeful, reciprocal, lifelong pattern.
- Change will take place one person, one small group, and one community at a time.
- Encouraging a dynamic, iterative, reflective practice.

GO TO SLEEP!

Marlowe, three years old at the time, held Sara hostage in his room, refusing to sleep. (Actually, who are we kidding? He still does this.) Sara was cranky, tired, and then, when she finally blinked into the light outside his dark room, relieved. Wanting music to match her mood, she asked her AI friend for help (figure 14.1). It came up with:

- "Mother's Little Helper" by The Rolling Stones.
- "Under Pressure" by Queen.
- "I Will Survive" by Gloria Gaynor.
- "Help!" by The Beatles.
- "You Can't Always Get What You Want" by The Rolling Stones.

Figure 14.1. *Resonant Minds. Line drawing by Debra Sherman.*

- "Mama Said" by The Shirelles.
- "Tired" by Adele.
- "The Kids Are Alright" by The Who.
- "Crazy" by Patsy Cline.
- "Manic Monday" by The Bangles.
- "It's Not Easy Being Green" by Kermit the Frog.
- "I'm So Tired" by The Beatles.
- "Chasing Pavements" by Adele.
- "In My Life" by The Beatles.
- "Stronger (What Doesn't Kill You)" by Kelly Clarkson.

Did Sara feel understood and seen after this playlist? Initially, no. Her gut reaction was, "What is this list?" Then she found humor in lyrics she wouldn't have listened to otherwise. "What a drag it is getting old" from the Rolling Stones had her smiling, and "Mama said there'll be days like this" made her feel less "under pressure" knowing "I will survive" even though "I haven't slept a wink and I'm so tired my mind is on the brink." Even when she wanted to scream for "help!" she knew that "this can only make me stronger."

So maybe the answer isn't no. While there were songs she would replace— perhaps "The Kids Are Alright" with "Walking in the Jungle"—the playlist made her smile, and perhaps the point is that it was a starting place to curate a playlist for mood and feelings. Although the list didn't include many songs that could be categorized as calming, the music lifted her mood, released some serotonin, and did exactly what it was supposed to do.

One colleague, a mother of four young adults, loved the idea of *Resonant Minds* as she confessed that when her children were younger, she wanted to sing songs to them but didn't have the background, expertise, or time to expand her repertoire beyond the few songs sung to her by her mom. What mom of four young children has time to collect, curate, and use songs for different times of the day, for different moods, and for different purposes?

If you do have a moment or two and want to get started on picking playlists that already exist, there are prompts you can ask AI, and the technology is fascinating. Learning from you, AI remembers your favorites and the songs you play most. Our position is that starting with the familiar is a good beginning point; however, we encourage you to keep going, to share ideas and lists, and to move beyond the familiar. As Marlowe said, "Listen to it first. See if you like it or not."

Music is a lever for more mindful action. The reason for incorporating music is clear—each person brings their own unique set of possibilities. Our goal is to encourage moments of reflection, where we ask ourselves how to make more conscious decisions about creating a broader, more inclusive music listening set. Executive functions are the skills needed to make decisions about the music that shapes lives.

As leaders of our own lives, we begin to understand how our choices impact others. The expanded playlists of our lives continue to grow and evolve. This reflects the reciprocal nature of habits of mind and life. To grow and sustain these feedback spirals of growth, we will share with communities and networks. Emerging technologies are already helping us discover new music and even create original compositions, further expanding the possibilities for personal and collective growth.

SO WHAT ABOUT AI?

We can't discuss playlists and purposeful selection of music without acknowledging the tiny computers in our hands, the Alexa and Google devices in our homes, and the Spotify and Apple Music channels catered to our listening habits.

AI has the potential to simplify or give us a head start. This technology can even surprise us with recommendations, but it doesn't always get it right.

During a conversation with Alex Kotran, founder and CEO of aiEDU, he reminded us how technology has the potential to create a negative "dopamine train." How do we stay mindful in a constantly evolving technological world with new discoveries and gadgets emerging daily?

Using AI prompts for playlists is a great start if you feel lost curating your own. However, these playlist generators usually feedback to us what is already familiar, what we've already listened to. While promising, research and development will soon offer more diverse options, for now, they tend to reinforce our existing tastes rather than push us toward new or unexpected music.

Our memories, our brains, create patterns and hold onto the familiar stories. Makes sense. We can't remember what we haven't experienced. So, if the general use of AI only captures those viewing and listening patterns, that's what you're going to get as listening suggestions.

What if we slow down a bit, open up without judgment, and are willing to hear what we thought we didn't like or we never imagined hearing. This is the point of reflection, of moving from existence to essence, of taking full advantage of the gifts of mindfulness.

We don't choose country music at the top of our playlist. That's our issue and our loss. Listening to country music wasn't something we grew up with. Matt, our baseball-loving relative, also loves country music, and now so do his children. Instead of reacting to Matt with, "Oh no. Country! How can that be?" a better reaction would be to respect him and try to expand our own understanding of this genre.

On the other hand, Matt was never exposed to classical music as a child. Now he is patient, listens, and doesn't make any unhappy faces or snoozing sounds when he visits. He is being mindful, even as he blasts his country music when he gets back in his car to go home. Small steps . . .

Bena Kallick shared with us that her husband, Charles, is not only a psychiatrist but also a player and lover of classical music. She is a lover and singer of show tunes. They shared their music with one another and grew to appreciate, and even like, the other's music.

Some of us grew up with Beatlemania or other new, popular forms of music. Now we have all these Swifties out there! It's so exciting that they are part of a very large, vibrant community.

What made us accept these new, and sometimes revolutionary, forms of music? We built on the familiar, found a groove, and found company with those who also liked the music, becoming a vibrant, exciting musical community.

Beyond popular music, there are so many times in our lives when we passively receive music selected by someone else for the common good. Wouldn't it be great if we could step into an elevator and ask for a playlist that would relax us on the way to a meeting or focus us before a presentation? Or how about taking a date to a restaurant where the music could set the tone for that romantic moment?

Is it so far off in the future that a group of mah jong players might have a device at their tables enabling them to pick the music being played, or even for technology to write a song to match the moment? We don't think so. Already, we have services that write personalized songs. We love that!

Yet, what if you want a whole playlist of songs for different purposes? Whether the mah jong player, the little league coach, a dad at home preparing dinner, or a business team who are meeting to plan for the year, music may be the right motivator.

That dream is a short way off from when individual jukeboxes were wired into the wall for each booth at a diner, but it's coming.

As long as we're writing about the positive use of AI and other technologies, we asked one of the open-source tools to write a poem for us about the future of AI, mindfulness, and music:

HARMONY OF TOMORROW

> In the digital dawn of days anew, where circuits hum and bytes accrue, AI, mindfulness, and music blend, A symphony of souls to mend.
> In the heart of machines, a mindful beat, Soft whispers in the silicon heat, Algorithms weave a tranquil thread, Guiding thoughts where calm is spread.
> Music flows from lines of code, A river where pure silence rode, Notes that soothe the weary mind, Melodies in patterns designed.
> Mindfulness, a gentle guide, AI stands faithfully beside, Together they craft a sacred space, Where thoughts find peace and hearts embrace.
> A future bright with rhythmic grace, Where human spirit finds its place, In the embrace of mindful tech, A world where hearts and circuits connect.
> The hum of servers, soft and clear, A digital mantra, drawing near, In this union, futures blend, Where healing notes and mindfulness send.
> AI learns the song of soul, Helping minds to be whole, Guiding through the noise of life, Easing stress, and soothing strife.
> In this realm of thoughtful sound, A harmony of hearts is found, Music, mindfulness, AI combined, A future where peace is intertwined.
> So let us dream of days ahead, Where technology and calm are wed, A world where every note and thought, In mindful harmony is caught.

We know that the use of AI to create music is controversial. Is it art? Without getting into that whole heated discussion, we know that AI will be available soon that will allow a movie director to create music for any length of time based on the script of the movie and the parameters the director would like to add. The same generative approach might be used at home for families celebrating birthdays or other special occasions.

The generative AI opportunities may take us from "Wouldn't it be nice" to "That was a perfect piece of music for this moment." While we're waiting for that technological magic to happen, we have plenty of opportunities to move from the familiar to the possibilities of expanded music in our lives.

As we look ahead to the exciting potential of all that technology will offer, we can reflect on the power of building community. To create lasting, mindful action, it takes more than just one song or an initial playlist—it requires motivation, consistent practice, and the formation of habits.

These elements are all crucial in long-term personal and cultural change, ensuring that technology supports not only innovation but also a deep sense of connection and purpose.

THE FRUSTRATING SILENCE

Five minutes on hold, maybe ten, and the same song is repeating again! This is an all-too-familiar experience. Would you prefer silence? Probably not. Silence on a call might make you think you've been disconnected. That sometimes frustrating music is the only connection you have to someone, somewhere who is going to pick up the line soon, and all you need to do is . . . wait.

Background music dates back to Ancient Greece and the Middle Ages, where music was used as a backdrop for early plays to enhance the plot. Gregorian chants would be used not to pray, but as a sonic landscape for religious rituals.

We've all made fun of elevator Muzak or commented on it to a stranger in an elevator. But Muzak is a real thing! Muzak Holdings LLC, founded in 1934, created purposeful background music designed to enhance your experience in places like department stores. With the rise of radio and television, mood music became common. During an intense scene, the music would turn dramatic, maybe speed up to help create the ambiance to go along with the story. This concept traces back to opera in the 1600s and was expanded by Richard Wagner in the nineteenth century with his use of leitmotifs—recurring themes associated with characters or ideas.

Music has a way of sneaking into our implicit memory, and many well-loved and familiar themes have done just that thanks to movie composers such as John Williams. Can you hum the tune for these characters?

- Darth Vader in Star Wars.
- "Hedwig's Theme" in Harry Potter.
- James Bond.
- "Super Mario Theme" song.

These themes were picked to enhance the audience's experience. They help you remember the character, create an emotional attachment to a theme, and once you hear the specifically composed music, you can think of the character before they even come on screen.

The idea of purposefully composing mood or character music goes hand in hand with enhancing your experience in the department store, where certain types of music might influence the buyer to spend more money. That's business!

Imagine making a phone call in 1962, and the telephone operator says, "Please hold while we connect your call," and you're met with silence. Silence! This lack of sound was a common experience until Alfred Levy, a factory owner, inadvertently discovered hold music when a loose wire picked up a radio broadcast. This serendipitous event led Levy to submit a patent for the Telephone Hold Program System, which stated:

> ... listening to a completely unresponsive instrument is tedious and calls often are abandoned altogether or remade which leads to annoyance and a waste of time and money.[1]

Similar to elevator music, a new system of hold music was born, which became a booming business as silence became the dreaded signal to hang up rather than wait. Companies started creating music designed to help people stay on the line, transforming hold times into a more bearable experience.

The famous Cisco phone system bought a song familiar to us all, "Opus Number One." With several million views on YouTube and countless plays on hold lines worldwide, this track has become iconic. In 1989, two friends, Tim Carleton and Derek Deel, came up with a song on a synthesizer and a drum machine. According to an interview on NPR, Carleton was a "Yanni-loving computer nerd, messing around with a drum machine and a synthesizer in his parents' garage in California."[2] When Deel went to work for Cisco in the early 1990s, he offered the song, and the next thing he knew, it was used on hundreds of millions of phones. Like most music artists experience at some point, they sold the product and never received any royalties for it.

Many companies now specialize in crafting hold music that is pleasant, non-repetitive, and keeps listeners engaged. The Experience Marketing Association board chair, David Green, has been working on hold music for over twenty years. He says that "small loops of music that repeat over and over at short intervals might subliminally or consciously make you count the intervals, and make you aggravated that you've heard it three or four or five times."[3] Finding the right music is crucial, and different companies have unique sound preferences to suit their brand and audience.

Since music can significantly impact the mood of the person on hold, companies like Beatsuite and On Hold Marketing Works advise companies on selecting music that acts as a soothing balm to the customer. Insurance companies are encouraged to use music that is not too happy or upbeat, given the serious nature of their services. According to Green, medical companies are advised to use "some very low, low, low beats-per-minute piano music, to take it down a little bit, and add messaging on the top that said to that caller, 'You may or may not owe this or the full amount on the bills sent to you. Please have your information ready, so we may help you work through this.'"[4]

How amazing is it that there are people out there mindfully picking playlists for us, even when we might find them annoying or repetitive? Companies like Apple allow customers to select their own hold music from a preselected list. Coming soon to a phone near you? AI will know your preferences and pick hold music for you. If it could read your mood and select music that will soothe your anxiety about being on hold, the experience could become much more personalized and enjoyable.

SO, WHAT IF?

We found many examples of opportunities and possibilities of technology assisting in and improving mindful action through music.

Hold music, elevator music, and doctors' offices are societal/cultural opportunities. Of course, there are others, many of which are commercially driven. Hop in a cab and watch a commercial. Pump some gas and watch a commercial. Open your social media or a website to a pop-up.

Maybe, just maybe, there's a chance to work some personalized and customized music into those experiences. We have no idea what some of those commercials cost at gas station pumps, but good for the companies that have figured it out. It's a clever marketing opportunity. We wonder what it would be like if they snuck in a piece of music to set a tone that reduces the anxiety of the day. Would customers feel better about coming back to a gas station that offers the commercials and some calm music at the pump?

The hustle and bustle of airports, from the moment of getting through security to waiting at the gate, usually have music playing. Not sure about you, but we don't remember hearing it. Regardless, the airports' strategy makes so much sense. The music played in airport waiting areas near the gates typically falls into a few categories, designed to create a calm, neutral, and pleasant environment for travelers. Airports often play instrumental or ambient music, which can include smooth jazz, classical, or new-age tunes.

This type of music is chosen because it is generally relaxing, unobtrusive, and unlikely to offend or distract passengers. The goal is to reduce stress and create a soothing atmosphere as passengers wait for their flights. Someone out there is trying to be mindful about music selections for air travelers.

Some airports work with music curators or services to create customized playlists that fit the airport's brand and the local culture. For example, an airport in Nashville might include more country music, while an airport in Miami might feature Latin rhythms.

The next step might be to offer options to tune into personalized music selections for each passenger, starting perhaps with a playlist but then having technology help with individualized selections.

BUILDING A MINDFUL MUSICAL MOVEMENT

The organic, individual use of music in a mindful manner should be supported and connected. Some may prefer to engage with music on their own, while others may join a small network or community. For those who want to become part of something larger, there are fascinating models of growth that have transferable principles.

Mid-twentieth century baseball, steeped in deep tradition, often looked at innovation with skepticism. Enter Bill Veeck, with his colorful personality and an unwavering belief in the power of the crowd. He set out to revolutionize America's favorite pastime.

Veeck had a knack for seeing beyond the diamond, understanding that the true essence of baseball lay in its fans—the passionate supporters who filled the bleachers, whose cheers and jeers echoed through the stadium. He knew that by listening to these fans and placing them at the center of the experience, he could create something extraordinary.

Often mingling with fans right in the thick of the action, Veeck chatted with them, listened to their stories, and absorbed their ideas.

This level of interaction made fans feel like they were part of the team, deepening their emotional connection to the sport.

We're not saying conductors have to walk into the audience, although some already do that. The lesson remains: when leaders—whether in education, healthcare, or parenting—can involve those they serve in decision-making, they create deeper, more mindful, and communal connections.

A great example of this approach is seen in the work of Dr. Craig E. Vigliante, an oral surgeon in Leesburg, Virginia. He talks with his staff about the music to be played during the day, adjusting it by patient, and he even talks to his patients about the music they might want to hear.

These examples reveal how building a movement of resonant minds through music requires creative approaches that prioritize connection and shared experience.

By drawing on the lessons from stories like those of Veeck and Vigliante, we can cultivate communities that celebrate music's power to inspire, heal, and connect. Through strategic initiatives and a commitment to integrating music into daily life—both in public spaces and at home—we can build a future where music is a unifying force, promoting mindful action and enriching the human experience.

Our movement begins with understanding the needs and desires of music lovers everywhere. Music has the power to evoke emotion, inspire action, and bring people together in ways that are both profound and lasting.

MUSIC AT HOME: CREATING A PERSONAL ECOSYSTEM

The heart of this movement lies within our homes, where music can transform everyday routines into mindful practices. A cozy corner filled with cushions and soft lighting, where the day's stress melts away to the soothing sounds of a favorite album, may be a starting point.

Headphones and earbuds are used by millions across all age groups. This is like taking that warm, cozy home corner wherever you go.

We don't have to run through every option to build on the familiar at home, with neighbors, family, and friends. We do want to encourage mindful action to go beyond the familiar.

MUSIC IN PUBLIC SPACES: A COMMUNITY AFFAIR

The *Resonant Minds* movement aims to transform public spaces into hubs of musical engagement. Schools, hospitals, and community centers become places where music is present, enhancing well-being and a sense of unity.

Imagine a hospital waiting room where gentle melodies soothe anxieties, or a school hallway filled with the sounds of student musicians performing for their peers. These musical microecosystems, inspired by Veeck's immersive stadium experiences, enrich the environment and bring people together in unexpected ways.

Just as Bill Veeck changed the face of baseball by listening to fans and prioritizing their experience, so the movement of *Resonant Minds* seeks to do the same for music.

AI today might not be the same as AI three years from now, so we can't limit ourselves to what we know now. We can be open to the idea that things will keep changing and that we can have the mindset to accept these tools as they change and adapt.

A MOVEMENT OF *RESONANT MINDS*

A movement of *Resonant Minds* will redefine how music is integrated into everyday life. This involves creating spaces where music is not just an occasional activity but a fundamental part of our social fabric. Here are a few ideas to begin incorporating the practice in various settings:

- Create a comfortable space where you can sit or lie down and focus on the music, allowing it to be a meditative and calming experience.
- Host regular family music nights where everyone shares their favorite songs or artists.
- Curate family playlists for different moods or activities, such as relaxation, focus, or energy.
- Implement music education programs that emphasize mindfulness and emotional connection.
- Start interactive music activities, such as learning a new instrument, songwriting, or engaging in family jam sessions.
- Transform schools, hospitals, and community centers into environments where music is constantly present. Background music in waiting rooms, live performances in common areas, and interactive musical experiences can enhance these spaces.
- Utilize technology to connect people through music. Online platforms and apps can facilitate shared musical experiences, allowing people to collaborate, create, and share music in real-time. Virtual concerts and streaming services can broaden access to diverse musical genres.
- Organize events that celebrate music's power to bring people together.
- Collaborate with musicians, artists, and cultural influencers to promote the movement.

Chapter 14

AI IS A TOOL TO HELP BUILD MINDFUL ACTION

Even as we protect and search for our essence, we're not afraid that AI will take over our existence. AI is a tool that should be cultivated to enhance the human condition, not just fill corporate tillers.

We also believe that the prompt exchange with your technology is a mindful action. Be clear about what mood, what energy, and what time of day it is.

Don't let the prompts *control* you; let them *expand* you.

Sample prompts to use with AI:

Mood-Based Playlists:
- "Create a playlist to help with relaxation and staying focused while working."
- "Suggest a playlist for deep concentration and productivity."
- "What songs are ideal for a focused study session?"
- "Give a playlist for a calm and peaceful working environment."
- "What are some instrumental tracks that enhance focus and attention?"

Emotion-Based Playlists:
- "What songs are suitable for processing emotions?"
- "Create a playlist for developing empathy and understanding."
- "Suggest a playlist for self-reflection and emotional growth."
- "What are some songs to help build resilience and emotional strength?"
- "Give a playlist for practicing mindfulness and emotional regulation."

Musical Memory/Attachments
- "Create a playlist with nostalgic songs from childhood."
- "What are some tracks that evoke strong memories and emotions?"
- "Suggest a playlist for creating new positive memories."
- "What songs are ideal for reminiscing about past experiences?"
- "Give a playlist that connects to significant life events and milestones."

Leadership and Community Building
- "Create a playlist with empowering songs for leaders."
- "What are some tracks that inspire teamwork and collaboration?"
- "Suggest a playlist for building a strong and supportive community."
- "What songs are suitable for fostering unity and togetherness?"
- "Give a playlist for motivating and energizing a team."

Movement Breaks
- "Create a playlist with upbeat songs for a quick movement break."
- "What are some tracks that get people moving and energized?"
- "Suggest a playlist for a short active break during work or study."
- "What songs are suitable for a refreshing dance break?"
- "Give a playlist for stretching and light physical activity."

PLAY ON

A future filled with possibilities. Mindful action through music, the use of technology, guided by executive functions, leads to habits of life.

A movement built from the familiar, building from the personal, developing communities.

As we continue the beginning of this journey, we reflect on how far we've come and are thrilled by what is ahead of us. The threads we've woven together—mindful music, executive function, personal growth, and the role of technology—lead to one place: the power of intentional action.

Margaret Mead's words remind us that *true change* happens when thoughtful, committed people come together. This principle is at the heart of what we've explored. Whether integrating mindful music practices into your daily routine, making technology work for you rather than overwhelming you, or taking steps toward building a community, the path forward is clear.

The conductor's baton is in your hands. Through music, mindfulness, and intentional choices, we cultivate habits that not only serve us as individuals but have a ripple effect on those around us. Our individual action is not just about one song, one playlist, or even several playlists. Change will happen through consistent practice, reflection, and connection.

So, what now? The answer is simple: take action. Start with a playlist, a moment of reflection, or a new mindful musical habit. Share it with your family, your community, and your networks. Maybe start by asking your partner, your children, or a friend to listen to a piece of music that you like and ask what they think. Ask them to share something with you. Take the first step. Play the first note. Play on (figure 14.2).

Figure 14.2. *Play On. Line drawing by Debra Sherman.*

NOTES

1. Sophie Haigney, "The Many Requirements of Hold Music, a Genre for No One," *NPR*, last modified September 5, 2019, https://www.npr.org/2019/09/05/757544079/the-many-requirements-of-hold-music-a-genre-for-no-one.

2. "516: Stuck in the Middle," *This American Life*, accessed September 15, 2024, https://www.thisamericanlife.org/516/transcript.

3. Haigney, "The Many Requirements of Hold Music, a Genre for No One."

4. Ibid.

Acknowledgments

To sit down day after day, Zoom after Zoom, page after page alongside the same person for countless hours with anyone is a daunting task. Now, when that same person is your father, those hours are laced with such deep history and understanding for one another, and anything can happen. For us, this time together was truly a gift.

The last several years, when I'd call my father and ask for his advice when leading professional development days at the United Federation of Teachers or when he'd hear me talk to my mom about students asking for advice on how to reach them better, he'd often say, "you're writing your book!" Perhaps, I'd think, but there's no way I would write a book alone.

Now, we all know fathers can be pushy, and mine isn't any exception. But he pushed me to be a better writer, to think more deeply about this work, and I learned I can push back! Sometimes, when I'd be deep in a hyper-focused work session on Zoom, he'd suggest taking a break, and my "Wait! What about this?" was often met with patience, grace, and another hour of thinking, writing, and deliberating together.

Truly, a gift. Thank you, Dad, for this time—this beautiful passion project that we both believe can make a meaningful impact on lives.

The real grounding presence through all of this was my mother. She'd pop in to say hello on Zoom, ensure we had meals during our in-person nonstop writing days, and served as our first reader. Not only that, as a beautiful artist (whose delicate artwork you see throughout) and a former special education teacher, her influence is deeply embedded in every page. Mom, may your patience and nurturing continue to be a grounding presence in *Resonant Minds* as it continues to evolve.

None of this would be possible without my children, Eva and Marlowe. As a baby, Eva was the reason why these interactive concerts came to life.

The interactive musical experiences started out for her, and in the years that followed, Marlowe and Eva have been patient guinea pigs for new programs and ideas. Their curious minds and love of music continually impact each and every program I put out into the world.

My partner, Amos, has been a supportive sounding board for this book and for all my wacky projects and ideas. He's been there to listen, put the kids to bed when I work late, and help put this work into action. How lucky I am to have a partner who has mindfully used music with me since our children were born, sparking ideas and challenging me to think deeper.

To my sisters—Adena and Rachel thank you for listening to endless discussions about this book, for being supportive when the writing got tough, and for singing *Les Misérables* and Carole King with me throughout our lives. This book wouldn't be the same without you.

Beyond family, the tens of thousands of children and their communities for whom I've had the honor of playing music, creating programs, and interacting with have inspired me most. Their shining eyes and curious minds give us hope for the future as we play on, and the work continues with them.

Countless thanks to:

- The loyal, dedicated Mozart for Munchkins audience—those who have been with us since their babies were eight weeks old, and now, with their eight-year-olds, still come, bringing along their younger siblings.
- The educators who have asked us to further their understanding of music and mindfulness, to create residency programs for their students and educators.

To the Mozart for Munchkins team—what an honor it has been to grow musically with you. I've learned so much from your dedication and passion for making music accessible to all audiences. Collaborating with our incredible team of musicians has been a source of immense joy over the years. I am deeply grateful to each of you. Thank you, thank you, thank you.

A special thank you to Goldie Hawn for starting MindUP and impacting the lives of countless children. The collaboration between Mozart for Munchkins and MindUP has helped bring this work out into the world, and it has taken flight ever since.

My life has been filled with music and mentors. Though my path has looked different from what we anticipated years ago, the gratitude I have for my lessons, the tears you witnessed over the piano, and the belief you always had in me has brought me to this moment. Veda, thank you for the formative experiences as a young musician and for being someone I can still reach out to decades later. Jeffrey Cohen, thank you for helping me find my voice at the piano and creating a space where I wasn't afraid to make mistakes. To Luba

Edlina Dubinsky, a survivor who instilled great discipline in me and planted the first seeds for deep, purposeful listening.

To our muses, encouragers, friends, colleagues, family, interviewees, commenters, readers:

- Ellen Galinsky
- Bena Kallick
- John Brown
- Shara Senderoff
- Terry Thoren
- Greg Hutchings
- Madison Strasburg
- Ethan Strasburg
- Aviva Adams
- Rebecca Adams
- Matt Strasburg
- Paul Goldstein
- David Levanthal
- Alan Goldblatt
- Kremena Bikov
- Indre Viskontas
- Rachel Black
- Peter DelGrosso
- Alphonso Horne
- Kathy Park
- Alison James
- Molly Lawlor
- Jessica Masanotti
- Rebecca Hershberger
- Juan Patino

Thank you, Carrie Brandon, editor, for your encouragement, patience, and trust.

Bibliography

Anderson, Chris. *The Long Tail: Why the Future of Business Is Selling Less of More.* Hyperion, 2006.

Aristotle. "Nicomachean Ethics." Translated by W.D. Ross. In *The Complete Works of Aristotle Vol. 2*, edited by Jonathan Barnes. Princeton University Press, 1984.

Atwal, Sanj. "Baby Shark Becomes First YouTube Video to Reach 10 Billion Views." Guinness World Book of Records. Last modified January 19, 2022. https://www.guinnessworldrecords.com/news/2022/1/baby-shark-becomes-first-youtube-video-to-reach-10-billion-views-689527.

Au, W. "High-Stakes Testing and Curricular Control: A Qualitative Metasynthesis." *American Educational Research Journal* 44, no. 3 (2007): 594–629. https://doi.org/10.3102/0013189X07306523.

Augustine of Hippo. *Confessions*. Translated by Henry Chadwick. Oxford University Press, 1991.

Barry, Ellen. "Are We Talking Too Much about Mental Health?" *New York Times*. Last modified May 6, 2024. https://www.nytimes.com/2024/05/06/health/mental-health-schools.html.

Berliner, Paul F. *Thinking in Jazz: The Infinite Art of Improvisation*. University of Chicago Press, 1994.

Bernstein, Leonard. *The Joy of Music*. Simon & Schuster, 1959.

Blair, Clancy, Douglas Granger, and Rachel Peters Razza. "Cortisol Reactivity Is Positively Related to Executive Function in Preschool Children Attending Head Start." *Child Development* 76, no. 3 (2005): 554–567. https://doi.org/10.1111/j.1467-8624.2005.00863.x.

Brennan, Caroline. "What Is Music Medicine?" *Cancerwise*. October 31, 2023. https://www.mdanderson.org/cancerwise/what-is-music-medicine.h00-159622590.html#:~:text=Studies%20have%20shown%20that%20intubated,biomarkers%20and%20improves%20hemodynamic%20stabilities.

Britton, Willoughby. "Can Mindfulness Be Too Much of a Good Thing? The Value of Moderation in Mindfulness Practice." *Current Opinion in Psychology* 28 (2020): 159–165. https://doi.org/10.1016/j.copsyc.2018.12.011.

Brown, Brené. *Rising Strong*. Random House, 2015.

Brown, Kirk Warren, Richard M. Ryan, and J. David Creswell. "Mindfulness: Theoretical Foundations and Evidence for Its Salutary Effects." *Psychological Inquiry* 18, no. 4 (2007): 211–237. https://doi.org/10.1080/10478400701598298.

Brownrigg, Mark. "Film Music and Narrative: How Music Works in Film." Thesis, University of Stirling, 2003.

Campbell, Patricia Shehan. *Music, Education, and Diversity: Bridging Cultures and Communities*. Teachers College Press, 2018.

Charry, Eric. *Mande Music: Traditional and Modern Music of the Maninka and Mandinka of Western Africa*. University of Chicago Press, 2000.

ClassicFM. "Soprano in Lockdown Passionately Sings 'Time to Say Goodbye' Over Italy's Rooftops." Last modified March 23, 2020. https://www.classicfm.com/discover-music/periods-genres/opera/soprano-lockdown-viral-time-to-say-goodbye/.

Conard, Nicholas J., Maria Malina, and Susanne C. Münzel. "New Flutes Document the Earliest Musical Tradition in Southwest Germany." *Nature* 460 (2009): 737–740. https://doi.org/10.1038/nature08169.

Confucius. *The Analects of Confucius*. Translated by Arthur Waley. Vintage Books, 1989.

Descartes, René. *Les Passions de l'âme*. Henry Le Gras, 1649.

Diamond, Adele, and Daphne S. Ling. "Conclusions about Interventions, Programs, and Approaches for Improving Executive Functions That Appear Justified and Those That, Despite Much Hype, Do Not." *Developmental Cognitive Neuroscience* 18 (2016): 35. https://doi.org/10.1016/j.dcn.2015.11.005.

Diamond, Adele, and Daphne S. Ling. "Review of the Evidence on, and Fundamental Questions about, Efforts to Improve Executive Functions, Including Working Memory." In *Cognitive and Working Memory Training: Perspectives from Psychology, Neuroscience, and Human Development*, edited by Jared M. Novick, et al. Oxford Scholarship online. (2020): 1–572. https://doi.org/10.1093/oso/9780199974467.001.0001.

Downey, Greg. *Learning Capoeira: Lessons in Cunning from an Afro-Brazilian Art*. Oxford University Press, 2005.

Doyon, Julien, and Habib Benali. "Reorganization and Plasticity in the Adult Brain during Learning of Motor Skills." *Current Opinion in Neurobiology* 15, no. 2 (2005): 161–167. https://doi.org/10.1016/j.conb.2005.03.004.

Dozier, Emily. "Taylor Swift Eras Tour 2024 Dates for U.S. Return: Ticket Prices, Cost, Full Schedule and More." *The Sporting News*. Last modified May 23, 2024. https://www.sportingnews.com/us/nfl/news/taylor-swift-tour-2024-tickets-prices-us-schedule-dates/612e97acae959d6de55ea896.

Dunbar, Robin. *Human Evolution: Our Brains and Behavior*. Oxford University Press, 2016.

Elpus, Kenneth. "Is It the Music or Is It Selection Bias? A Nationwide Analysis of Music and Non-Music Students' SAT Scores." *Journal of Research in Music Education* 62, no. 2 (2013): 175–194. https://doi.org/10.1177/0022429413485601.
Fancourt, Daisy, and Saoirse Finn. "What Is the Evidence on the Role of the Arts in Improving Health and Well-being? A Scoping Review." *World Health Organization*. Regional Office for Europe, Health Evidence Network synthesis report, no. 67. 2019. https://www.ncbi.nlm.nih.gov/books/NBK553773/.
Foulkes, Lucy, and Jack Andrews. "Are We Talking Too Much about Mental Health?" *New Ideas in Technology* 69 (2023). https://doi.org/10.1016/j.newideapsych.2023.101010.
Freeman, Walter J. *How Brains Make Up Their Minds*. Columbia University Press, 2000.
Galinsky, Ellen. *Ask the Children: The Breakthrough Study That Reveals How to Succeed at Work and Parenting*. Quill, 2000.
Galinsky, Ellen. *The Breakthrough Years: A New Scientific Framework for Raising Thriving Teens*. Flatiron Press, 2024.
Galinsky, Ellen, Jackie Bezos, Megan McClelland, Stephanie M. Carlson, and Philip D. Zelazo. "Civic Science for Public Use: Mind in the Making and Vroom." *Child Development* 88 (2017): 1410. https://doi.org/10.1111/cdev.12892.
Galinsky, Ellen, and Kimberlee Salmond. *Youth and Violence: Students Speak Out for a More Civil Society*. Families and Work Institute, 2002. https://youthtoday.org/2002/09/youth-violence-students-speak-out-for-a-more-civil-society/.
Galinsky, Ellen, Stacey Kim, James T. Bond, and Kimberlee Salmond. *Youth and Employment: Today's Students Tomorrow's Workforce*. Families and Work Institute, 2003.
Geiringer, Karl, and Irene Geiringer. *Haydn: A Creative Life in Music*. University of California Press, 1982.
Gross, James J., and Ross A. Thompson. "Emotion Regulation: Conceptual Foundations." In *Handbook of Emotion Regulation*, edited by James J. Gross. Guilford Press, 2007.
Gudmundsdottir, Helga. R. "Mothers as Singing Mentors for Infants." In *The Oxford Handbook of Music Education (Vol. 2)*, edited by R. C. Taylor. Oxford University Press, 2015.
Habibi, Assal. "Musical Brainwaves." *Edinburgh Culture Summit, Brain & Creativity Institute*. University of Southern California, 2020. https://www.youtube.com/watch?v=4qJ7VEAw7mU.
Habibi, Assal, Antonio Damasio, Beatriz Ilari, Ryan Veiga, Anand A. Joshi, Richard M. Leahy, Justin P. Haldar, et al. "Childhood Music Training Induces Change in Micro and Macroscopic Brain Structure: Results from a Longitudinal Study." *Cerebral Cortex* 28, no. 12 (2018): 4336–4347. https://doi.org/10.1093/cercor/bhx286.
Habibi, Assal, Beatriz Ilari, Kevin Crimi, Michael Metke, Jonas T. Kaplan, Anand A. Joshi, Richard M. Leahy, et al. "An Equal Start: Absence of Group Differences in Cognitive, Social, and Neural Measures Prior to Music or Sports Training in

Children." *Frontiers in Human Neuroscience* 8, no. 690 (2014). https://doi.org/10.3389/fnhum.2014.00690.

Haigney, Sophie. "The Many Requirements of Hold Music, a Genre for No One." *npr*. Last modified September 5, 2019. https://www.npr.org/2019/09/05/757544079/the-many-requirements-of-hold-music-a-genre-for-no-one.

Hallam, Susan. "The Power of Music: Its Impact on the Intellectual, Social and Personal Development of Children and Young People." *International Journal of Music Education* 28, no. 3 (2010): 269–289. https://doi.org/10.1177/0255761410370658.

Hallam, Susan, John Price, and Georgia Katsarou. "The Effects of Background Music on Primary School Pupils' Task Performance." *Educational Studies* 28, no. 2 (2010): 111–122. https://doi.org/10.1080/03055690220124551.

Hankins, Thomas L., and Robert J. Silverman. *The Glass Armonica: Musical Innovation and the Politics of Sensibility.* American Philosophical Society, 1995.

Hanno, Emily C., Jorge Cuartas, Luke W. Miratrix, Stephanie M. Jones, and Nonie K. Lesaux. "Changes in Children's Behavioral Health and Family Well-Being during the COVID-19 Pandemic." *Journal of Developmental and Behavioral Pediatrics* 43, no. 3 (2022): 168–175. https://doi.org/10.1097/DBP.0000000000001010.

Hanover Research. *AASA – Developing Resonant Resilient Nimble Leaders.* Hanover Research, September 28, 2022. https://www.hanoverresearch.com/reports-and-briefs/k-12-education/aasa-developing-resonant-resilient-nimble-leaders/.

Hargittai, Eszter. "Digital Na(t)ives? Variation in Internet Skills and Uses among Members of the 'Net Generation.'" *Sociological Inquiry* 80, no. 1 (2010): 92–113. https://doi.org/10.1111/j.1475-682X.2009.00317.x.

Hargreaves, David J., and Adrian C. North. "The Functions of Music in Everyday Life: Redefining the Social in Music Psychology." *Psychology of Music* 27, no. 1 (1999): 71–83. https://doi.org/10.1177/0305735699271007.

Harvey, Alan R. *Music, Evolution, and the Harmony of Souls.* Oxford University Press, 2019.

Hawn, Goldie. *A Lotus Grows in the Mud.* Berkeley Books, 2005.

Hennessy, Sarah L., Matthew E. Sachs, Beatriz Ilari, and Assal Habibi. "Effects of Music Training on Inhibitory Control and Associated Neural Networks in School-Aged Children: A Longitudinal Study." *Frontiers in Neuroscience* 13, no. 1080 (2019). https://doi.org/10.3389/fnins.2019.01080.

Hess, Juliet. "Equity and Music Education: Euphemisms, Terminal Naivety, and Whiteness." *Action, Criticism, and Theory for Music Education* 16, no. 3 (2017): 15–47. https://doi:10.22176/act16.3.15.

Hilliard, Russell E. "Music Therapy in Hospice and Palliative Care: A Review of the Empirical Data." *Evidence-based Complementary and Alternative Medicine* 2, no. 2 (2005): 173–178. https://doi.org/10.1093/ecam/neh076.

History.com editors. "Doris Kearns Goodwin on Empathy." *History*. Accessed September 18, 2024. https://www.history.com/topics/us-presidents/doris-kearns-goodwin-on-empathy-video.

Hudson, Ray. "Regions and Place: Music, Identity and Place." *Progress in Human Geography* 30, no. 5 (2006): 626–634. https://doi.org/10.1177/0309132506070177.

Hughes, Langston. "A Sacred Symphony," from *The Collected Poems of Langston Hughes*. Vintage Books, 1994.

Hulbert, Ann. "Cover to Cover." Last modified November 2013. https://www.theatlantic.com/magazine/archive/2013/11/the-soundtrack-of-your-life/309527/.

Huxley, Aldous. *Music at Night and Other Essays*. Chatto & Windus, 1931.

IFPI. "Engaging with Music 2021." *International Federation of the Phonographic Industry*. 2021. https://www.ifpi.org/wp-content/uploads/2021/10/IFPI-Engaging-with-Music-report.pdf.

IFPI. "Engaging with Music 2022." *International Federation of the Phonographic Industry*. 2022. https://www.ifpi.org/ifpi-releases-engaging-with-music-2022-report/.

IFPI. "Global Music Report 2022: State of the Industry." *International Federation of the Phonographic Industry*. 2022. https://luminatedata.com/.

Juslin, Patrick N., and Daniel Västfjäll. "Emotional Responses to Music: The Need to Consider Underlying Mechanisms." *Behavioral and Brain Sciences* 31, no. 5 (2008): 559–621. https://doi:10.1017/S0140525X08005293.

Kabat-Zinn, Jon. *Wherever You Go, There You Are: Mindfulness Meditation in Everyday Life*. Hatchette, 2005.

Kalinak, Kathryn. *Film Music: A Very Short Introduction*. Oxford University Press, 2010.

Karageorghis, Costas I., and David-Lee Priest. "Music in the Exercise Domain: A Review and Synthesis (Part I)." *International Review of Sport and Exercise Psychology* 5, no. 1 (2012): 44–66. https://doi.org/10.1080/1750984X.2011.631026.

Kearns Goodwin, Doris. *Team of Rivals: The Political Genius of Abraham Lincoln*. Simon & Schuster, 2005.

Keltner, D., and J. Haidt. "Approaching Awe, a Moral, Spiritual, and Aesthetic Emotion." *Cognition and Emotion* 17, no. 2 (2003): 297–314. https://doi.org/10.1080/02699930302297.

Kennedy, John F. "Remarks at Amherst College." October 26, 1963.

Kenney, William Howland. *Recorded Music in American Life: The Phonograph and Popular Memory, 1890–1945*. Oxford University Press, 1999.

Koelsch, Stefan. "Towards a Neural Basis of Music-Evoked Emotions." *Trends in Cognitive Sciences* 14, no. 3 (2010): 131–137. https://doi: 10.1016/j.tics.2010.01.002.

Koen, Benjamin D. *Beyond the Roof of the World: Music, Prayer, and Healing in the Pamir Mountains*. Oxford University Press, 2009.

Lakes, Kimberley D., and William T. Hoyt. "Promoting Self-Regulation through School-based Martial Arts Training." *Journal of Applied Developmental Psychology* 25, no. 3 (2004): 283–302. https://doi.org/10.1016/j.appdev.2004.04.002.

Lama, Dalai, and Howard C. Cutler. *The Art of Happiness: A Handbook for Living*. Riverhead Books, 1998.

Langer, Susanne. *Philosophy in a New Key*. Harvard University Press, 1951.

Langer, Susanne. Quoted in Dacher Keltner. *Awe: The New Science of Everyday Wonder and How It Can Transform Your Life*. Penguin Press, 2023.

Launay, Jacques, Bronwyn Tarr, and Robin I. M. Dunbar. "Synchrony as an Adaptive Mechanism in Human Social Bonding." *Ethology* 122, no. 10 (2016): 779–789. https://doi.org/10.1111/eth.12528.

Leuchtenburg, William E. *Franklin D. Roosevelt and the New Deal: 1932–1940.* Harper & Row, 1963.

Levitin, Daniel J. *This Is Your Brain on Music: The Science of a Human Obsession.* Dutton, 2006.

Ludke, Karen M., Fernanda Ferreira, and Katie Overy. "Singing Can Facilitate Foreign Language Learning." *Psychology of Music* 42, no. 3 (2014): 389–403. https://doi.org/10.3758/s13421-013-0342-5.

Lumet, Sidney, director. *Network.* Metro-Goldwyn-Mayer, 1976. 2 hr., 1 min. https://www.youtube.com/watch?v=ZwMVMbmQBug.

Magsamen, Susan, and Ivy Ross. *Your Brain on Art: How the Arts Transform Us.* Random House, 2023.

McPherson, James M. *Battle Cry of Freedom: The Civil War Era.* Oxford University Press, 1988.

Merlock Jackson, Kathy, ed. *Walt Disney: Conversations.* University Press of Mississippi, 2006.

Millard, Andre. *America on Record: A History of Recorded Sound.* Cambridge University Press, 1995.

Mithen, Steven. *The Singing Neanderthals: The Origins of Music, Language, Mind, and Body.* Weidenfeld and Nicholson, 2005.

Miyake, Akira, N. P. Friedman, M. J. Emerson, A. H. Witzki, A. Howerter, and T. D. Wager. "The Unity and Diversity of Executive Functions and Their Contributions to Complex 'Frontal Lobe' Tasks: A Latent Variable Analysis." *Cognitive Psychology* 41, no. 1 (2000): 49–100. https://doi.org/10.1006/cogp.1999.0734.

Molnar-Szakacs, Istvan, and K. Overy. "Music and Mirror Neurons: From Motion to 'E'motion." *Social Cognitive and Affective Neuroscience* 1, no. 3 (2006): 235–241. https://doi:10.1093/scan/nsl029.

Monson, Ingrid. *Saying Something: Jazz Improvisation and Interaction.* University of Chicago Press, 1996.

Mozart, Wolfgang Amadeus. "12 Variations on Ah, vous dirai-je, Maman." K. 265. 1781–1782.

Mozart, Wolfgang Amadeus. *The Letters of Mozart and His Family.* Edited and translated by Emily Anderson. Penguin Books, 1966.

National Academies of Sciences, Engineering, and Medicine. *The Promise of Adolescence: Realizing Opportunity for All Youth.* National Academies Press, 2019. https://doi.org/10.17226/25388.

National Center for Complementary and Integrative Health. "National Health Interview Survey 2017." Last modified September 15, 2024. https://www.nccih.nih.gov/research/statistics/nhis/2017.

National Center for Education Statistics. "About One-Quarter of Public Schools Reported That Lack of Focus or Inattention From Students Had a Severe Negative Impact on Learning in 2023–24." July 18, 2024. https://nces.ed.gov/whatsnew/press_releases/7_18_2024.asp.

National Endowment for the Arts (NEA). "The Arts and Achievement in At-Risk Youth: Findings from Four Longitudinal Studies." Washington, DC, 2012. https://www.arts.gov/impact/research/publications/arts-and-achievement-risk-youth-findings-four-longitudinal-studies.

National Scientific Council on the Developing Child. "Building the Brain's 'Air Traffic Control' System: How Early Experiences Shape the Development of Executive Function." Working Paper No. 11. Center on the Developing Child at Harvard University. Last modified February 2011. https://developingchild.harvard.edu/resources/building-the-brains-air-traffic-control-system-how-early-experiences-shape-the-development-of-executive-function/.

NeuroArts Blueprint. "NeuroArts Blueprint: Advancing the Science of Arts, Health, and Wellbeing. International Arts + Mind Lab." *NeuroArts Blueprint Report.* Johns Hopkins University, 2022. https://neuroartsblueprint.org/blueprint-report/.

Nielsen Music/MRC Data. *Nielsen Music Reports, 2017–2021.* https://www.nielsen.com/.

North, Adrian, and David Hargreaves. *The Social and Applied Psychology of Music.* Oxford University Press, 1997.

Northouse, Peter G. *Leadership: Theory and Practice, 8th Edition.* Sage Publications, 2018.

Obama, Barack. "Message to the World Choir Games." Shaoxing, China, 2010.

Ontai, Lenna L., and Ross A. Thompson. "Patterns of Attachment and Maternal Discourse Effects on Children's Emotional Understanding from 3 to 5 Years of Age." *Social Development* 11, no. 4 (2002): 433–450. https://doi.org/10.1111/1467-9507.00209.

Paine, Albert Bigelow. *Mark Twain: A Biography: The Personal and Literary Life of Samuel Langhorne Clemens. Vol. 3.* Harper & Brothers, 1912.

Patel, Aniruddh D. *Music, Language, and the Brain.* Oxford University Press, 2008.

Peterson, Linda, John Brereton, Joseph Bizup, Anne Fernald, and Melissa Goldthwaite, eds. *The Norton Anthology 13th Edition.* W.W. Norton & Company, 2011.

Pink, Daniel H. *To Sell Is Human: The Surprising Truth about Moving Others.* Riverhead Books, 2012.

Putnam, Robert D. *Bowling Alone: The Collapse and Revival of American Community.* Simon & Schuster, 2000.

Rabkin, Nick, and Eric C. Hedberg. *Arts Education in America: What the Declines Mean for Arts Participation.* National Endowment for the Arts, 2011.

Rauscher, F. H., G. L. Shaw, and K. N. Ky. "Music and Spatial Task Performance." *Nature* 365, no. 611 (1993). https://doi.org/10.1038/365611a0.

Repacholi, Betty M., and Alison Gopnik. "Early Reasoning about Desires: Evidence from 14- and 18-Month-Olds." *Developmental Psychology* 33, no. 1 (1997): 12–21. https://doi.org/10.1037/0012-1649.33.1.12.

Rodrigues-Gomez, Diego Alejandro, and Claudia Talero-Gutierrez. "Effects of Music Training in Executive Function Performance in Children: A Systematic Review." *Frontiers in Psychology* 13, no. 968144 (2022). https://doi.org/10.3389/fpsyg.2022.968144.

Rogers, Fred. *The World According to Mister Rogers: Important Things to Remember.* Hyperion Books, 2003.

Roorda, Debora L., Helma M. Y. Koomen, Jantine L. Spilt, and Frans J. Oort. "The Influence of Affective Teacher–Student Relationships on Students' School Engagement and Achievement: A Meta-Analytic Approach." *Review of Educational Research* 81, no. 4 (2011): 493–529. https://doi.org/10.3102/0034654311421793.

Sacks, Oliver. *Gratitude.* Pan Macmillan, 2015.

Sacks, Oliver. *Musicophilia: Tales of Music and the Brain.* Knopf, 2007.

Salimpoor, Valorie N., Mitchel Benovoy, Kevin Larcher, Alain Dagher, and Robert J. Zatorre. "Anatomically Distinct Dopamine Release during Anticipation and Experience of Peak Emotion to Music." *Nature Neuroscience* 14, no. 2 (2011): 257–262. https://doi.org/10.1038/nn.2726.

Schachner, Adena, et al. "Spontaneous Motor Entrainment to Music in Multiple Vocal Mimicking Species." *Current Biology* 19, no. 10 (2009): 831–836. https://doi.org/10.1016/j.cub.2009.03.061.

Schellenberg, E. Glenn, and César F. Lima. "Music Training and Nonmusical Abilities." *Annual Review of Psychology* 75 (2024): 87–128. https://doi.org/10.1146/annurev-psych-032323-051354.

Schickele, Peter (PDQ Bach). *The Short-Tempered Clavier and Other Dysfunctional Works for Keyboard.* Vanguard Classics, 1965, compact disc.

Schlesinger Jr., Arthur M. *A Thousand Days: John F. Kennedy in the White House.* Houghton Mifflin, 1965.

Scientific American. "It Turns Out We Were Born to Groove." Last modified January 10, 2024. https://www.scientificamerican.com/article/it-turns-out-we-were-born-to-groove/.

Scott King, Coretta. *My Life, My Love, My Legacy.* Henry Holt and Company, 2017.

Senderoff, Shara. "Biography." *Shara W. Senderoff.* Accessed September 18, 2024. https://www.sharawsenderoff.com/bio.

Sinek, Simon. *Leaders Eat Last: Why Some Teams Pull Together and Others Don't.* Penguin Publishing Group, 2014.

Skinner, B. F. *About Behaviorism.* Vintage Books, 1976.

Squire, Larry R., and Andrew J. O. Dede. "Conscious and Unconscious Memory Systems." *Cold Spring Harbor Perspectives in Biology* 7, no. 3 (2015). https://doi.org/10.1101/cshperspect.a021667.

Stafford, William. "The Way It Is." In *The Way It Is: New and Selected Poems.* Graywolf Press, 1998.

Stamberg, Susan. "Denied a Stage, She Sang for a Nation." *NPR.* Last modified April 9, 2014. https://www.npr.org/2014/04/09/298760473/denied-a-stage-she-sang-for-a-nation.

Sterne, Jonathan. *MP3: The Meaning of a Format.* Duke University Press, 2012.

Swift, Taylor. "Shake It Off." August 19, 2014. Big Machine Records. Compact Disc.

Tarr, Bronwyn, Jacques Launay, and Robin I. M. Dunbar. "Music and Social Bonding: 'Self-other' Merging and Neurohormonal Mechanisms." *Frontiers in Psychology* 5 (2014): 1096. https://doi: 10.3389/fpsyg.2014.01096.

Thaut, Michael H., David A. Peterson, and Gerald C. McIntosh. "Temporal Entrainment of Cognitive Functions: Musical Mnemonics Induce Brain Plasticity and Oscillatory Synchrony in Neural Networks Underlying Memory." *Annals of the New York Academy of Sciences* 1060, no. 1 (2006): 243–254. https://doi.org/10.1196/annals.1360.017.

Thaut, Michael H., G. C. McIntosh, R. R. Rice, R. A. Miller, J. Rathbun, and J. M. Brault. "Rhythmic Auditory Stimulation in Gait Training for Patients with Parkinson's Disease." *Movement Disorders* 12, no. 1 (1996): 219–227. https://doi.org/10.1002/mds.870110213.

Thaut, Michael H., and Volker Hoemberg, eds. *Handbook of Neurologic Music Therapy*. Oxford University Press, 2014.

The Institute for Habits of Mind. "What Are the Habits of Mind?" Accessed September 18, 2024. https://www.habitsofmindinstitute.org/learning-the-habits/. The authors would like to acknowledge Catherine Costa-Jones and express gratitude for her thoughtful ideas and editorial contributions.

The Troggs. "Love Is All Around Me." October 1967, Lion Records, vinyl.

This American Life. "516: Stuck in the Middle." Accessed September 15, 2024. https://www.thisamericanlife.org/516/transcript.

Thoma, Myriam V., Roberto La Marca, Rebecca Brönnimann, Linda Finkel, Ulrike Ehlert, and Urs M. Nater. "The Effect of Music on the Human Stress Response." *Psychoneuroendocrinology* 38, no. 1 (2013): 133–141. https://doi.org/10.1371/journal.pone.0070156.

Thompson, William F. *Music, Thought, and Feeling: Understanding the Psychology of Music*. Oxford University Press, 2014.

Threadgold, Emma, John E. Marsh, Neil McLatchie, and Linden J. Ball. "Background Music Stints Creativity: Evidence from Compound Remote Associate Tasks." *Applied Cognitive Psychology* 33, no. 5 (2019): 873–888. https://doi.org/10.1002/acp.3532.

TicketSmarter. "New York Philharmonic Tickets." *TicketSmarter*. Accessed September 19, 2024. https://www.ticketsmarter.com/p/new-york-philharmonic-tickets.

Tilson Thomas, Michael. "Music and Emotion through Time." TED2012 official TED Conference, March 2012. Video, 19 min., 56 sec. https://www.ted.com/talks/michael_tilson_thomas_music_and_emotion_through_time?subtitle=en.

Tolstoy, Leo. *What Is Art?* Translated by Aylmer Maude. Hackett Publishing Company, Inc., 1996.

Tunstall, Tricia. *Changing Lives: Gustavo Dudamel, El Sistema, and the Transformative Power of Music*. W.W. Norton & Company, 2012.

Twain, Mark. *A Connecticut Yankee in King Arthur's Court*, edited by M. Thomas Inge. Oxford University Press, 2006.

U.S. Census Bureau. "Income and Poverty in the United States: 2021." Last modified September 13, 2022. https://www.census.gov/library/publications/2022/demo/p60-276.html.

Vittes, Laurence. "Exclusive Interview with Yo Yo Ma on the Spirituality of Music." *Huffpost: The Blog*. Last modified September 30, 2012. https://www.huffpost.com/entry/yo-yo-ma_b_1920286.

"Walt Disney's Words: Quotations of Walt Disney." Compiled by Kathy Puckett. 2001.

Warren Brown, Kirk, Richard M. Ryan, and J. David Creswell. "Mindfulness: Theoretical Foundations and Evidence for Its Salutary Effects." *Psychological Inquiry* 18, no. 4 (2007): 211–237. https://doi.org/10.1080/10478400701598298.

Warren Brown, Kirk, Robert J. Goodman, Richard M. Ryan, and Bhikkhu Anālayo. "Mindfulness Enhances Episodic Memory Performance: Evidence from a Multimethod Investigation." *PLoS One* 11, no. 4 (2016). https://doi.org/10.1371/journal.pone.0153309.

Washington, George. "General Orders, June 4, 1777." In *The Writings of George Washington from the Original Manuscript Sources, 1745–1799, Vol. 8,* edited by John C. Fitzpatrick. United States Government Printing Office, 1931.

Weineck, Kristin, Olivia Xin Wen, and Molly J. Henry. "Neural Synchronization Is Strongest to the Spectral Flux of Slow Music and Depends on Familiarity and Beat Salience." *Elife* (2009). https://doi.org/10.7554/eLife.75515.

Witek, Maria A. G., et al. "Syncopation, Body-Movement and Pleasure in Groove Music." *PLoS ONE* 9, no. 4 (2014). https://doi.org/10.1371/journal.pone.0094446.

Yalch, Richard, and Eric R. Spangenberg. "The Effects of Music in a Retail Setting on Real and Perceived Shopping Times." *Journal of Business Research* 49, no. 2 (2000): 139–147. https://doi.org/10.1016/S0148-2963(99)00003-X.

Yazzi-Mintz, Ethan. "Voices of Students on Engagement: A Report on the 2006 High School Survey of Student Engagement." *Center for Evaluation and Education Policy, Indiana University.* 2006. https://eric.ed.gov/?id=ED495758.

Zander, Benjamin, and Rosamund Stone Zander. *The Art of Possibility: Transforming Professional and Personal Life.* Harvard Business Review Press, 2000.

Zatorre, Robert J., and Valorie N. Salimpoor. "From Perception to Pleasure: Music and its Neural Substrates." *Proceedings of the National Academy of Sciences* 110, no. 2 (2013): 10430–10437. https://doi.org/10.1073/pnas.1301228110.

Zelazo, Philip David, Clancy B. Blair, and Michael T. Willoughby. *Executive Function: Implications for Education.* NCER 2017-2000. National Center for Education Research, Institute of Education Sciences. U.S. Department of Education, 2016.

Zelazo, Philip David, Destany Calma-Birling, and Ellen Galinsky. "Fostering Executive-Function Skills and Promoting Far Transfer to Real-World Outcomes: The Importance of Life Skills and Civic Science." *Current Directions in Psychological Science* 33, no. 2 (2024): 121–127. https://doi.org/10.1177/09637214241229664.

Zelazo, Philip David, and Stephanie M. Carlson. "Hot and Cool Executive Function in Childhood and Adolescence: Development and Plasticity." *Child Development Perspectives* 6, no. 4 (2012): 354–360. https://doi.org/10.1111/j.1750-8606.2012.00246.x.

Zentner, Marcel, and Tuomas Eerola. "Rhythmic Engagement with Music in Infancy." *Proceedings of the National Academy of Sciences* 107, no. 13 (2010): 5768–5773. https://doi.org/10.1073/pnas.1000121107.

About the Authors

Morton Sherman is the retired senior associate executive director of AASA, known for his visionary leadership during a twenty-five-year career as a superintendent dedicated to elevating academic standards and promoting equitable education. Throughout his career, Mort championed initiatives that addressed achievement gaps and empowered communities, leaving a legacy of systemic change and a commitment to fostering inclusive, impactful learning environments.

Sara Leila Sherman is a distinguished classical musician and educator, renowned for her work in making music accessible to young audiences through her children's concert series, Mozart for Munchkins, and the nonprofit Little Mozart Foundation. Blending music and mindfulness, she has pioneered innovative approaches that empower educators and parents to use music as a tool for mindful learning and personal growth at esteemed institutions such as Lincoln Center Kids, The New York Public Library, and Hudson Yards to ensure music is available to all communities.

www.ingramcontent.com/pod-product-compliance
Lightning Source LLC
Chambersburg PA
CBHW021809220426
43662CB00006B/244